MORAL IMAGINATION

MORAL
IMAGINATION

DAVID
BROMWICH

PRINCETON UNIVERSITY PRESS

Princeton and Oxford

Published by Princeton University Press,
41 William Street, Princeton, New Jersey 08540

In the United Kingdom: Princeton University Press,
6 Oxford Street, Woodstock, Oxfordshire OX20 1TW
press.princeton.edu

Library of Congress Cataloging-in-Publication Data

Bromwich, David, 1951–
[Essays. Selections]
Moral Imagination : essays / David Bromwich.
    pages cm
  Summary: "Spanning many historical and literary contexts, Moral Imagination brings together a dozen recent essays by one of America's premier
cultural critics. David Bromwich explores the importance of imagination and
sympathy to suggest how these faculties may illuminate the motives of human
action and the reality of justice. These wide-ranging essays address thinkers
and topics from Gandhi and Martin Luther King on nonviolent resistance,
to the dangers of identity politics, to the psychology of the heroes of classic
American literature. Bromwich demonstrates that moral imagination allows
us to judge the right and wrong of actions apart from any benefit to ourselves,
and he argues that this ability is an innate individual strength, rather than a
socially conditioned habit. Political topics addressed here include Edmund
Burke and Richard Price's efforts to define patriotism in the first year of the
French Revolution, Abraham Lincoln's principled work of persuasion against
slavery in the 1850s, the erosion of privacy in America under the influence of
social media, and the use of euphemism to shade and anesthetize reactions to
the global war on terror. Throughout, Bromwich considers the relationship
between language and power, and the insights language may offer into the
corruptions of power. Moral Imagination captures the singular voice of one of
the most forceful thinkers working in America today" —Provided by publisher.
  Includes index.
  ISBN 978-0-691-16141-9 (hardback : acid-free paper)
  I. Title.
  PS3552.R637A6 2014
  813'.54—dc23   2013038596

British Library Cataloging-in-Publication Data is available

This book has been composed in
Baskerville 10 Pro and Bodoni At Home

Printed on acid-free paper.
Printed in the United States of America
1 3 5 7 9 10 8 6 4 2

To Jeffrey Stout

Th'abuse of greatness is when it disjoins
Remorse from power.

—Shakespeare, *Julius Caesar*

CONTENTS

PREFACE

THIS IS A BOOK ABOUT WORKS OF THE MIND OF VARIOUS sorts, and the people who wrote or spoke them. The common subject of the essays is the relationship between power and conscience. A politician like Lincoln or a political writer like Burke, as much as the author of a novel or a poem, is engaged in acts of imagination for good or ill. At the same time, he is answerable to the canons of accuracy that prevail in the world of judgment between person and person. These writers and several others whom I deal with recognize that the will of the powerful can induce a blindness to the nature of their actions which is one of the mysteries of human life. All of the essays in this book are concerned with that mystery, too.

Much of my subject matter was dictated by the end of the Cold War. I have been troubled by the thought that America, in these years, was bypassing an opportunity to resume a connection with our most generous ideals: respect for the dignity of the person, and a commitment to improve the justice of a society that looks to its own welfare and liberty. The United States has at times sought to be exemplary. We have unfortunately become evangelical; and part of the reason is the wish to stand unopposed at the center of the world. This ambition is conventional, not particularly democratic, and in no way imaginative. It is driven by energetic fantasies.

I write to defend the human faculty which several of the writers I most admire—Wordsworth, Ruskin, Gandhi, Virginia Woolf, and Martin Luther King, among others—have made us think of as *moral imagination*. This is the power that compels us to grant the highest possible reality and the largest conceivable claim to a thought, action, or person that is not our own, and not close to us in any obvious way. The force of the idea of moral imagination is to deny that we can ever know ourselves sufficiently to settle on a named identity that prescribes our conduct or affiliations. Moral imagination therefore seems to me inseparable from the freedom that is possible in society.

Cultural identity, on the other hand—the subject of the second essay here—presumes and works to reinforce a social fixity that obstructs imagination. Accordingly, I would rank it among the fictions that Francis Bacon described as "idols." He divided them in his *New Organon* into four kinds: *Idols of the Tribe*, *Idols of the Cave*, *Idols of the Market Place*, and *Idols of the Theater*. Idols of the tribe are the offspring of the human love of order: the conceit that "man is the measure of all things" and confidence that the world is more orderly than it actually is. Idols of the cave, market place, and theater are the products of distortions of mind that spring from personal disposition or preoccupation; from vacuous belief induced by the vulgar and fanciful misuse of words to convey a counterfeit sense; and from systems of religion and metaphysical philosophy, abetted by false science. It will be seen that in Bacon's view, the idols of the tribe command all the rest; and I concentrate on the idols of the tribe in their contemporary forms. In our time, when the measure of man is subdivided into ethnic, racial, or national man, idols of the race, nation, and ethnic group enjoy a special authority. Everyone, it is said, needs to belong to a tribe of some sort. I give reasons to doubt the truth of this as a premise of sociology, or as an insight into psychology.

"The Meaning of Patriotism in 1789" offers a pertinent comment on a related theme: the recent acceptance of the inevitability of nationalist loyalties. At the moment that marked the launching of the highest hope for individual rights and democracy, an argument for sympathy without regard to nation or person, and an argument for loyalty to a significant group, were debated by Richard Price and Edmund Burke at a memorable depth on both sides. Price and Burke asked whether loyalty to one nation could matter as it once had, now that democratic rights appeared on the verge of obtaining general assent. A merely national loyalty—which Burke defended more subtly than is often realized, and which Price ranked below the impartial love of liberty—was not, in 1789, lightly supposed to deserve the assent of free minds.

The next three essays concern some particulars of American morale that emerged forcibly in the 1850s. Lincoln and Whitman are the heroes of this part: I write about them at length because I believe that the debates of the 1850s in America, like those of the 1790s in Britain, by force of historical circumstance and the accidents of genius produced discoveries of lasting value concerning the relations of men and women in society. The accurate imaginings of Emerson, Thoreau, Melville, Dickinson, Whitman, and many others still run ahead of our own conventions of thought; but many Americans feel a peculiar closeness to Lincoln and Whitman. I think this order of affection is justified, and, beginning with "Lincoln and

Whitman as Representative Americans," the essays joined in this section offer a provisional attempt to say why.

"Lincoln's Constitutional Necessity" looks at his political thought in the context of an ideal of individual freedom and a principled belief in equality—ideals to which Lincoln held firmly and which he did much to interpret definitively for his time and our own. The essay also tries to account for the potency of a leader at a moment of choice, and for Lincoln's apparent belief in historical necessity as an impersonal force. "Shakespeare, Lincoln, and Ambition" puts to the test of practical criticism my belief that the versions of imagination employed in politics and in literature are not separable. It shows Lincoln exemplifying in words and action, whether consciously or not, a self-knowledge and a wariness that were a resource available to him from Shakespeare's tragedies.

"The American Psychosis" renews a question that has perplexed me as it has other commentators on American society and literature. From the humblest to the most original and erudite talents, why have so many American artists been captured by the belief that your soul may "absolve you to yourself" (to borrow Emerson's words)? Why does the typical hero of American fiction so often seem to fit D.H. Lawrence's characterization, "hard, isolate, stoic, and a killer"? The answer relates to a Protestant conviction of the inviolability of the self: a belief that is necessary to the strength of a liberal society but fatal when treated as a guide to the conduct of life. "How Publicity Makes People Real" brings out an opposite tendency of American culture, which nonetheless draws on the same compulsion and anxiety. It is not enough for us to be real to ourselves, within ourselves. We want to be completely special, yet we want to be completely normal.

All of the data of mass culture conspire to persuade us that we hardly exist outside the social world in which we are most visible.

Self-absorption and uninhibited aggrandizement are familiar extremes of character in the United States. They have also marked the character of the nation as a whole. "The Self-Deceptions of Empire" is an appreciation of a theologian and social critic, Reinhold Niebuhr, who saw more searchingly than others at mid-century the combined effects of the belief in America's uniqueness and a commitment to worldwide expansion. Niebuhr wrote to chasten the assumption that we are good (uniquely good) and that we are therefore situated to punish our enemies, enlighten our friends, and mobilize the diffusive benefits of the global market. Many readers who believe they are following Niebuhr's wisdom have gotten his emphasis wrong. They think he said, "There's evil out there in the world, and we must act correspondingly with a practical sense of the limits of our ability to correct it." On the contrary: he said that we harbor in ourselves both good and evil, just as other people do. I admire him as an iconoclast of the jargon of exceptionalism.

As the first section of the book introduces a contest between habitual loyalties and imagination, the final section points to the persistence of the contest today. My subject here is the intellectual environment in which contemporary varieties of patriotism and the American war on terror have flourished. The idea of the West as one side of a clash of civilizations forms a large part of that environment, and in "What Is the West?" I consider the version of the relevant history recounted by Niall Ferguson. "Holy Terror and Civilized Terror" urges the adoption of a rigorous definition of terrorism. We ought to describe as "terrorist" any act of deliberate violence that compasses the deaths of innocent persons in order to achieve a political end. State terror, such as Britain practiced in Kenya, Russia in Chechnya, and the U.S. in Iraq—state terror, as exemplified by our own state among others—differs morally in no way from the terror of the people we are in the habit of calling terrorists. Moral imagination affirms the kinship in evil of these two sorts of violence.

We pretend that our violence is not violence, that our conquest is not conquest, that a client state, because it belongs to us, is on the way to democracy. "Euphemism and Violence" interprets some linguistic symptoms of this bad faith. But new illustrations crop up every day. Think of the phrase "signature strike" to denote the purposeful killing of a possibly innocent person whose identity we do not know, on the ground that his pattern of contacts, movements and so on, his "signature," makes him look like an enemy. Again, with a boyish privilege D. H. Lawrence would have understood well, prosecutors of the war on terror like to speak of the enemy as "bad guys." No further definition is thought to be necessary. The fact that we hide our actions from ourselves ought to give us heart, in one sense, for it suggests that shame is still doing its proper work. But the prevalence of euphemism allows the self-deception of the powerful and the deception of the populace to continue. I have included at the end four additional comments on the predicament in which American democracy has found itself in the years since 2001. These are part of a journalistic commitment that I associate with the civic concerns outlined in the essays on moral imagination, cultural identity, and patriotism.

Two essays in this book require an additional prefatory word because their timeliness belongs to an earlier time.

To begin with "A Dissent on Cultural Identity": it has been argued that the spirit of national unity from the war on terror broke the charm of "culturalist" doctrine once and for all. Did I then overstate an ephemeral trend? An opposite challenge might be raised concerning the prediction of the effects of social media in "How Publicity Makes People Real." This has been so spectacularly borne out by the growth of the digital-internet complex that the pessimistic view I offered may now seem an instance of scholastic understatement.

And yet, the preoccupation with identity still pervades the academy, even if more quietly than before. A triumphant faith sounds calmer than a militant faith. I was arguing chiefly against two single-minded theorists, Charles Taylor and Michael Walzer, and the political dangers I pointed to in their thinking still seem to me considerable. I have allies here—more than I found the space to acknowledge at the time. Anthony Appiah, in an early response to Taylor's proposal of "cultural recognition" as a *right*, observed that no distinct line can separate the well-meant politics of recognition from the politics of compulsion. By every step you take in adding to the prestige of identity cultures, you contribute to make identity a political need with political leverage. From bureaucratization of the need comes official subsidy and supervision, and thereby an additional check on individual thought and action. This is never done without a cost to freedom, and it adds to the uneasy sense that a merely individual identity is not enough.

On the face of present-day discussions, cultural identity may have taken an underground course, but it remains in fact as influential as ever. Beyond the boundaries of the multicultural debates in North America, the ideology of identity has been deployed in the creation and definition of new states in the Balkans, in the former Soviet republics, and in the Middle East. Liberal believers in cultural identity, trained in part by the writings I discuss, have drafted constitutions for those countries. Thus the orthodoxy of the 1990s has made a lasting impact on the practice of American foreign policy, as well as on the rules and sanctions of American society. Nor have the effects been altogether happy. Assurance by American legal experts that a democratic constitution for Iraq should be based on tribal identities (Shiite, Sunni, and Kurdish) did not check but excited the violent disorder of 2004–2006. That was an admonitory instance of translating cultural recognition into political practice.

In the eighteen years since I wrote, the theorists of cultural identity have not altered their views so much as they have widened the grounds on which they seek to carry conviction. In the recent and ambitious writings of Walzer on comparative politics, for example, one detects a convergence between the treatment of revolutionary nationalism and of religious piety. Walzer is struck by the extent to which movements of national liberation have been driven by religious enthusiasm. This was the subject of his first book, *The Revolution of the Saints*, an analysis of the Puritan revolution in which political radicalism and religious zeal were shown to go hand in hand; yet the revised view comes close to saying that radical politics can never transcend the religious motive from which it springs. Walzer plainly regrets this finding; he would prefer a secular radicalism; but he presses hard the inference that nonreligious politics in a new nation are a lost cause. Modern militants bring with them, into the revolutions they lead and into the states they forge, more of the old beliefs than they realize.

Or what comes to the same thing: they have to deal with people who are attached to the old beliefs. Revolutionary radicalism in politics is thus shown to be secular only on the surface of events, and only for a generation, at most.

More expansively, Taylor has argued in his recent work that secularization itself was not secular. Whig history and the habits of reductive social science may have deceived us into omitting religion from the common understanding of modernity; but professed faith and the "lived religion" of pious communities in modernity were always much closer to the heart of the Enlightenment project than we were led to suppose. Along these lines, in *A Secular Age* Taylor develops a historical background for his argument on cultural identity and recognition; and it is clear that the political and historical projects go together. In a lecture given in the early 1990s, at Yale Law School, he announced that the peoples of the former Soviet Union had come out of a "deep freeze"; the revived ethnic enthusiasm was the result of a thaw that returned the tribes to their deepest instincts. The implication was that the natural state of man *is* one of ethnic identification—mere politics being as unfriendly as ice to the human touch. The context left no doubt that the freeze had not been the result of the oppressive artifice of totalitarian politics alone. A similar derangement would be imposed by any politics that sought to free itself from the thick or robust identity conferred by culture. For culture is the authentic reality. And politics? A superimposed set of hopeful expectations. Close to the heart of any authentic politics must be religious practice, which is part and parcel of the real enlightenment of secular modernity.

Both of these provocative and influential writers assent to the theory that a bond exists that is more humanly compelling than the moral duties of men and women toward each other in the light of our shared condition on earth. I do not acknowledge any such deeper obligation, and rather cast my vote with the Huxley of *Ends and Means* and the Orwell of *1984*. I see no point in trying to maintain a distinction between ideology and religion. Ideology is religion that has not built its church, and religion is ideology grown lofty and distinguished. This was the common view of the educated in liberal societies half a century ago. If it remains so today, we who hold the belief have lost our voice. The fiction of cultural identity is now so well entrenched that it has been possible for recent advocates of civil rights to argue that sanctions against "hate speech" are justified, since insult, carried by words alone in the absence of physical menace or a threat to livelihood, tends to impair the self-esteem of individuals. They say it does so by lowering the collective self-image of the group. Yet this argument presumes that the vulnerable persons have always already delegated their identity, their morale, and their empirical consciousness to the named identity of the group. At home and abroad, such an assumption reinforces the virulence of the same fixed identities it says it wants to reform.

Is there a connection between group identity and the destruction of privacy? I think there is. "How Publicity Makes People Real" was written several years before the invention of Facebook, but it offered an almost self-evident projection from tendencies by then impossible to mistake. Broadcast therapy and reality TV had accustomed people to finding themselves most real when most revealed. Two goods were supposed to be accomplished in this way. The confessing person is spared anonymity and what is said to be the loneliness that makes anonymity a curse. Also, he or she is put in immediate and visible contact with a circle of helpers. I am writing two months after the revelation that the national security bureaucracy of the United States is far on the way to collecting all possible information about every person in the United States and much of the rest of the world: friends, habits, patterns of consumption, assets and debts, travels, tastes in reading and eating and music, political orientation, random curiosities, financial and medical history. Young people may have lived all of their conscious lives with the assumption that these things were known already, or could be known; but the storage of a comprehensive pool of secret data under secret laws is consistent with neither enlightenment nor democracy.

So extended a regime of publicity can only serve to undermine and degrade personal autonomy: my conscious ability to govern my actions. Considered as an aesthetic experience, the virtual boards and walls and rooms and screens and links may yield a new way of making your life a work of art. The destruction of privacy gives a window into a theoretically unlimited number of lives and the pleasure of a mediated experience that can be enhanced and intensified to the limit of waking existence. But the knowledge that comes from a web of personal communications overseen by the state assures the transparency of a one-way mirror. You may look with pleasure at the new accessories, applications, constituents of yourself, but the state takes in your look. One recalls the warning of Bacon that the minds of men and women are a haunted mirror, "an enchanted glass, full of superstition and imposture, if it be not delivered and reduced." There may be an inward connection, after all, between the discipline of moral imagination and the patience required to draw back from our appetite for images.

Bacon spoke for half of the critical calling of imagination when he noticed the susceptibility of the mind to waking dreams and wishful thinking: a temptation the more seductive when the illusions are pleasing to collective self-love. Whitman spoke for the other half when he said that a recovery was always possible through acts of inspired judgment: acts, he would have us realize, in which an unswerving self-trust may accompany an ingrained self-suspicion.

> Somehow I have been stunned. Stand back!
> Give me a little time beyond my cuffed head and
>   slumbers and dreams and gaping,
> I discover myself on a verge of the usual mistake.

One would like to live in a country that could say this to itself.

"Shakespeare, Lincoln, and Ambition," which appears for the first time in this book, was part of a Spring 2012 commemorative series organized at Yale University by David Kastan. Several of the other essays began as public lectures, and I am especially grateful to Richard Levin and Anthony Kronman of Yale for the chance to contribute "Lincoln and Whitman as Representative Americans" to the 2001 DeVane Lectures on Democratic Vistas; to Ralph Lerner and Nathan Tarcov at the University of Chicago for proposing the seminars in Fall 2001 at the Committee on Social Thought which became "The American Psychosis"; and to Akeel Bilgrami for the invitation in 2007 to give the Edward Said Memorial Lecture at Columbia University on "Moral Imagination." Discussions with the abovementioned friends and colleagues brought sharper detail and qualification to my arguments. I have revised most of the essays lightly to correct errors and infelicities and keep redundancy to a minimum. Two exceptions are "A Dissent on Cultural Identity" and "Holy Terror and Civilized Terror," both of which have been checked in these smaller ways and also cut to rid them of local emphases that seem dated. Conversations with Dudley Andrew, George Kateb, Edward Mendelson, Steven Smith, and Georgann Witte deepened my understanding of many of the topics; and discerning comments by an anonymous reader for Princeton University Press convinced me to revise and expand the preface. I am grateful to Jackson Lears at *Raritan*, Robert Silvers at the *New York Review of Books*, Michael Walzer at *Dissent*, and Mary-Kay Wilmers at the *London Review of Books* for steady interest and encouragement. Alison MacKeen, at Princeton University Press, thought of the title and helped to shape the contents, and the book has greatly benefited from her advice.

Essays have previously appeared in the following journals, in some cases under a different title: "Moral Imagination," *Raritan,* vol. 27 no. 4 (2008); "A Dissent on Cultural Identity," *Dissent*, Winter 1995 (with replies by Michael Walzer and Charles Taylor); "The Meaning of Patriotism in 1789," *Dissent,* Summer 2011; "Lincoln and Whitman as Representative Americans," *Yale Review,* Spring 2002, reprinted in *Democratic Vistas: Reflections on the Life of American Democracy,* ed. Jedediah Purdy (Yale University Press, 2004); "Lincoln's Constitutional Necessity," *Raritan,* vol. 20 no. 3 (2001); "The American Psychosis," *Raritan,* vol. 21 no. 4 (2002); "How Publicity Makes People Real," *Social Research,* vol. 68 no. 1 (2001); "The Self-Deceptions of Empire," *London Review of Books,* October 23, 2008; "What Is the West?" *New York Review of Books*, December 8, 2011; "Holy Terror and Civilized Terror," *New Republic,* January 23, 2006; "Cheney's Law," *Huffington Post,* October 20,

2007; "Euphemism and Violence," *New York Review of Books*, March 5, 2008; "William Safire: Wars Made out of Words," *Antiwar.com,* October 1, 2009; "What 9/11 Makes Us Forget," *Huffington Post*, September 10, 2011; "The Snowden Case," *London Review of Books*, June 21, 2013.

ONE

CHAPTER 1

MORAL IMAGINATION

MORALITY AND IMAGINATION HAVE SOMETHING TO DO with each other, and both have something to do with the human power of sympathy. Probably most people would grant that much. The difficulty comes when we try to decide how and where to bring morality and imagination together. From the seventeenth century onward, *morals* denotes the realm of duties and obligations, of compulsory and optional approvals and regrets, the rewards and sanctions properly affixed to human action. Imagination applies to things or people as they are not now, or are not yet, or are not any more, or to a state of the world as it never could have been but is interesting to reflect on. Morality, we say, is concerned with the real and its objects are actual. Imagination conjures up fictions and its objects are, at most, probable: we could believe them real in a world that otherwise resembled our own. The sense that morality and imagination are closely allied— that they might not belong to separate categories—is initially as puzzling as the idea of "moral imagination" that is my subject.

Imagination, in its dominant sense in the sixteenth and early seventeenth centuries, referred to an extravagant and undependable faculty of the mind that fetched ideas from afar. This was the imagination of Philip Sidney and Fulke

Greville, and of Francis Bacon when in the *Advancement of Learning* he remarked that the mind of man was "like an enchanted glass, full of superstition and imposture." Hobbes, with his scientific and reductionist program, defined imagination as "decaying sense," and among the extraordinary short definitions at the start of *Leviathan*, you find none at all of morals; but Hobbes's drift can be inferred from his observation that conscience is the coming together of two or more opinions. Thus conscience and imagination are equally unreliable, for Hobbes. Of all the writers of the period, Shakespeare has, if not the gentlest, the least indifferent things to say for imagination; yet when Theseus utters his sententious speech at the close of *A Midsummer Night's Dream*—"The lunatic, the lover, and the poet, / Are of imagination all compact"— the well-tuned words of praise do not wholly vindicate imagination:

> The poet's eye, in a fine frenzy rolling,
> Doth glance from heaven to earth, from earth to heaven;
> And as imagination bodies forth
> The forms of things unknown, the poet's pen
> Turns them to shapes, and gives to airy nothing
> A local habitation and a name.

The idea that the poet gives to things "a local habitation and a name" makes a handsome compliment; but Theseus is only saying that such particulars help the idle coinage of the brain to carry credit. For what the poet dreams of can never be checked, since it lies in the realm of things unknown; while the shapes that emerge from poetry begin as "airy nothing" and are not expected to have a permanent life in the mind of a rational person. Shakespeare does not take us far from Hobbes after all.

Both the division between morals and imagination and the common distrust of imagination itself have to be recalled if we are to realize what a strange yoking of contraries is signaled by the very idea of moral imagination. The departure comes in the later eighteenth century and without much foreshadowing. If you think of Romantic poetry and the criticism and writings on morality that it sponsored, you may find yourself taking moral imagination for granted. By the middle of the nineteenth century —in Heine, in Hugo, in George Eliot—the idea seems to be everywhere. And it shows a vitality that has persisted in the thinking (even the tactical thinking) of movements of social reform and political resistance in the twentieth century. Yet there was nothing inevitable about the rise of this idea, which offers to society no equipment for living and no pragmatic measure of its own consequences.

The first writer to use the phrase "moral imagination" was Edmund Burke in *Reflections on the Revolution in France*. The passage occurs in his meditation on the crowd that forced the king and queen of France to move from Versailles to Paris; close up, the phrase comes out of Burke's report of the assault on the queen in her bed chamber, a disgrace of which he says: "I thought ten thousand swords must have leaped from their scabbards to avenge even a look that threatened her with insult." But the time when that could happen is past; the age of chivalry is gone, and with it the moral conditions that made such a response possible: the spirit of religion, and the spirit of a gentleman. What has replaced them, Burke says, is the morale of a "perfect democracy," which is "the most shameless thing in the world." He adds: "As it is the most shameless, it is also the most fearless." Burke thinks the age of chivalry was admirable because it did not bring moral duties under the institutional control of majority suffrage; and in seeking to give an adequate picture of an older regime of judgment, he arrestingly joins the words morality and imagination. By a total revolution like that of France, all will now be changed:

> All the pleasing illusions, which made power gentle, and obedience liberal, which harmonized the different shades of life, and which, by bland assimilation, incorporated into politics the sentiments which beautify and soften private society, are to be dissolved by this new conquering empire of light and reason. All the decent drapery of life is to be rudely torn off. All the superadded ideas, furnished from the wardrobe of a moral imagination, which the heart owns, and the understanding ratifies, as necessary to cover the defects of our naked shivering nature, and to raise it to a dignity in our own estimation, are to be exploded as a ridiculous, absurd, and antiquated fashion.

This celebrated passage is by no means easy to interpret. Burke sets on one side metaphors of the ancient, the pleasing, the bland and beautiful; the assimilable, the dignified; modesty and softness and concealment. On the other side are metaphors of destruction and iconoclasm; shining a light to expose what is hidden; tearing away a veil or a piece of clothing; ridiculing; exploding. The essence of things seen without prejudice or illusion, by the cold light of reason or of pretended enlightenment, is shown to be unendurable: it leaves us naked, shivering, helpless, and stripped of dignity. Things are made humanly bearable and assimilable only as they are modified by habit and custom, enhanced by "superadded ideas," made pleasing by the work of illusion. We need the coverings that enlightenment and reason to want to strip away.

Notice that "moral imagination," as Burke here uses the phrase, is an entirely conventional process. "All the superadded ideas, furnished from the wardrobe of a moral imagination"—the wardrobe furnishes *habitual* ideas that, item by item as they are picked out and worn, protect our shivering nature and make us know our duties. I exhibit a moral imagination when I act rightly by my selection from a pre-existing array of approved habits. There is nothing original or individual about moral imagination on this view. It is the means by which possible motives of action are winnowed in advance; so long as I choose with a moral imagination, I cannot but choose well. By the same measure, I cannot but act in a way that is familiar and precedented. This does not mean that my action is a matter of sheer reflex. It is a conscious choice, which the heart owns and the understanding ratifies: Burke put the last words in the sentence because he wanted to be sure that we would view the possessor of a moral imagination as obeying the conscience through an act of will. Yet the result that I achieve must be the same result as would predictably come to anyone rightly brought up. If we compare imagination in its high Romantic sense, there is nothing imaginative about this version of moral imagination; nor is there anything moral about it, in either the Kantian or the utilitarian understanding of morals. The moral imagination simply offers wisdom without reflection.

Various motives conspired to produce the eloquence of this orthodox account. The object of Burke's sympathy, the Catholic queen of France, was a surprising and in some ways an unconventional choice for a Protestant writer in a country that went to war with France nearly once a decade in the eighteenth century. The reverence with which he treated the queen appeared, to most of Burke's English contemporaries, startling both in degree and in kind. By portraying the French revolution, in a nearby description, as a leveling and calculating agency, an instrument of democratic modernization and ascendant finance capitalism, he suggests that our continued reliance on a moral imagination may have something heroic about it, just because it is now under challenge. What was once a safe and rehearsed response has become a defensive assertion of faith, requiring moral and physical courage. Yet what stands out most is Burke's elaboration of a curriculum of imagination: he makes us see that to imagine morally is a labor of the social will whose success is proved only when woven into the conduct of each person. The instructions I am to follow are already there, but they must act through me in order to be realized. Each individual is tested at every moment of a revolutionary age. Burke himself is on the line, and so is the reader. The words of the passage finally say more than the logic of his thinking should have made Burke want to say. The sense is orthodox, but the stance is critical, dramatic, inquisitive, disturbed.

Of the poems Wordsworth published in *Lyrical Ballads* in 1798, the one that exposed him to most derision and reproach was "The Idiot Boy." Yet Wordsworth set particular store by this poem; and he was right to do so. To capture the radicalism of its sympathy, one has to summarize a story that is chiefly remarkable for what does not happen in it. Betty Foy sends her child, an idiot boy named Johnny, to fetch a doctor to the bedside of her friend Susan Gale, who is sick with a high fever. Hours pass, Johnny does not return, and gradually his mother's thoughts turn from care for her friend to anxiety that her boy is lost—and, since he does not know his way, lost forever. She goes to ask the doctor for help but, roused from sleep after midnight, he resents the intrusion. Betty herself sets out, in despair of finding Johnny:

So, through the moonlight lane she goes,
And far into the moonlight dale;
And how she ran, and how she walked,
And all that to herself she talked,
Would surely be a tedious tale.

In high and low, above, below,
In great and small, in round and square
In tree and tower was Johnny seen,
In bush and brake, in black and green;
'Twas Johnny, Johnny, every where.

She comes upon Johnny sitting on his horse, near a waterfall, and when she hugs him Johnny laughs and makes his excited noise *Burr.* She asks him what he has done all night, what he has seen and heard, and he answers: "The cocks did crow to-whoo, to-whoo, / And the sun did shine so cold!" The owls he turns to cocks, the moon to the sun at night—a metaphor with the incongruity and truth of poetry. Meanwhile Susan Gale has been miraculously cured of her fever.

Readers at the end of the eighteenth century would not have been shocked by the mere presentation of a character like the idiot boy. The appearance of such figures in ballad or fiction was almost a cliché: a madwoman, Madge Wildfire, a few years later was placed by Scott near the center of the plot of *The Heart of Mid-Lothian.* If anything, in Romantic writing the presence of a mad man or woman supplied an occasion for exotic coloring. Wordsworth's readers might indeed have been more satisfied had they been told more about Johnny's feelings from inside. But the treatment of Johnny is matter-of-fact: we hear nothing about his feelings except the concluding words about the sun and the cocks; about his condition we learn nothing apart from the words of the title. As for the melodramatic interest that is set up—the answer to the question, Will Susan Gale obtain her cure by this unreliable messenger or by some other means?—it is scuttled twice, almost casually, and introduced at the end as a matter of incidental concern. What Wordsworth attends to, rather, are the feelings of Johnny's mother about her wayward son. The portrayal of a mother's cares, as deeply as such feelings can be imagined, and with the idiot boy as their object: this was the choice that drew the scorn and incredulity of respectable critics. Wordsworth was felt to have abused the name and nature of human feelings by portraying the mother's affection for an aberrant instead of a normal person. Surely, they said, readers could be brought to sympathize with a woman like Betty Foy without distraction by the unsuitable match of her feelings with so embarrassing a cause.

To critics and to a young disciple, John Wilson, who complained of the emotional demands of the poem, Wordsworth replied by insisting on the humanity of Johnny as it comes to be known through his mother's love. It mattered to Wordsworth's realism that he had chosen to read the subject not by a pretended empathy with Johnny himself, but rather "by tracing the maternal passion through many of its more subtle windings" (as he wrote in the preface to *Lyrical Ballads*). And here we touch on a discovery announced by his mode of treatment: moral imagination is not to be found in the reliable sentiment anyone may be supposed to have on such an occasion, the sentiment shared by every person who knows what the appropriate emotions are regarding a boy like Johnny. The orthodox question—What kind of feeling ought he to elicit?—has been replaced by the question, What can *I* feel about him? Wordsworth thought it was possible for the reader to have feelings other than generous pity for a human aberration. Yet we come upon our feelings here through Betty Foy's attachment to Johnny. We are made to feel as she does; and the integrity of her feelings is seen to constitute its own defense.

The axis of imagining has shifted as we moved from a third-person to a first-person question, from a rehearsed response of pity for children like this to a sense of Johnny's actual dignity. Pity, let it be added, might lead here to action on behalf of its object, as pity often does: the settling of Johnny into a home for such boys, to make sure that he has company, for example; or the issuing of a reprimand to Betty Foy for letting him go dangerously unsupervised. Our sense of his dignity, by contrast, leads apparently nowhere. That is one of the odd things about it. In trying not to feel as Johnny does, even if that were possible, but, instead, as his mother does, I choose to call human the things that one *can* have human hopes and fears about. Possibly Wordsworth would go even further. He would say, I become human by the self-knowledge acquired in coming to recognize that I have such feelings. (That is the sense of one of Wordsworth's greatest lines, a line that floats almost free of its context in "Resolution and Independence": "By our own spirits are we deified.") My attention to Johnny ultimately says something about him; but it does so only after it has said something about me. A dignity I withheld from him I would at once have failed to confirm in myself. According to Wordsworth (if I have his doctrine right), the only relevant evidence is the mark of respect and self-respect that is shown or stinted.

"The great secret of morals," wrote Shelley in *A Defence of Poetry*, "is love; or a going out of our nature, and an identification of ourselves with the beautiful which exists in thought, action, or person, not our own." One remarkable thing about this definition is its refusal to confine the object of identification to a person; we may equally sympathize with an action or a thought: an extension and decomposition of the idea of sympathy that seems consistent with Shelley's most original poetry. But notice that on his view—which Shelley derived from Wordsworth's early poems and the preface to *Lyrical Ballads*—the more unlikely or remote the path of sympathy, the surer the proof of moral imagination. Thus, to sympathize with someone like myself is commendable, perhaps, but it shows nothing much. It is a plausible extension of the future-regarding aspect of ordinary egotism, and the scriptural warning applies: "For if ye love them that love you, what reward have ye?" (Matthew 5:46). But to feel with the mother who has lost her idiot boy, or, as in *Frankenstein*, with a monstrous creature who must learn humanity from people even as he finds that people turn away in horror and disgust—these are truer tests of "a going out of our nature."

So far, I have been discussing the theory of moral relations: a topic outside the realm of practical morality. But one extension to our ideas of justice seems clear. What I owe to people like me is a duty whose performance comes easily. Carrying it out is like paying dues. By contrast, justice to those who are not my kind is surprising, unrehearsed. The idiom of seventeenth- and eighteenth-century moral philosophy—as shown in the characterization of moral duties by writers like Samuel Pufendorf and William Paley—understates the contrast when it calls an "imperfect" rather than a perfect obligation a prosperous person's giving of shelter to a miserable houseless man. Whatever we may call it, Wordsworth and Shelley place conduct of this sort in a separate category; they find it a source of wonder and admiration that they deny to a thought, action, or person similar to one's own. The moral imagination here takes an interest in people it cannot call "neighbors" without enlarging the meaning of a neighbor. I turn now to Burke once more, for a different kind of example, in which the metaphor of a wardrobe could not possibly have served his purpose.

In 1783, when Burke began in earnest his prosecution of the British East India Company, the company itself was the government of Bengal. It had enjoyed an official sanction from the 1760s onward whose peculiarity has been captured in recent histories by P. J. Marshall, Frederick Whelan, and Nicholas Dirks, among others. The company was a trading power, which a series of ad hoc adjustments had vested with political authority: "a state in the disguise of a merchant," as Burke called it. Its operations were handled by the members of a governing counsel in Bengal, itself answerable to the directors in London; but the council could hire agents to collect rents and taxes, and it could recruit mercenary or tribal armies to fight the wars of a company whose sovereignty was identical with that of Britain. It also effectively controlled a supreme court that had recently been appointed to dispense laws of a British severity to the native subjects of India.

Several plausible cases of misconduct or criminal action were brought before Burke and other India reformers in the House of Commons in the early 1780s; it was understood that their response would affect the control of the future governance of India. Earlier Burke himself had rejected calls for an inquiry into the finances and management of the company, on the ground that this would constitute an intrusion on a corporate charter. By 1783 he had changed his mind; and Fox's East India Bill, which he now supported, would have assigned all authority over the company to two government commissions, one for administration and one for commerce, to run their terms regardless of changes of ministry. Whatever one thought of their plan, it was, as the historian Richard Pares observed, the first time in the reign of George III that someone had tried to take the politics out of an interest that had always been purely political.

What could justify so radical a step? Burke starts his answer by pointing out that the East India men are corrupting the government of England by the wealth they extract from India and use for self-aggrandizement.

> Arrived in England, the destroyers of the nobility and gentry of a whole kingdom will find the best company in this nation, at a board of elegance and hospitality. Here the manufacturer and husbandman will bless the just and punctual hand that in India has torn the cloth from the loom, or wrested the scanty portion of rice and salt from the peasant of Bengal, or wrung from him the very opium in which he forgot his oppressions and his oppressor. They marry into your families; they enter into your senate; they ease your estates by loans; they raise their value by demand; they cherish and protect your relations which lie heavy on your patronage; and there is scarcely an house in the kingdom that does not feel some concern and interest that makes all reform of our eastern government appear officious and disgusting; and on the whole, a most discouraging attempt. In such an attempt you hurt those who are able to return kindness, or to resent injury.

14

If you succeed, you save those who cannot so much as give you thanks. All these things show the difficulty of the work we have on hand: but they show its necessity too. Our Indian government is in its best state a grievance. It is necessary that the correctives should be uncommonly vigorous; and the work of men, sanguine, warm, and even impassioned in the cause. But it is an arduous thing to plead against abuses of a power which originates from your own country, and affects those whom we are used to consider as strangers.

Here, the test of the justice of a moral imagination turns out to be justice to a stranger. Burke is closer, in fact, to Shelley than he is to himself in his writings on France. Yet, Burke confesses with bewilderment, there is a puzzle about acting on someone's behalf across so wide a distance: a puzzle that perhaps in the nature of empire cannot finally be solved.

The people connected with India whom one comes to know in England are those who have profited from the company's trade, rent, and less official exactions, those who convert their financial gain into social standing and political power at home. They have injured the people of India, but the cries are lost over the thousands of miles of ocean that separate England from the subcontinent it governs by proxy. Friendship and association with the former plunderers are inviting to the English at home. They "marry into your families" and "enter into your senate" and give out loans that protect your relations; the benefit you can realize from their crimes is now familiar and conspicuous. Meanwhile, whatever gratitude the Indians may feel for the defense of their rights is valueless, since it is the gratitude of people without political strength, and it cannot be heard across the barriers of language and race. Given the illicit pressures on opinion in England and the censorship of perception, Burke's motive for addressing the fate of India must have had a deeper basis than conventional good breeding and the "wardrobe of a moral imagination" in his later sense. To share his urgency regarding the reform of British India, one must break out of the domesticating habits for which the wardrobe served as a metaphor—the socialized forbearance toward neighbors and their fortune, with no questions asked—and recover a natural indignation on behalf of the oppressed of every race. One must make one's own the pleasures and pains of the Indians as members of the same species as oneself. If I think as a citizen of the empire, under this moral imperative, I must suppose they are people who have as much right as I have not to be ruled by a government that in its best state is a grievance.

Burke says that only men of warm passions can initiate so thoroughgoing a change. This emphasis implies that one cause of the evil may be a wrong or weak imagining: the sort of thinking that assumes that the Indians need a certain way of life, about which they may receive instruction from a political or economic theory or a proper historical understanding. Burke, on the contrary, has not come to assist the Indians mainly from a sense of their suffering; rather, what strikes him is that his own country is the cause of their suffering: he identifies himself with the transgressions of Britain in order to accuse his neighbors. Burke seems to say that the motive for sympathetic action must come from learning the work of truth and constancy that is becoming to one's own dignity. It is not a question of what I owe to the sufferer but of what I owe to myself. A usual mistake of imagination—especially when heated by ambition—is to think of other people as moral objects while regarding oneself as a moral actor. Burke's deep intimation is that the momentum of commerce, the insolence of power, and an empire's appetite can only be checked if the rulers of Britain now resolve on what they will *not* permit themselves to do.

I do not know how much of Burke's writing Lincoln had read, but he showed a similar grasp of political psychology in one important respect. Characteristically, Lincoln traced people's collective actions to a basis in shared customs, sentiments, and habits of thought. Like Burke, he knew that he was living in a revolutionary time, and he believed any radical change, if it was to be a change for the better, had to draw on moral commitments and social practices with a long past. If one opposed slavery, one ought not to say that the Constitution was a covenant with death and an agreement with hell, but rather say that the words "All men are created equal" really meant to include all men, and that the Constitution, however imperfectly at first, always existed to realize this promise of the Declaration of Independence. Lincoln understood as Burke did a singular truth about moral persuasion in politics: that an injustice you aim to correct had better be seen not from the point of view of the victim, but from the perspective of the agent who commits the injustice, the person who profits from it. The sense of pity, whatever need it satisfies, is practically useless to the cause of reform, but the particulars of self-accusation may be useful. With Lincoln on slavery, as with Burke on empire, the pressure for reform comes from a redefinition of self-respect or sympathy with myself. Some contrast between what I am and what I ought to be startles me and leads to self-discontent, which then issues in remedy or redress.

The most instructive passages come from the years 1856 and 1857, when Lincoln was starting to draw the line between two possible futures for the United States, in one of which the states would be all slave, and in the other all free. The following passage deals only with the feelings, manners, and expectations of white people:

> Can men vote truly? We will suppose that there are ten men who go into Kansas to settle. Nine of these are opposed to slavery. One has ten slaves. The slaveholder is a good man in other respects; he is a good neighbor, and being a wealthy man, he is enabled to do the others many neighborly kindnesses. They like the man, though they don't like the system by which he holds his fellow-men in bondage. And here let me say, that in intellectual and physical structure, our Southern brethren do not differ from us. They are, like us, subject to passions, and it is only their odious institution of slavery, that makes the breach between us. These ten men of whom I was speaking, live together three or four years; they intermarry; their family ties are strengthened. And who wonders that in time, the people learn to look upon slavery with complacency?

You cannot vote truly, Lincoln says, in a state or territory where one kind of person has inordinate influence, and where the slave owner, with his human property and the power it confers, himself contributes to a brutalization of manners. In a sense, the more amiable the slave owner is, the worse his influence on society, since, by the effects of his wealth and his kindness together, his example weakens the natural aversion people generally feel toward slavery (if they have not been inured to it from childhood). Now suppose that the vicious habits of the slave system— contempt for the rights of some people, acceptance of inequality, and accommodation to the spectacle of arbitrary power—suppose these habits are taken into the wardrobe of a moral imagination. What then becomes of the morale of a free people? We shall come to look on slavery with complacency; but from the moment we do, "our progress in degeneration" is "pretty rapid" (as Lincoln says in a letter about this time.)

A second passage may be read as completing the same thought; but it belongs to a different context. Chief Justice Taney's majority opinion in the Dred Scott case presented a new theory about the meaning of the Constitution. It said the framers never contemplated the admission of Negroes to citizenship; that none of the rights of citizens had been intended to apply to Negroes; and that the rights of property of a slaveholder were such that no new territory could legally exclude slavery. There was a reason why Lincoln called this finding "an astonisher in legal history." He believed that the founders of the United States did have in their minds the significance of the words "All men are created equal" when they framed the Constitution a decade after they signed their names to the Declaration. And Lincoln thought they gave those words the same sense that most readers give them. But if the Negro is a human being and if, knowing that he is one, we in our own minds ratify the wrong of the Dred Scott decision, what are we doing to ourselves?

All the powers of earth seem rapidly combining against [the black man]. Mammon is after him; ambition follows, and philosophy follows, and the Theology of the day is fast joining the cry. They have him in his prison house; they have searched his person, and left no prying instrument with him. One after another they have closed the heavy iron doors upon him, and now they have him, as it were, bolted in with a lock of a hundred keys, which can never be unlocked without the concurrence of every key; the keys in the hands of a hundred different men, and they scattered to a hundred different and distant places; and they stand musing as to what invention, in all the dominions of mind and matter, can be produced to make the impossibility of his escape more complete than it is.

To the extent that we support the decision as the law of the land, we ourselves become the jailers of a man locked behind the doors of a prison bolted with a hundred keys, and the keys in a hundred hands. Imprisonment without any means of redress or accountability by the jailer meets the commonest definition of tyranny. And as with British India in the 1780s, so with America in the 1850s: respectable society comes to the assistance of the jailer. Money, political ambition, conventional morality, theology, all play their parts; and for Lincoln this proves the moral bankruptcy of the arrangements to which American society has given way. A contemporary who read these passages and placed them side by side might start to ask questions. Are we happy to be the prosperous jailers of a significant portion of humanity? If we consent to oppressions like these and profit from them directly, as in the South, or indirectly, as in the North, who and what are we?

And yet, once again, as in Burke's description of the misery of British India, we are not quite put into the minds of the sufferers, though Lincoln comes a little closer than Burke: instead of the cloth torn from the loom or the rice taken out of someone's mouth, he gives us the extended image of the prison and the lock and keys. The omission of anecdote and detail points to a salient feature of Lincoln's morality that has not been much noticed. He speaks about slavery more often from the perspective of the master than from that of the slave. His resistance to slavery is founded less on horror and pity than on a conscientious belief in the good of renouncing mastery. "As I would not be a slave," he wrote in a journal note, "so I would not be a master. This expresses my idea of democracy. Whatever differs from this, to the extent of the difference, is no democracy." Almost nowhere does Lincoln speak with contempt of slaveholders—a remarkable fact when you consider that he maintained steady contact with the abolitionists and admired their moral commitment if not their tactics. From the Peoria speech of 1854 through the final speech on reconstruction, Lincoln says "our Southern brethren" have had the bad fortune to inherit an institution that has made them oppressors. If we of the North, he adds, had grown up with slavery as a permitted practice, we would be no better than they are; and if they had grown up in a section free of slavery, they would be no worse than we are.

Behind much oppression and behind the complacency with which we abridge our knowledge of suffering lies a force in human nature as pervasive as habit; namely the force of inhibition, of willful imperceptiveness and self-censorship; a benign-seeming, coercive instinct that aims to bring uniformity to experience and to leave us comfortable and free of doubts. In a central passage of *Mrs. Dalloway*, Virginia Woolf introduces her readers to the god "proportion" whose severe standard guides the clinical practice of the psychiatrist Sir William Bradshaw. Proportion assists Sir William in his important work of sculpting society in order to trim it clear of unseemly shapes:

Proportion, divine proportion, Sir William's goddess, was acquired by Sir William walking hospitals, catching salmon, begetting one son in Harley Street by Lady Bradshaw, who caught salmon herself and took photographs scarcely to be distinguished from the work of professionals. Worshiping proportion, Sir William not only prospered himself but made England prosper, secluded her lunatics, forbade childbirth, penalised despair, made it impossible for the unfit to propagate their views until they, too, shared his sense of proportion. . . .

But Proportion has a sister, less smiling, more formidable, a Goddess even now engaged—in the heat and sands of India, the mud and swamp of Africa, the purlieus of London, wherever in short the climate or the devil tempts men to fall from the true belief which is her own—is even now engaged in dashing down shrines, smashing idols, and setting up in their place her own stern countenance. Conversion is her name and she feasts on the wills of the weakly, loving to impress, to impose, adoring her own features stamped on the face of the populace. . . . But Conversion, fastidious Goddess, loves blood better than brick, and feasts most subtly upon the human will. For example, Lady Bradshaw. Fifteen years ago she had gone under. It was nothing you could put your finger on; there had been no scene, no snap; only the slow sinking, water-logged, of her will into his.

What Sir William's god despises, what it seeks as far as possible to obliterate, is all evidence of idiosyncrasy, every sign of an individual will that turns aside from the drift of the group. This specialist on mental disorders is a well-adapted priest of power and unconscious privilege —or perhaps one should say, of a privilege whose cost and reward is unconsciousness. The connection Woolf draws between his professional status and social authority and the oppression of marriage seems to me far from arbitrary. She has in mind a tacit authority that recruits us to its ends and incorporates us before we can know what we might be without its intervention. And the suicide of a main secondary character of the book, Septimus Warren Smith, the young poet returned from the war, seems to be a direct emanation of the will of Sir William. When Smith has his recurrent fantasy of a brutal and predatory nature under the cover of society—which he signals to himself by the shadowy epigram, "Once you stumble, human nature is on you"—what really haunts him is the confident bad art of Sir William. Though Smith hardly knows why, he knows he must defect from the rule of proportion and conversion; and he is satisfied even to part from life, so long as suicide frees him from the burden of these gods.

The names "proportion" and "conversion" are drawn by Woolf from different idioms—proportion from aesthetics, conversion from religion and morals. By her choice of terms, I take her to be saying that lack of imagination is a necessary condition for keeping up a society based on subordination, a society in which balance and stability are valued more than justice and liberty. We do not want to think so, of course; and we use other names: mental hygiene, sanity, propriety, decency. But the end is to tyrannize by the imposition of uniformity, suavity, compliance—all those estimable qualities that serve to polish experience and to give it every quality of art except courage and surprise. The fate of those whom society crushes or the state overrules is suffered first and last in the mind of the individual. Woolf connects this fact with the loss of identity in marriage because proportion and conversion, working together, turn every two into one. Society is worse because it crushes more than two at a time.

There are conversions so public and voluntary we may feel they deserve a different name. Let us call them transformations, without supposing that we have brought to light an altogether different phenomenon. An example within living memory was Martin Luther King's "A Time to Break Silence," delivered at Riverside Church, New York, in April 1967. It may be symptomatic of our own love of proportion that this has not become one of King's best-known speeches or writings. Yet "A Time to Break Silence" marks a courageous choice by a leader of a movement to pass beyond his parish and speak for people whose sufferings he had no formal obligation to address. King was pleading here not for the rights of black people, but against abuses of a power that originated from his own country, and that affected those whom we were used to consider as strangers.

> What do the peasants think as we ally ourselves with the landlords and as we refuse to put any action into our many words concerning land reform? What do they think as we test our latest weapons on them, just as the Germans tested out new medicine and new tortures in the concentration camps of Europe? Where are the roots of the independent Vietnam we claim to be building? Is it among these voiceless ones?
>
> We have destroyed their two most cherished institutions: the family and the village. We have destroyed their land and their crops. We have cooperated in the crushing of the nation's only non-Communist revolutionary political force—the unified Buddhist church. We have

supported the enemies of the peasants of Saigon. We have corrupted their women and children and killed their men. What liberators!

Now there is little left to build on—save bitterness. Soon the only solid physical foundations remaining will be found at our military bases and in the concrete of the concentration camps we call "fortified hamlets." The peasants may well wonder if we plan to build our new Vietnam on such grounds as these. Could we blame them for such thoughts? We must speak for them and raise the questions they cannot raise. These too are our brothers.

This is an argument against destruction, on behalf of the great secret of morals which is love, or mercy. King imagines himself in the position of the Vietnamese under the bombing sorties of B-52s, or the casualties of what was called the "pacification program." He imagines the situation of people who watch their society destroyed for their own sake to yield a better and more modern and liberal society.

King asks his listeners to look at what is actually happening; but he does so without firsthand testimony by the sufferers. Indeed, his description, unlike Lincoln's, is not even heightened by metaphor; yet its purpose comes out plainly in his repetition of the most important word of the passage, *we*. What have we done? Who are we that have done this? It is a summons to a personal and national inquest. King said in an interview about this time that he could no longer segregate his protest against injustice at home from his knowledge of the injustice his country was doing abroad. He supposed this was an issue in which black and white Americans together were implicated. Self-respect, he says, forbids us from seeing ourselves as the authors of these deeds. What then shall we do to become ourselves again?

A critical feature of the moral imagination I have been exploring is that justice to a stranger comes to seem a more profound work of conscience than justice to a friend, neighbor, or member of my own community. This goes against the premise, shared by political conservatives and moral conservatives (some of whom are political liberals), that every person builds up loyalties and public affections from the inside out, the circle of those closest to me naturally taking priority over the circle of those who are less close. But one can penetrate the falseness of that communitarian diagram simply by recalling any strong feeling one has ever had of the reality of a person about whom one knew very little. One may conclude that, to acquire such reality, it is not necessary for a stranger to be defined or made to acquire "thickness" by the data of ethnicity, race, or class.

This rejection of remedial action from a predigested idea of people's needs may serve to bring into view a second feature of moral imagination. Its authority calls on me to act in accord with my own constitution. An ideal of virtuous conduct, to borrow a thought from Pindar, offers guidance by this maxim: "Become what you have learned yourselves to be." So I refuse to treat myself as less than a moral judge and agent; every action becomes a matter also of my duties toward myself. For needs and sufferings, when entered into from the point of view of the sufferer, are liable to be mischievous; they excite an impulse toward relief that can justify any improvement, any therapeutic cure, any act of assimilation or conquest. They vindicate my choice by a generous picture of myself as a doer. In this way, the evangelical doer of the nineteenth century was excited to action by regarding himself as an agent of civilization. The doer of the twenty-first century may achieve a similar result by regarding himself as an agent for the global market, or for the spread of universal rights. The moral imagination warns against such complacent self-regard.

To pass from Burke as a critic of empire to Martin Luther King on the duties of non-violent resistance is not so long a stretch as most people imagine. Both were faithful to a particular constituency—the Rockingham Whigs, the Southern Christian Leadership Conference—and by their apparently divergent acts of protest, they did not suppose they were undermining that constituency. Still, in their campaigns against the Vietnam War and the East India Company they went against the prudent advice of many who had been close to them. I have stressed the perception that they could not do otherwise and still be themselves. But one must also record an impression that every biographer of both men has been struck by. Burke and King alike were possessed of an elemental keenness that made them angry at the sight of injustice. They did not, like so many public men, avert their eyes from such exposure; and when it came unbidden, they registered a shock. King resolved to give his best energies to opposing the Vietnam War from the moment when in the January 1967 issue of *Ramparts* he saw pictures of Vietnamese children burned by napalm. It happened over breakfast and the reaction was almost physical. Something similar occurred when Edmund Burke first read the accounts of British officials approving the torture of the Begums of Oudh in order to obtain their treasure. The Begums were Indian princesses, under a foreign code of conscience, but when Burke saw their story he recoiled as he would from an assault on an

English lady, and spoke as if he would avenge even a look that threatened them with insult. In King and Burke, the sense of anger at injustice is strong and perpetual: we come to feel they have sharper sight for the abuses of power than ordinary men and women; we also feel that an injustice they witness calls out to them instantly. It is as if a layer of insensibility that normally weakens, muffles, and protects us, were missing from their composition.

Both King and Burke had in view a difficult-to-persuade audience like ourselves. Why difficult? The liberal contract theory of the seventeenth and eighteenth centuries pictured the citizen as one who proves the reality of natural rights by binding himself to other members of society. This theory rests on an idea of both individual and collective freedom in which rights tend to implicate needs (the right of property as acquisition, the need for property as protection). To the extent that the political contract is sealed by its responsiveness to needs, it is interventionist regarding the conscience of the individual. For the same reason, liberal theory gives support to the psychology of intervention in a larger sense. I draw here on a recent paper by Uday Mehta, "The Language of Peace and the Practice of Non-Violence," which traces a consistent challenge to the contract theory of collective legitimation from Gandhi's idea of conscientious non-violent resistance.

Since, observes Mehta, the contract supposed by the state-of-nature theorists must be seen to confer benefits equally on all, it requires sufficient power—including a possible resort to violence—to overcome opposition to those benefits or to remove the sufferings imposed by people who obstruct the full reach of the benefits. To secure that object, the state is awarded a monopoly on violence, and it takes as one of its proper functions the making of war for the sake of preserving peace. What then becomes of the individual? He is called on, from time to time, to approve or cooperate with the violence of the state. It may seem that the pragmatic good performed by a limited constitutional state more than offsets the evil of this encroachment. Yet Gandhi's objection to the theory, as Mehta interprets it, cannot be met in this way, for the assimilation of each person into the plan of benefit, improvement, and clearance of distress, itself embodies a trespass against individual conscience: at the very least it presumes that all the work of conscience can be done collectively. The individual is absolved of both credit and blame, because the decision has been routed through the imperative of the common good. By contrast, non-violent resistance, which relies on persuasion and excludes force, may favor a collective life distrustful of violence and not prone to interventions that place us outside ourselves.

The modern morality in which the person, and then the state, are supposed to sympathize with the needs of the sufferer, is vitiated by an original error. For this theory removes from the scene the actor, the doer, who is called upon to confer the benefits or relieve the suffering. He can easily come to think that his conscience is not on the line, since the machine of collective remedy triggers a suitable attention to reform. All the interventions take care of themselves without regard to the integrity of the person who acts. Indeed, that person is emancipated to commit violence without remorse. But there is surely something wrong with this exemption; one cannot help feeling that mischief could come of it. For it treats the ideal of the common good with a half-conscious cynicism, as if the common good might be achieved without the virtue of integrity.

In a remarkable essay, "Gandhi, the Philosopher," Akeel Bilgrami suggests that the distinctive mark of Gandhi's thinking is a tension between personal integrity and a communal participation that evades or dissipates conscience. Regard for integrity, as Bilgrami points out, tends to awaken conscience, or the actor's awareness of his individual constitution. It informs conduct and brings action into coherence with judgment. At its bidding, I do not hope to implicate, improve, organize or modernize other people as a consequence of the adequacy and rightness of my judgment; nor do I condemn them if they decline to follow me. I reserve to myself the duty to resist any invitation or compulsion to follow *them* when they do wrong. Integrity, to the extent that it influences others, works by example and not by precept or conversion. Nonviolent protest is thus a tactic that becomes more than a tactic, since its self-sufficiency and its restraint may have an exemplary power. Something of this train of thought is familiar to American readers from Thoreau's essay "Civil Disobedience."

It is only a step from Gandhi to Martin Luther King by way of Thoreau; and only another step when we turn to the source Gandhi acknowledged for his thinking about integrity: Ruskin's pamphlet on the duties of commerce, *Unto This Last*. Ruskin here contests what he thinks is the central maxim of modern political economy, "Buy in the cheapest market, and sell in the dearest"—a maxim in which he discerns the essence of moral anarchy. Whatever the adepts of economic correctness may say, there is a radical fault in a system that, as the cost of distributing the benefits of the market, turns each buyer and each seller into a knave. At the heart of Ruskin's critique is the immoralism of the capitalist market, when measured against an ideal of chivalric honor. He makes this plain in the opening essay of *Unto This Last* when he numbers the ancient professions of soldier, pastor, physician, lawyer, noting the existence of a good bestowed by each and a corresponding harm that each must be willing to die to prevent. The soldier must risk his life rather than desert his post; the physician must risk his life rather than violate his oath as a healer. And the merchant?—"What," says Ruskin, "is *his* 'due occasion' of death?" If the merchant does not know the duties in the service of which he would sacrifice himself and his fortune, how can he know what good he serves?

> Buy in the cheapest market?—yes; but what made your market cheap? Charcoal may be cheap among your roof timbers after a fire, and bricks may be cheap in your streets after an earthquake; but fire and earthquake may not therefore be national benefits. Sell in the dearest?— yes, truly; but what made your market dear? You sold your bread well to-day: was it to a dying man who gave his last coin for it, and will never need bread more; or to a rich man who to-morrow will buy your farm over your head; or to a soldier on his way to pillage a bank in which you have put your fortune?
>
> None of these things you can know. One thing only you can know: namely, whether this dealing of yours is a just and faithful one, which is all you need concern yourself about respecting it; sure thus to have done your own part in bringing about ultimately in the world a state of things which will not issue in pillage or in death.

"The Roots of Honor" was the name that Ruskin gave to one chapter of *Unto This Last*—an homage to a phrase of Burke's describing chivalric virtue in *A Letter to a Noble*

Lord. So we are thrown back again on the analysis by an eighteenth-century reformer of a company that acts in the place of a government and fails to know what pillage or plunder it ought to deny itself.

I think that there is in fact a continuous coherence in the thought about public duty and conscience that passes through Burke, Wordsworth, Lincoln, Ruskin, Woolf, Gandhi, and King. Different as they are, I take all of them to be saying one thing. We are lifted wrongly out of ourselves by the idea of a system that absolves us before the fact, whether that system is an empire, a Union, an economy, or a national security state in the grip of perpetual emergency. I do not mean by these examples to suggest that global commerce or mass democracy or the profession of psychiatry or the contract theory of government is, in itself, an enemy of integrity, or that there is a reflex passage from any of these to proselytism for state violence and the abuses of empire. None of these entities is in every imaginable form an evil. The use of moral imagination is to gauge the self-deception that intervenes when in the apparent service of highminded aims we come to describe our appetites as needs.

The human creature loves to justify itself. It will generate adequate explanations of any conduct, however brutal, in order to show itself uncontaminated by the evil it has set out to cure. In this endless adventure of rationalization, pity serves as a unique and trusted assistant, since the presence of pity assures us that we can feel generously. Yet pity can be made agreeable to selfishness. Blake prophesied in "The Human Abstract":

> Pity would be no more
> If we did not make somebody Poor

And Mercy no more could be
If all were as happy as we.

And mutual fear brings peace,
Till the selfish loves increase:
Then Cruelty knits a snare,
And spreads his baits with care.

He sits down with holy fears
And waters the ground with tears;
Then Humility takes its root
Underneath his foot.

The pity of Jesus was spontaneous, gratuitous, the mover of conscience to acts of mercy. It was a human and divine going out of his nature on behalf of the miserable. What the projectors of nation, empire, and the rational market did, according to Blake, was to conventionalize pity and set it to regular work. The good it brought could then be seen as a fortunate by-product of the evil with which it cooperated. This symmetry, of vicious policy with virtuous compensation, gave a pleasing odor to the poison of heartlessness. The Christian virtue that instructs us to relieve those in adversity is corrupted by the satisfaction it takes in the persistence of misery and the sheer accidents of inequality. No inequality, no pity.

And mutual fear brings peace. Hobbes had thought this a scientific law of politics among individuals ruled by a sovereign—a law that could assure individuals remaining at peace anyway with each other. Blake replies that the passions of love and hate cannot be deployed so mechanically and still assure the negation of their likely effects: the fear to which you become accustomed in one realm, foments cruelty in another. Public life and private morality are in this way not insulated from each other's effects. Cruelty knits his snare even for instincts not initially disposed to cruelty, and it waters them with "holy fears"—the threat to our happiness and our property comes to be seen as a threat to something higher, for which human sacrifice is warranted; a sacrifice we might shrink from offering, but for the conviction that the fears are holy. The final perversion of moral feeling, says Blake, is to cover with humility those acts of collective self-will that involve collective sacrifice. I, too, suffer for the cruelty I commit; I suffer in thinking that others must suffer at my hands; I weep for the fact that I am the chosen instrument of necessary violence; I shed holy tears for torments brought into being by a system that humbles me as it tramples others.

What is lost in this human process of self-justification? The answer is everything Blake means by "The Divine Image"—the title of the poem he wrote as the companion and antithesis of "The Human Abstract." Dignity, magnanimity, every inward relation to the content and consequence of the acts I perform or ratify by an act of will, these are the things that are lost as I dwindle into a tool. That Blake was a believer in non-violence may be doubted in view of his poems on the French and American revolutions; but as a moral psychologist, he was of the party of Gandhi and King. He says that resistance to cruelty begins with resistance to oneself. That is the sense of his proverb, "Without contraries is no progression"; and also, "Opposition is true friendship." Actual enemies do exist, yet perpetual brooding on the identity of friend and enemy is a disease that chokes all roads to self-knowledge. Besides, there is a difference between thinking that some part or aspect of a person is at enmity with my interests, and believing myself possessed of a science so perfect and preemptive that I am forbidden to think about the person and am allowed only to plan his destruction (or what comes to the same thing, his total absorption into my enterprises).

Such deformations of morality come from a love of power that may be indistinguishable, in practice, from the compulsion to be doing something—knowing, conquering, and never letting be. In *Orientalism,* Edward Said wrote memorably about Flaubert's mockery of the nineteenth-century European dream of total knowledge and the concomitant dream of empire; and he remarked with bafflement the indifference of the ideologists to the botched debris of their dreams: "failed revolutions, wars, oppression." However balked by failure, they kept up their incorrigible "appetite for putting grand, bookish ideas quixotically to work immediately." This craving for immediate effect is essential, also, to the diagnosis of power I have borrowed from the writers on moral imagination. Said went on to say of the achievements of nineteenth-century orientalist scholarship: "What such science or knowledge never reckoned with was its own deeply ingrained and unself-conscious bad innocence and the resistance to it of reality." That is a striking formulation: bad innocence; an innocence that denies reality. How can innocence be bad? Blake would answer, By wishing to perpetuate itself as innocence; by remaining impervious to the intractable particulars of reality. Power rarely persists in the face of constant contradiction, but, when helped by bad innocence, there is no mischief or wickedness of which it is not capable. The writers in the tradition I have been recalling are all in this sense destroyers of bad innocence.

My argument rests on an intuition of moral psychology. The aim has been to find a source of resistance to the most elusive of vices, self-deception. And the place to look for self-deception, the writers I have quoted all agree, is in the texture of human conduct, in our manners or habits of self-regard. But how to guard against a mystification of manners? Why should manners be as consequential as these writers say they are? It might seem that they are themselves often a mask for the real relations of privilege and privation; that they cover more than they disclose; that, when appeased, they produce a semblance of good conscience that excuses the worst oppressions of society. Is it not possible that we conceal from ourselves, precisely through the softening hygiene of manners, the cruelties we ourselves commit? Do we not, by a thoughtless choice of approved relations, absolve ourselves of our crimes against strangers? Complicity in a system of accepted feelings—including the outlets of accepted reform—in this way might be seen to abet our blindness to the actual harm we do.

The criticism is more than plausible. A regime of honest oversight, for example, such as Burke proposed for the British in India, could render the exactions of power all the more insidious. The view that it *tends* to do so is broadly accepted by recent postcolonial scholars, many of them influenced by Michel Foucault; and the tone of Burke's protective warning about men who "marry into your families" can be made to interpret Lincoln's warning about our acceptance of the slave owner as a neighbor. We may only abate an evil in order to guard ourselves against pollution; such a concern with domestic morale, so it is said, falsely narrows the culprit; and in that sense, all emphasis on corruption of manners may lighten the burden of conscience by picturing an evil that is not systemic. And yet Burke and Lincoln impart a constant wariness of the adjustments by which we square a public abuse with ourselves by removing a symptomatic part of its façade. They constantly bring their questions closer to home. On the other hand, the non-moral critique of moral imagination, offered by Foucault and others, issues from a reluctance to speak at all of such things as integrity and conscience. This reluctance is premised on the belief that the foundations of social action lie in relations of status and power that are impenetrable by our knowledge of persons.

To grant that premise is to deny that every man and every woman embodies an integral principle, a coherence. But once you begin to regard yourself as an end and think of what it is to constitute yourself, the data of manners appear no longer an affair of the surface but the marrow of conduct: they command interest at every point, and nothing rivals their claim to give substance and stress to experience. A state constitutes itself by a framework of laws, we say; but it does not make itself just as it pleases. It presumes the constitution of the person, the vitality and sustaining presence of individuals who have gone to the work of creating themselves. This stubborn faith accounts for the way that Burke, Lincoln, and Woolf, especially, ask their readers or listeners to put themselves on the line: every gesture, they seem to say, must be tallied and answered for. They would like to hold each person responsible at every moment. They are pointing to a sense in which the fashionable saying, "The personal is the political," might turn out to be true and important. In this way they look to reverse a tendency they see in the modern state and society: a tendency to subdue the individual to a point that leaves every person both impotent and exonerated. As the corrupt Christian pleads, "I sinned, but I can put it off on Jesus," so the corrupt citizen is tempted to say, "I did not refuse, but my yes was meaningless, it was the system that did it."

The use of moral imagination as a source of resistance is clearest when one tries to think in opposition to collective enterprises such as the manipulation of sentiments to pump up a war of aggression. The person who sees himself as a doer, sees others, and, *a fortiori*, other nations as worthy or unworthy objects of his moral will. It is an expansive feeling, quite without the pressure of self-inquiry, and it naturally falls in with expansive policies. Such a person has in view a great civilizing good. The logic of benevolent imposition need not be looked at too closely. The person, on the contrary, who sees himself as both doer and object, who asks what a given act is doing to himself and his neighbors, is less a prey to an imagination heated by proselytism and war. For humanitarian wars and other such projects gather adherents chiefly from an impression that the good they bring is more than personal. The end of human action becomes a horizon formed by the profiles of the beneficiaries of all our actions; and as we act for them and act again, that horizon continually recedes. Gandhi was speaking against this justification of cruelty by success, this process of self-confirming rationalization, when he asked the "Reader" of his dialogue on Indian Home Rule, *Hind Swaraj*, to resist "the argument that we are justified in gaining our end by using brute force because the English gained theirs by using similar means. It is perfectly true that they used brute force and that it is possible for us to do likewise, but by using similar means we can get only the same thing that they got. You will admit that we do not want that." Those words may make a credo for all who act from moral imagination. Whether by the ruses of philanthropy, enlightenment, conversion, or war, there is no escaping the question, What shall we be? But even as we ask it, we must admit it to be a weak translation of another question, repeated many times over. Who shall I become?

2008

CHAPTER 2

A DISSENT ON CULTURAL IDENTITY

HUME SAID THAT ABSOLUTE MONARCHY WAS "THE EASIEST death, the true *Euthanasia*, of the British constitution." I offer some notes and questions about a line of political apologetics that if pursued far would lead to the euthanasia of liberal society. In the past two decades, an argument first ventured in academic circles, which associates human dignity with cultural identity, has made deep inroads toward acceptance by liberal theorists. The theorists assent to the culturalist argument from a belief that we ought, as a matter of democratic duty or international realism, to widen our support for acts of membership in identity-cultures. It is understood that in the course of doing so we shall have to modify our idea of the proper duties of the liberal state, in keeping with the demands of two constituencies: the speculative thinkers who "construct" the individual to accord with the supposed priority of the group in the making of identity; and the various sects, clans, and dormant nations that serve as bearers of the revived racial and religious enthusiasms clamoring for recognition and for authority throughout the world today. The call is loudest in states without a tradition of liberal government. It would be a good thing, we are asked to agree, for liberal states to answer the call early, and as fully as possible when they feel it close to home.

"Culturalism" is the thesis that there is a universal human need to belong to a culture—to belong, that is, to a self-conscious group with a known history, a group that by preserving and transmitting its customs, memories, and common practices confers the primary pigment of individual identity on the persons it comprehends. This need, culturalism says, is on a par with the need to be loved by a father and a mother, and with the need for a life of friendships and associations. As I will be compelled to say again and again in these pages, the idea seems to me trivially true. But, taken in the strong sense in which alone it is worth discussing—the sense in which "my culture" is a fact endowed with a dignity and deserving of a respect comparable to the dignity and respect I would claim for myself—the idea seems to me a lie.

The culturalist story acquires its pathos in the usual way, by the personification of an abstract entity. Why would a liberal theorist embrace such an idea? Here I am at a loss; but it is possible to characterize what the theorists are doing when they write with sympathy for the idea of culture. They are trying to shed a habit of irony. They are heeding a wish for compassion from people whose ways, and needs, they are frankly unequipped to understand. The shedding of irony is a gesture that they hope will be taken seriously. Irony, however, seems to be the natural condition of the social critic; and the culturalist idea has imposing consequences for one's sense of what social criticism can be. It brings a characterization of the critic as someone who owes his first loyalty to the community in which his thought, being, and social identity have matured. The critic derives his language, it is said, from this community. Every effort he makes toward a reform of its life and habits will presuppose the critic's rootedness and his desire for continuing membership. The critic works to reform a culture from within the culture. How else *could* he work, if he knows nothing personally that he does not know culturally?

Michael Walzer has defended this conception of the social critic in three books: *The Company of Critics, Interpretation and Social Criticism,* and *Thick and Thin.* A similar picture can be inferred, as I will show, from the writings of Charles Taylor on modern politics and secularization. But I give most attention to Walzer for a particular reason. I have a practical interest in social criticism, and view it as far less "connected" to the expectations of a community than Walzer believes it to be. Critics, and reformist leaders such as Edmund Burke, Abraham Lincoln, and Martin Luther King, often startled or shocked their audiences, opted out of the terms set by a given community or a going debate, and thereby changed the meaning of community by enlarging it. As I see it, a decent appreciation of such critics requires that we reject the culturalist idea. To achieve their ends, they worked from a sense of community that was generous because it had been thinned of its racial and religious and, in some cases, its national connections.

Within liberalism, a congeniality toward illiberal societies *so long as they are real communities* might seem to involve a strange accommodation. If the writers I discuss end up persuading many others that such congeniality is a good thing, it will make a lasting difference to what liberalism takes itself to be. I said "illiberal societies." And yet, at just this point the writers in question shift their stress. Community was a baggy enough word, with an admonitory function in a selfish decade, the 1980s. Now we want a word with more substance, and *society* will not do: it suggests a sharp look at social arrangements, at the workings of the judicial system, the state of tax regulations, and so on. *Culture* is more piquant, if shiftier. In practice it gets its force from a literal correlation with region, religion, and race, in ascending order of importance. These visible markers of culture are emphasized by the liberal culturalists, with an eye on their liberal audience, as if the terms actually mattered in descending order. Race, that *sine qua non* of culture-makers, is frequently left quite out of account, though one may come across delicate mentions of "blood-ties." Culture meanwhile picks up some happier, though still vague, associations from a friendly acquaintance with Mardi Gras, museums of folklore, and ethnic musical groups in universities. Culture becomes the province not so much of the knife-wielding warlords bent on expelling monsters from the outer regions, as of the necklace-carving, lullaby-singing grandparents whose full-blooded ministrations give an ancient resonance to the idea of "home." As the argument proceeds, I will try to keep in mind those necklaces and lullabies. I ask my readers to listen for the sounds of knives being sharpened.

The first attempt by Walzer to sketch a theory of cultural recognition came in his 1990 Tanner Lecture "Nation and Universe." The case was for a universal right to "human flourishing," which can only be understood in the medium of this or that local variant. Each culture is said to "reiterate" in a different way the general hope or yearning. But the differences of expression count, and are to be honored as large differences. This varied and "reiterative" universalism is set over against the Kantian, or "covering-law" universalism, according to which every choice by an individual ought to be made as if against a background of the twin ideas of autonomy and freedom shared by humanity as a whole. A judgment can be agreed on, Kantian universalism seems to say, no matter how wide the distance between the judge and other potential judges in other settings. By contrast, reiterative universalism points out the difficulties of translation enforced by physical or anthropological distance. At the same time, it reserves a place for the particular adaptations or cultural idioms by which ends are realized that may turn out to be universal after all. We iterate (each according to our group's custom) the goods we care about. We look different as we do so, but we are looking differently for something iterable in other idioms. What this comes to, it appears, is universalism with a plea for "thick description" of the variants.

It is not clear at first glance what practical difference separates this view from liberal ideas about enlightened judgment that have a less thoroughly culturalist shading. I suspect one main disagreement is at stake. The demand of culturalism is to heighten continually the moral burden of attention to the expressive phenomena of the group. With this demand goes a tactical subordination of, and a growing incapacity to do even rhetorical justice to, the data of personal and temperamental differences. Indeed, I do not see what to make of the shift of attention unless it backs a hypothesis with practical force: that the individual differences which liberalism existed to protect may be less important, because to our eyes less expressively marked, among people who have grown up in illiberal cultures.

What those people want, what their leaders assure us they want, seems to be group distinction above all. (At least, that is how it looks in translation.) We therefore do them wrong to impose assumptions about individual personality that we take for granted. But which is the grosser paternalism: to say, "None of our brute individualism for you, in your otherwise flourishing, value-filled cultures?" or to say, "We believe personal autonomy to be the final freedom, the aim of the least wicked way of life we can imagine?" Walzer, plainly, would prefer to be neither sort of paternalist, but he is struck by the immodesty of the second assertion. His wish to do justice at all costs to the good of cultural coherence may be traced in many of his choices of words.

A pair of key sentences in "Nation and Universe" sketch a view of the particulars of life that matter most:

> However things are with divine creativity, the values and virtues of human creativity can best be understood in the reiterative mode. Independence, inner direction, individualism, self-determination, self-government, freedom, autonomy: all these can be regarded as universal values, but they all have particularist implications.

The word *particularist* has here been brought in to split the difference between individuals and cultures; the effort is really *to claim the virtues of an individual life for individual cultures*. The particularisms are those of separate peoples, but we are asked for the moment to suppress our knowledge that it is from just such collective agencies as this that personal identity is most at risk. As, in the usage here, *particularism* claims individual traits for a *culture*, so elsewhere *people* will transfer to separate peoples the traits of a *person*. This last transposition occurs in the following sentence: "People have to choose for themselves, each people for itself." Grammatically, the structure is ablative absolute, close to the jimmied-out variety known as a commasplice: two clauses join in a rush, they mimic the speed of a single thought. In the sentence above, however, the comma-splice is also a thought-splice.

Reading for consistency with the singular subject, we come up with "People have to choose for themselves, each person for himself." On the other hand, for consistency with the plural: "Peoples have to choose for themselves, each people for itself." But look at what Walzer actually wrote. Person (singular) and people (a culture) are brought into play in the first clause, in the second only people is cashed, yet we are made to feel that we have learned something important about *persons* (the synonym for people in the first clause, uncashed but kept in play). My experience as a reader is that turns of phrase like this are too subtle in what they accomplish to be a product of conscious planning. When he wrote the sentence—"People have to choose for themselves, each people for itself"—I believe the proper logic for a people was in Walzer's mind. But he did not want to seem to ignore the imperative of personal, or individual, choice; and this gave the misleading cue that undermined the grammar. As it gets worked out, choice is quickly transferred to the culture, its "particularism" being the only relevant one. There may be historical situations, as well as grammars, in which the comma cannot be spliced.

Something similar happens in his use of the phrases *a life* and *a way of life*. An (individual) life has its setting in a (communal) way of life. Does it follow that the way of life supplies the particularities any of us would look for in a life? "In fact," writes Walzer, "it is entirely possible to inherit a life and still possess it as one's own." One might, that is, make the way of life one's own, give it the coloring of a life one says one has chosen. In a complex being the process will not be one of mere ratification. Yet

to attend to all that occurs in such acts of taking possession is beyond the scope of the cultural interpreter, on
Walzer's view. The matter is too intricate. What can rea-
sonably be expected is that the interpreter should evince
a proper regard for a given way of life as it is refracted in
the medium of a shared commitment. "Neither the same
fellowship nor the same idea of respect will be universally
shared—and then what demands respect is only indirectly
the individual himself; it is more immediately the way
of life, the culture of respect and concern, that he shares
with his fellows." The individual will be respected to the
exact degree that he shows his markings by belonging to
a "culture of respect and concern." Contextualized, he is
worthy; alone, he evades our instruments—he must consent to pass unremarked. Notice how cunningly, in this
scheme of thought, the culuralist outcome is clinched in
advance. Every way of life is somebody's way; it did not
come from nowhere. Yet so long as the very possibility of
"respect and concern" is at stake, any individual would be
misguided and possibly heartless to offer a description of
a culture in terms not derived from that culture. If such
descriptions were given credence, we might not consent to
call "a way of life" a life.

Since, argues Walzer, justice itself has been variously
invented, being merely "one more product of human creativity," we ought not to expect "a singular and universal
justice" for all. "Why should we value human agency if we
are unwilling to give it any room for maneuver and invention?" Room for maneuver and invention here denotes
the scope of choice allowed to a particular culture in con-
stituting its *texture*. I draw this last word from aesthetics,
with Walzer's sanction, for he likens the self-invention of
a culture to the creativity of a playwright. A too-liberal

structure of laws, such as might impede the culture from exerting creative control in shaping its members, he compares to the censorship that would prevent the playwright from assuming control of his craft. Thus, in the name of liberal values, the believer in liberal justice is obliged, as an act of cultural faith, to let the good particularism of the culture take charge of its members—their way of life, their life, and their lives, which are different names for the same thing.

"When we think of the nation," concludes Walzer, drawing on Benedict Anderson's *Imagined Communities*, "we are led to think of boundaries . . . and then we are led to think of other nations: this is a useful intellectual progress." Those last words are evasive. It is indeed a mark of intellectual refinement to say to someone: "You are an X and Xishness is real to me," rather than to say "You are a does-not-compute, hence unreal." But that form of progress has no implications for what we may choose to *do* about the X (the person) or Xishness (the culture), once we have admitted either phenomenon to exist. Affectively, it is not clear that the thought of boundaries, a conviction of the otherness of the other side, is any improvement on the despised Kantian model of progress, by which one passes from self-respect to respect for others by saying "You resemble me in the most important way I can imagine: by being similarly human."

"Nation and Universe" was an anthropology and epistemology of the culturalist idea. In a later essay, "The New Tribalism," the bearings are more worldly: what ought to be the liberal response to the struggles for cultural identity and nationhood in Eastern Europe, the Balkans, and elsewhere? "I imagine," writes Walzer in opening, "tens of thousands of old men and women whispering to their grandchildren, singing folk songs and lullabies, repeating ancient stories." They have come out of the deep freeze, they are here to stay, and he must say what he can on their behalf, for "The left has never understood the tribes." Cultural self-definition will prove to be, thinks Walzer, what Communist totalitarianism was not: an eternal fact of human nature. We had better understand it, if only to coexist with it. Neutrality enforced by the state, toward religious and ethnic identity, "is likely to work well only in immigrant societies where everyone has been similarly and in most cases voluntarily transplanted, cut off from homeland and history. In such cases—America is the prime example—tribal feelings are relatively weak." One might choose to treat America as the rare case of normal humanity and not therefore eccentric. Sanity too can be rare. This was the idealism that made Whitman write, in his preface to *Leaves of Grass*: "America does not repel the past or what it has produced under its forms or amid other politics or the idea of castes or the old religions." Whitman added, regarding all those forms that have earned the name of culture, that America "perceives that the corpse is slowly borne from the eating and sleeping rooms of the house." We ought to treat the cultures with respect, as befits the recognition that they are dead and we are living. We ought to treat them with respect, reply the culturalists, in the knowledge that they give us what life we have.

Yet Walzer concedes that all cultures are artificial. The illusion of a natural unity or origin comes from a founding that has receded far enough in the past for its chaotic details to be forgotten. What, then, are we to make of the expedient by which late-coming tribal feelings are evoked to build up a strong conviction of *natural* identity? What do we make of it when the expedient is worked out specifically in relation to government subsidies, educational ideology, the provision of public and forensic space for the cultivation of ethnic identities? Let us hold these questions in mind. For the time being, we are encouraged by Walzer to suppose the confusion will press against natural limits, because "Obviously, there is such a thing as inauthentic tribalism." Obviously? He instances the Katangese secession of 1961.

Speaking as someone who would like to de-authenticate as many ideologies as possible, I see nothing obvious about the process of sorting the authentic from the spurious tribes. Shall duration be the sole criterion? What then of duration that includes an interval of lapsed tribal memory followed by a reassertion from the ground of recovered memory? James Clifford dealt with such a case in "Identity in Mashpee," drawing the moral that, for a *legal* claim of tribal status, the difficulties were apt to be formidable in the eyes of a late, liberal, artificial culture. Shall we judge authenticity then by countable rituals? Or by the number of initiates? With women included? Whether or not the tribe itself counts women? Or by the perishability of its system of belief in the absence of help from a liberal government inspired by culturalist theory? Self-sufficiency might easily be considered evidence of authenticity and hence of worthiness of support. On the other hand, only tribes without self-sufficiency will have the need or the desire for support.

I grind out the paradoxes to show that the claim of authenticity is in this context tautological to the point of inscrutability. Tribalism being a category of authenticity, what is posited in the defective case seems to be an inauthentic authenticity. Can one be sure about Katanga? Had that inauthentic secession worked out politically, it is a fair surmise its backers would seem in a hundred years as authentic as the Irish in Great Britain or the Slovenes in Yugoslavia. Really, the shortest way back to a grasp of authenticity is by a consistent reversion to natural rather than artificial ideas of community. That must mean continuity of blood (such as could be verified under a slide); or of folk depth (such as could be verified by an archaeologist or an ethnomusicologist). The courtroom case for identity in Mashpee was that a tribe in possession again of a custom it had forgotten for generations had as much identity with itself as a person who loses contact with the data of identity while asleep. The trouble with invoking authenticity at all—we shall see by-and-by how irresistible the category has been for the culturalists—is hardly that it fails to contain enough specimens. The applicants are an almost endless array. Many contemporary forms of Satanism are likely to be survivals of the lapsed-identity sort, the most potent of their customs often many centuries old. On the present view, what reason could we cite for barring their adherents from tribal status?

Having in mind the Eurasian republics, Bosnia, and many other recent examples, Walzer remarks: "Rather than supporting the existing unions, I would be inclined to support separation whenever separation is demanded by a political movement that, so far as we can tell, represents the popular will." Still, why not put it the other way: "Rather than support separation, I would be inclined to support the existing unions except when . . . ?" A disposition to favor the separatist claim in practice seems to be an irresistible effect of having granted in theory a superior reality to "particularism." We ought to try to find some good in the separations, if possible; good wherever they convincingly represent the popular will, so far as we can tell. "Let the people go who want to go," Walzer continues. "Many of them won't go all that far." I confess I cannot share the mood of that sentence. Geographically, scarcities of transportation will contract the space in which an exclusionist pilgrimage is executed. Considered any other way, "Many of them won't go all that far" is an astonishing euphemism. In length of atrocious cultural self-invention, the peoples of Bosnia have gone very far while going nowhere.

"If," Walzer affirms, "there turn out to be political or economic disadvantages in their departure, they will find a way to reestablish connections." That would seem to depend on how many links have been severed. How many were the assassinations? How frequent the random killings of civilians? How brutal the tortures, the rapes, the religious and racial propaganda strewing the path of the defeated? In the light of facts like these, "They won't go all that far" is an apothegm almost parental, and generalized from the experience of a parent in a lucky family. It brings poor comfort to the recalcitrant member of the departing tribe, who may have felt driven to go because claimed by her kind, and claimed in a setting where the ugliness of that appropriation was one degree less intolerable than the certain death promised by the culture-hardened members of the rival tribe. Now, what (if any) are the duties of a liberal toward this particular person, whom we are urged to surrender to the vivid particularism of the culture?

The reservation that my question implies has been anticipated in a reserve clause of "The New Tribalism": "I don't mean to underestimate the nastiness of tribal zealots. But weren't the zealots of the religious wars equally nasty?" For "nasty," read "murderous"—but what should follow from such knowledge? The only lesson drawn appears to be that we have an obligation not to interfere with the popular force of a nation coming late to its sovereign cultural identity; on no account may we make it the beneficiary of the lesson we learned from religious wars: that the thing to do with a cultural identity is to keep it to yourself. On what ground do we refrain from speaking to the tribes with *this* understanding? Perhaps we hold back from a simple decency and modesty; and why not, if the stakes are low? To judge by the tenor of these articles, Walzer is fairly sure that religious wars are a thing of the past. I think they could well erupt again. Two highly favorable points about religious wars may as well be admitted. They give a meaning to life, and they give pleasure to many people. Historical experience suggests that one can, with hard persuasive work, shame people out of the brutal pleasure of the violence, since most human beings have other sources of excitement. The best shaming device is the suggestion that cultural identity is nothing to be puffed up about—that there are persons, whose approval is to be desired, who respect people less for their collective self-image than for other traits. My inclination to put the matter in this way must mean I share the Enlightenment prejudice against religion rather more than Walzer does. I share rather less the Enlightenment belief in the inevitability of progress. Anyway, the version of progress he invokes, which manages to encompass progress both toward universality and toward tribal intensities of feeling, is out of my imaginative reach.

What can it mean for liberals, holding the beliefs we hold about politics, to say without a contest: "Let the people go who want to go." Individual interests, even our enlightened interests, may be more exacting than that. Walzer believes (in a formulation I paraphrased earlier) that "the commitment of individuals and groups to their own history, culture, and identity . . . is a permanent feature of human social life"; but in assessing the tribes, his emphasis falls on the history, culture, and identity of groups. It is different when we come to the "divided selves" of the members of the commercial democratic societies. As a citizen of such a society, Walzer says, "I will acquire a more complex identity than the idea of tribalism suggests. I will identity myself with more than one tribe; I will be an American, a Jew, an Easterner, an intellectual, a professor." Only one of these names denotes what most people would call a tribe; the difference here has not been split with very much care. But what must strike anyone reading this characterization of the mobile, multi-essential, divided life of the liberal tribalist is how consciously impoverished it is.

Suppose one described the same citizen as a man of a subtle scholarly temper, with a driving affection toward friends and family, and active benevolence toward many others; animated by a strong impulse of gentleness in all his recorded dealings; a wholly anti-theatrical person with a tacit but deep antipathy to all dramatic displays; one whose appetite to be a spectator at any catastrophe is an absolute zero, but whose aversion to violence leads him to underrate the cost and the infectious nature of violence itself; one whose imagination of disaster may in consequence be cooler than is sometimes desirable in predicting the dark developments of a bad time. This makes, at least, a different and a possible description of the author we have surveyed. It is novelistic rather than abstract and socialized. It aims at the individual rather than the race, and it tries to capture the peculiarities of a temperament.

That cultural identity is "a permanent feature of human life" is trivially true. We all come from somewhere. *Naturam furca expelles, tamen usque recurret*: though you drive out nature with a pitchfork, yet it will come back all the way. It is with culture as with nature: the word, if it means anything, suggests a second nature grafted upon the first until the two become indistinguishable. But why must each of us be more than matter-of-fact in committing our lives to our history, our culture, our identity? They—culture, history, identity—have done many things for us and many things to us. What makes us affect gratitude instead of anger in return? A culture may be like a family. Are we therefore to presume it is a happy family?

We owe nothing to any object or condition as a mere forced consequence of its permanence. Many permanent features of human life are bad and partly eradicable: envy comes to mind. Some features are worth trying to discourage. William Blake would not have agreed that cultural identity is a necessary feature of human life, though he believed that art was and that nature was. How much, Blake asked, that we care for and how much that we habitually associate with culture does *not* come from art, from "mental fight," from the personal imagination that the culturalists ask us to bind down to its origins in culture?

> Every Time less than the pulsation of an artery
> Is equal in its period and value to Six Thousand Years,
> For in this Period the Poet's work is done . . . .

To the culture, there is no substitute for six thousand years. Yet Blake declares that the artist is any man or woman, that his or her particulars are sufficient material for reflection: nothing is faster than thought and nothing weighs more. Does he set the human standard unrealistically high? Do we want to set it realistically low? We had better admit from the first that we are touched by individuals, and by the idea of their lives, and that it is by association with these alone that we ever come close to imagining a race or *its* way of life. Those who would *like* to be moved directly by the latter are sentimentalists; and their effort to be moved is an emotional exertion with a practical correlative. They are preparing themselves by delusive affection for the empty charity of war.

Charles Taylor has long been impressed (as he remarks in an introduction to his *Philosophical Papers*) by "the way in which an individual is constituted by the language and culture which can only be maintained and renewed in the communities he is part of." Though delivered in the tones of common sense, the claim is extreme, and we should digest it slowly. The individual is not merely influenced and partly shaped by language and culture. These things "constitute" the individual. And yet for Taylor the highest ideal of life is "self-realization"—an ideal that has heavily marked the strain of German romanticism that descends from Herder. Self-realization presumes a negative freedom from constraint, but the ideal at its full reach must go beyond that; it touches "some of the most inspiring terrain of liberalism" (as Taylor put it in an essay of 1979, "What's Wrong with Negative Liberty"). To realize oneself is to pass from false into true consciousness. We may each make the passage distinctly, yet, for all of us, self-realization is a discovery of the meaning of life. The quest for self-realization, or self-fulfillment, as Taylor also calls it, is not undertaken by the individual alone. He is given a language by a culture, and his success is contingent on his work in the medium of that language. Self-fulfillment thus belongs, as a local product, to a larger and endless process for which culture supplies the tools. Individual and culture are alike expressive. In works of art, we can say, the individual has his flowering; in the long past of culture and custom, he has his soil. A main duty of the state is to see that the course of cultivation is allowed to go unimpeded.

What is initially puzzling about this view is that it should want to call itself liberal. But perhaps its liberality is assured by the assumption that culture itself is progressive. Taylor appears to have misread Lionel Trilling's *Sincerity and Authenticity* as a narrative of progress, and to have felt the propriety of extending an idea of authenticity to describe culture as well as its constituent persons. All that remained was to find a method by which the routines of authentication could be decently bureaucratized. This method Taylor in fact supplies, with a proposal that liberal societies invent a new legal right: the right to cultural "recognition." The proposal is worked out in some detail in his essay of 1992, "The Politics of Recognition," a secondary purpose of which may be to suggest what the tribes will look like once their struggles for power are reduced from wars for sovereignty to contests for political representation. Before assessing the argument, I must warn that I find Taylor's idea of "recognition" elusive. Its translation from idealist metaphysics to republican politics is an uneasy affair, in ways the translator has not always taken into account. More palpably here than in Walzer, we are confronted with an idea of political fulfillment that is borrowed from aesthetics. There is a revealing moment in Taylor's essay on negative liberty when he observes that freedom without a positive idea of self-realization is "philistine."

Recognition names a gesture or ritual on which Taylor would like to confer legal force. By recognition, a state says to a culture, or a culture says to another culture: "I admit that you have a being (an identity, a collective self) capable and worthy of realization." A piece of extra-curricular knowledge may be useful here. Taylor has been a major public participant in discussions of the separa-tion of Quebec, and he is a declared optimist regarding the probable consequences of separation. His essay is in some ways a Canadian sermon for sympathetic readers in the United States. The cultural negotiations under way in Canada are brought forward as a strenuous but not dis-couraging example of what the future holds for the North Atlantic commercial democracies generally. And on the whole, this prototype compares favorably with such alter-natives as Bosnia and Ireland. Knowing his audience well, Taylor, by the mere evocation of national tranquility, is able to sidestep the challenge of liberal secularism to *all* bargains with cultural identity.

He agrees with Walzer in one large prescriptive assump-tion. We must by no means look skeptically on the claims of a culture—a race, a religion, a tribe, or a not yet rec-ognized nation. Rather, the culture and its claims are legitimate until proved otherwise. But Taylor is willing to specify, more tender-mindedly than Walzer, the harm that may ensue upon "misrecognition"—an idea I confess to finding unintelligible, which Taylor associates with evils quite apart from physical abuse, economic exploitation, and social subordination (for all of which the liberal state already has sanctions). "Real damage, real distortion," says Taylor, can come from misrecognition. What, one might ask, is real recognition? Must it be justified by testimony from solid sources to prove its connection with our old friend authenticity? Can there be wrong but well-meaning recognitions that do less than real damage? These matters are left unaccounted for, but they are in any case *a posteriori* considerations, for it is plain to people of moral intelligence that "the withholding of recognition can be a form of oppression." The premise Taylor requires for this axiom is that human beings are dialogically constituted. We may believe in the dialogue of the mind with itself, or other forms of inner colloquy, but these emerged from an internalization of a public process: they are the forming and reforming of a self-image that was always already social.

My identity is defined, observes Taylor, "as an individual, and also as a culture." Yet the form of that statement is misleading. In his argument, priority is granted again and again to the culture. Personal dignity is mediated by cultural recognition. I learn to value who I am by coming to know that others value the sort of person I am—"sort" being determined not imaginatively or whimsically but from the available social science categories. Race, religion, and native language take precedence over profession, region, and political affiliation. This is a new kind of assumption for a liberal theorist to make. It is not yet firmly entrenched, but Taylor writes as if it were and thereby invites consideration of the question: what would it be like if many liberals came to think like this? When I look into the meaning of the assumption, I am first troubled, then baffled. But Taylor himself soon aborts the inquiry. Instead of the construction of a person by a culture, the topic becomes "the importance of cultural survival." The last word unpredictably changes the tenor of the discussion.

Adequate representation for a culture may have seemed an extension of democratic rights. But, with cultural *extinction* on the line, a plea for cultural entitlement acquires much of the urgency of an appeal for human rights as such. We feel one way about people interested in recognition as a group—another way about a group of people on the brink of dying out as a group. What will become of these people? we ask, and we sympathize. As with the shifts of grammar in Walzer, a collective entitlement is here asserted by soliciting attention to the fate of *persons* (their commitments, their sufferings), but then the appeal is transferred to the *people* to whom the persons belong. In this transposition, Taylor actually goes a step further than Walzer. People, he says, who are bent on the difficult project of cultural survival will want to explore a "politics of difference" based on "judgments about what makes a good life—judgments in which the integrity of cultures has an important place." To ascribe to a culture the virtue of integrity is an exorbitant choice for a left-wing theorist. (For a blood-and-soil conservative or fascist, such a move would be commonplace: ascription of integrity is what is needed to get irredentist politics off the ground.) Suppose, then, that an individual culture requires integrity. What are the consequences for the individual person who requires validation by a culture? Surely the person had better not be skeptical, puzzled, or unresolved on the question of cultural identity.

In reading "The Politics of Recognition," one may feel some doubt whether the author is narrating a development of which he heartily approves or one which he would prefer to qualify, reform, argue with, or in some measure retard. In the following passage an appearance of detachment almost topples into satire:

> What is new . . . is that the demand for recognition is now explicit. And it has been made explicit in the way I indicated above, by the spread of the idea that we are formed

by recognition. We could say that, thanks to this idea, misrecognition has now graduated to the rank of a harm that can be hardheadedly enumerated along with the ones mentioned in the previous paragraph.

The previous paragraph had mentioned "inequality, exploitation, and injustice"; and I find it impossible to grasp "cultural misrecognition" except as a description inclusive of such harms as the above, to which they alone give a pragmatic meaning. Consider misrecognition of a personal kind: it might be expressed in acts of ostracism, which would be a form of injustice. If there were no such result, what could qualify as evidence that misrecognition had even taken place? The strangest word in the passage is "hardheadedly." Are we to understand the misrecognized as hardheaded, in the sense of calculating, when they deliver their complaint? Or are the sympathizers hardheaded, in the sense of cynical, when they decide the complaint must be met and the bargainers recognized?

When Taylor comes to describe the goods of an identity-culture, he is not far from characterizing the goods already associated with the life of a liberal society.

> Merely on the human level, one could argue that it is reasonable to suppose that cultures that have provided the horizon of meaning for large numbers of human beings, of diverse characters and temperaments, over a long period of time—that have, in other words, articulated their sense of the good, the holy, the admirable—are almost certain to have something that deserves our admiration and respect.

The few qualities listed above that do not belong to the usual ascriptive traits of "democratic character" are such as might be fostered by any society that functions *as* a society. In short, the mesh is at once too fine and too wide. Nazi Germany, the extreme case of an integral culture, did have a well-articulated sense of "the good, the holy, the admirable." This is an example the liberal theorists of culturalism want very much not to see brought into view, but the Nazis were great pioneers of identity culture; without the massive resistance and sacrifice of Russia, their culture might have been strong enough to outlast the Second World War in Europe; and in that case, their conquering way of life would simply have become "life," for a great many people. If it went on to survive a hundred years or more, any culturalist would be compelled to admit that it was indeed a culture with a horizon of meaning.

Within a picked corps of rulers, given a freedom comparable to what the SS enjoyed during the war, one can imagine a certain diversity of character persisting in that culture—within limits of course, but our diversity too has limits. There seems no sure way of discriminating the integrity of a total politics from the integrity of a self-sustaining culture. If it be answered "But theirs was not authentic," one can note the weirdness of adopting a Nazi criterion of worth in an attempt to invalidate Nazi culture. The way out is to renounce tribal concern and respect as an act of idolatry that wants to extract an ethical good from religious and aesthetic phenomena. And yet, to make that admission is to break again into the language of non-culturalist liberalism: a language in which we refuse to say that culture is the definitively naturalizing fact of life, or that it represents a humanization of the social artifice in a way that mere politics fails to accomplish.

One sure sign of the triumph of a theory is that it comes to be treated as common sense. The acceptance of culturalism, no longer as a speculation but as a necessary premise of social thought, was attested in 1994 by "Multicultural-ism: A Liberal Perspective," a major essay by the liberal theorist Joseph Raz. The purpose of Raz's argument is to complete the transition from Walzer's "understanding" and Taylor's "recognition" to a full-scale adoption of *multicultural toleration* as a natural right of citizens in a liberal democracy. Liberal toleration of persons, who of course may be members of various cultures, turns out not to have been enough. The new natural right will belong to a new liberalism, says Raz: a liberalism of "affirmation." The people who do the affirming are, once again, groups. But what could it mean for a liberal society to add its affirmation of the cultures to their affirmation of themselves? They do a fair job of it in any non-repressive society, and their affirmations come at the expense of many other things.

Where Walzer's construal of the priority of culture had a source in twentieth-century anthropology, and Taylor's seemed a late version of German romantic organicism and expressivism, Raz draws his conception from a reading of Wittgenstein on games. Our "core options" in life, he asserts, have the structure of a game like chess. The metaphors that Walzer and Taylor borrowed from art, Raz borrows instead from the domain of craft or skill. The options turn out to include—in a generic and unspecifying list— "cultural, sporting, and other interests we develop" as children and grownups. Add these up and they may be seen to form a culture within liberal society. It follows that society—its important constituents now taken to be *cultures*—must appear as the bearer of individual traits that once were linked with personal character. We have seen this operation twice before, but let the difference of idiom speak for itself: "Only through being socialized in a culture can one tap the options that give life a meaning."

Suppose I state now an opposite thesis. *Nothing* gives life a meaning—nothing except the socially illegible or arbitrary energy of a person. He, or she, does not know the meaning of that energy. With luck, one may hope fate and fortune conspire to keep a mind and a body on the move, and one may hope that, with the unselfish instincts allowed to run the same race as the selfish ones, a decent and useful life will emerge. I make this credo as non-robust as I can, and it is not yet finished because no first-person wants it to be: the story of oneself is made by second and third persons (including oneself in some future, where one might as well be a second or third person). The "options," on this view, do not precede the person. To suppose that they can is a version of the bad faith of supposing the essence of a person can precede the existence. No final understanding is attainable of what I am: this axiom of Mill's may even have been shared by Wittgenstein. Science will not do it, poetry will not do it, psychoanalysis may produce the desired assent but that, too, constitutes no more than a provisional understanding, and what none of these things can perform, no ideology or system of life is likely to achieve. And yet, Raz seems to affirm that culture can do it. But what do we mean if we say that culture *constitutes* identity? For Raz, we mean that culture explains the encounter between the self I have become and my "options" along the way. But that conclusion is plausible only if the self is defined, as it need not allow itself to be defined, in wholly cultural terms.

We are now in a position to appreciate the vexing involutions of an effort to match the politics of cultural identity with the maxims of prudence in a pluralist democracy. Raz sees no special difficulty here because he thinks exclusionist cultural self-images are much the same thing as divergent vocational temperaments. "Philosophers do not make good generals, and generals do not make good philosophers." Ku Kluxers do not make good Lubavitchers, and Lubavitchers do not make good Ku Kluxers, but the compatibility of their values can be understood on the analogy of a society that incorporates both generals and philosophers. The plurality of cultures is just a plurality of callings. As a matter of experience, I think this argument is wrong. Competing cultures do not claim simply "the virtues of the competing ways of life," where we can read ways-of-life as a synonym for skills, routines, acquired itineraries. For cultures come to us frankly professing to give a meaning to life. Still tracking the flexible continuous analogy of games and skills, Raz declares that "liberal multiculturalism" is not "opposed to the assimilation of one cultural group by others." It would seem the cultures themselves can be trusted to guard against that; but the acceptance of assimilation is at odds with Taylor's worry about integrity and survival. If the cultures are assimilated by a liberal society, they will surely suffer extinction (however involuntary) and thereby suffer also a loss of integrity to each member. The truth is that faithful culturalism must be opposed to assimilation in practice if not in principle.

The fact that many of the cultures a new-modeled theorist may have to endorse are themselves illiberal was discussed in passing by Walzer and hardly at all by Taylor. Raz is the most candid of these three writers, and the most troubled when he looks at that prospect. His solution is to build liberal protections into the cultures that bear the illiberal threat: "Multiculturalism urges respect for cultures that are not themselves liberal cultures. . . . But it does so while imposing liberal protections for individual freedom on those cultures." The suggestion is ingenious but preposterous. On this plan, liberalism is required to integrate, into the self-understandings of other cultures, the political freedoms that make liberalism what it is; the hypothesis being that the cultures will allow it and that, having seen the good of the principles, they will nonetheless prefer to remain on the whole illiberal. If one ever sought to enforce such a plan, its effect would be either to crush the orthodox heart of the cultures or to repel every effort to assert the liberal right of exit. In short, a century of crises like the integration of Little Rock in 1957, made infinitely repeatable by a government that refuses to deny the legitimacy of Governor Orval Faubus.

So equivocal an experiment of thought can only appeal to someone whose ideas of cultural membership are at once benign and detached. In the work of the liberal culturalists, all the efforts to define a non-parochial form of recognition suggest that their thinking has been inoculated against bigotry by a previous exposure to liberalism; yet the unconditional good of this element of liberal practice is allowed to pass without more than perfunctory acknowledgement. "Some people," observes Raz, "fear, consciously or unconsciously, that if our culture is not superior to others, we are not entitled to love it as much as we do." This embarrassment, or fear, must be the other side of the unsuspecting confidence Raz supposes one might cherish regarding a culture. Can we then imagine someone saying, "Even though my culture is inferior to others, I love it unshakably"? Or, "Granted my culture seems impoverished beside the neighboring culture I am coming to know, still I prefer to be forever attached to mine"? Inferior and superior are not ascriptions that people commonly make of cultures; they would be unlikely to do so even if stupefied by theorists into thinking of themselves only in the context of culture. But let anyone imagine what it would be like to engage in the comparison suggested by Raz. Is this a state of mind that has ever been attained?

We are to suppose someone thinking, with love, of his own culture and thinking at the same time that it is not the only culture imaginable from inside. I am to reflect my culture as member and to reflect on it as nonmember and to conclude that from my point of view it is permissible though perhaps false to love it unquestioningly. (Raz compares the unconditional character of this attachment to the love we feel for our children. Enlightenment theorists of culture like Burke tended to compare it instead to the love we feel for a grandparent. The shift is one more symptom of the *tenderness* culture now admits among the debts that are properly owed to it once personified.) To repeat: I do not believe that the imputed state of mind has occurred or that it can occur in the nature of culture and in the nature of the way people use culture. The thoughts, "This culture is deeply mine," and "This culture is perhaps inferior," simply do not coexist in a single mind. The person who thinks, "My culture is perhaps inferior," has begun to think his way into a different culture, and is dangerously close to the thought that "No culture is worthy of my love in the way that humanity, and particular human beings, are."

Anyway, the fear of inferiority is an other-people's-fear. I doubt that Joseph Raz has felt it. Neither has Michael Walzer or Charles Taylor. Rather, they think that cultural identity is necessary for the others. It is all they have. We, the argument seems to say, know better, or rather some part of us knows. But as for the others—even "oppressive" cultures deserve *our* support for *their* sake because those oppressive cultures "provide many of their members with all that they can have." All they can have of what? Of goods. And as we know, all goods are at bottom cultural goods. But in the name of what principle, conviction, or value of our own do we wish upon others the good of the oppressive culture that is all they can have? One thing we can be sure of. In sympathizing with an oppressive culture, and forging a bond to prove the substance of our sympathy, we condemn to deeper oppression by that culture the very rebels against it whom liberal principles adjure us to admire.

Among the primary commitments of a liberal society is not to infringe on the rights of unaffiliated talent. A thinker may choose, as Spinoza once did, or an artist may choose, as Naipaul and Rushdie have, to cease to belong as reclaimable property to the culture that "constitutes" them. They are doing something that Walzer, Taylor, and Raz agree is epistemologically impossible. Nevertheless, they are doing it. And liberal theorists in the past affirmed a commitment to respect the claims of such persons against the culture they were making less sure of its integrity. I do not finally see how to assess the culturalist argument except as a weakening of this commitment in favor of other affirmations. The reply of the Enlightenment liberal must be that the case for the shift of principle has not been made. Its plausibility has come from throwing around the idea of culture a sympathetic haze that owes its charm to a reminiscence of the atmosphere of a person. Every pragmatic suggestion of culturalism betrays itself in a forcing together of two, mutually repellent, hypotheses: that the tribal cultures will abate not a jot of their property in each member whom they own; and that they are sufficiently flexible proprietors to allow us a spotless conscience as we commit to their care individuals of the many nations and nations-within-nations tending now toward dissolution.

I began by saying that liberal culturalism is a lie, a gesture of shrugging off irony adopted late by persons who think habitually as ironists. I have to recur to the same note more somberly. The theorists of cultural identity are hatching dragons. The nest belongs to a kind of creature they have never imagined, but there they sit and brood, with care and concern, thinking what comes will possibly look a good deal like themselves. The fire may scorch us in the years to come. By the self-evasion and the pandering of our belief in culture as the maker of identity, we rob the cultures with whom we profess to sympathize of the very clue that has made liberal democracy the distinct entity we are growing every day uneasily convinced it is. If the manners of a liberal society are not inherited by successive generations in the prospering democracies, if their incompatibility with certain other options is not understood, talk will be at an end regarding the right of exit we fondly hope to attach to the illiberal societies in return for our recognition of their right to be just what they are. At some point the irony must be re-engaged. The right of exit unconditionally recognized by every truly vital culture is the right to be a nonperson, the right to permanent exile, the right to be killed by a flourishing community of unimpeded members. Liberal culture, if we can call it a culture, is the only one that has ever disclaimed property in the persons of its members. Maybe that is another way of saying it is not a culture after all. And so much the better for liberalism.

1995

CHAPTER 3

THE MEANING OF PATRIOTISM IN 1789

IF YOU LOOK AT RECENT ACADEMIC DISCUSSIONS ABOUT THE good and bad energies brought into play by patriotism, you are struck by a certain elusiveness regarding the commitment of the commentators. Patriotism, the love of our country, is sometimes presented as a profound requirement of human nature; yet it is admitted that some people are more urgently moved by patriotism than others, and that the feeling is acquired and not innate. More often, patriotism is treated as a contingent good. The analogy is with religious belief. It is said that good people do not need to believe in God, but most people cherish such a belief, and it acts as a restraint on the viciousness of people who are not good, so we ought not to speak against religion. Indeed, we ought to encourage it as an engine of moral unification and restraint.

So too with the love of one's country. It is often defended or deferred to by scholars as a contingent good, beneficial to many people and not to be shunned by anyone who would preserve the reputation of a reliable neighbor. Richard Rorty argued in *Achieving Our Country* that a pragmatic liberalism in America ought to rely on patriotic sentiments to encourage Americans to live up to our ideals. Michael Kazin, in a recent essay in the *New Republic*, "Stuff of Legend," suggested that the luck that made America exceptional could be invoked by Barack Obama for a higher "exceptionalism" to spur generous action toward people less lucky than ourselves. The truth is that a great many famous evocations of patriotic sentiment have been tactical in a similar sense. George Kateb in "Is Patriotism a Mistake?" speculated that Lincoln, during the Civil War, had used the word "Union" in preference to "emancipation" because, though the cause he cared for was the removal of slavery, he knew that masses of people would only fight for the Union. There is considerable evidence to support that surmise.

At an outer edge of the consensus, one finds the communitarian idea that patriotism is a proof of our social nature; that people who lack such feeling or decline to display it are thin-blooded in some way, or missing an essential element of gregarious virtue and decency. George Orwell in his remarkable essay "Notes on Nationalism" tried to enforce a distinction between patriotism, the attachment to a particular way of life that "one believes to be the best in the world," and nationalism, which he supposed "inseparable from the desire for power." Orwell's was a brave attempt, but I doubt that the distinction can be maintained. What I call my patriotism, someone else will unmask as nationalism, and vice versa. The broad terms of this familiar discussion seem not to have changed much since 1789 and 1790, the years of publication of the two works with which I will be concerned.

When, in the spring and summer of 1789, the political protests and popular disorder in France began to be called a revolution, Richard Price was known as a moral philosopher, Dissenting preacher, honorary doctor of divinity at the University of Glasgow, and pamphlet writer on economic questions. He had supported the American Revolution and praised the long stride taken by Americans in establishing the rights of liberty of conscience and freedom of speech. On November 4, 1789, at the Dissenting chapel in the section of London called the Old Jewry, Price delivered his "Discourse on the Love of Our Country." It was, in fact, a political sermon, for Price had been invited, on the 101st anniversary of the Glorious Revolution, to address the Society for Commemorating the Revolution in Great Britain; and he went out of his way to link the honor and bloodless fame of the English revolution of 1688 with his hopes for the revolution in France. Both events, as Price saw them, were chapters in the progress of society toward enlightenment and the abolition of cruelty and superstition. The progress was cosmopolitan because it knew no bounds and could hardly recognize a standard of justice that varied with national boundaries. Benevolence was morally admirable only to the extent that it did not favor certain human beings over others. Loyalty to our own country was a partial good unless it was placed in the service of humanity.

Price today is remembered in the history of political thought, rather narrowly and unfairly, because his sermon supplied the pretext for Edmund Burke's *Reflections on the Revolution in France, and on the Proceedings in Certain Societies in London Relative to that Event, in a Letter Intended to Have Been Sent to a Gentleman in Paris* (1790). The second clause of Burke's title alludes to Price's sermon: Burke meant to cast doubt on the patriotism of "certain societies." In the one-hundred-page polemic that opens his treatise, Burke denies that the English people agree with three central affirmations on which Price had taken his stand: the right to choose our governors, the right to cashier them for misconduct, and the right to frame a government for ourselves. All of these political rights were still controversial in 1789, and Burke sharpens his attack by omitting two additional rights from the Revolution Society's list that would have been less controversial: liberty of conscience and the right to resist power when abused. But these are subordinate details, for the core of Burke's attack on Price is not political but sentimental. As he presents the radical doctrine of "the Reverend Dr. Price" and the Revolution Society, their promulgation of new rights springs from a failure of natural feeling.

A month before Price delivered his discourse, the king and queen of France had been harassed by a mob and taken forcibly from Versailles to Paris. Natural feeling, says Burke, should command sympathy with the victims in such a scene of molestation and violence. And nothing but a want of natural feeling could have led Richard Price, in the face of that open insult to grace and nobility, to celebrate the merely political significance of a "king led in triumph, and an arbitrary monarch surrendering himself to his subjects." Why, asks Burke, "do I feel so differently from the Reverend Dr. Price?" and he answers: "For this plain reason—because it is natural I should." Burke was also struck by the millenarian fervor of Price's conclusion: "Lord, now lettest thou thy servant depart in peace, for mine eyes have seen thy salvation." These words (from the gospel of Luke and the Book of Common Prayer) Burke took to endorse a sentiment of brotherhood that would abolish all distinctions between nations and would not scruple to achieve universal benevolence by violent means. Price's language had laid him open here, for he spoke of "the ardor for liberty catching and spreading" and "a blaze that lays despotism in ashes and warms and illuminates Europe!" Illumination may have been an abstract idea for Price, but, as Burke read the signs of the times, France was threatened with actual destruction.

The debate between Burke and Price can seem to turn on a question of manners. Burke thought it was psychologically unnatural of Price to accept and even approve of the indignity to which a reigning king and queen were subjected by a mass of the people. And as Burke saw it, this ill-advised approval had everything to do with Price's rejection of ordinary patriotism, his conviction that political justice could bypass the customary channels of moral sentiment and become a simple deduction of generous feeling toward mankind at large. But did Burke not agree with Price that universal benevolence was possible and desirable? And did Price not agree with Burke that general moral feelings must have a particular origin? The distance between their positions has been overestimated by every commentator I have read. Both were interested in the good of mankind at large. Yet from similar ideas of the work that reason must perform upon the materials of habit and memory, and with a similar ranking of public over private virtue, they drew opposite conclusions.

Price begins his discourse with a text from Psalm 122 on the good of prayer for Jerusalem: it is for "my brethren and companions' sakes" that peace may rightly be requested. This mode of address, says Price, emerged as an expression by the psalmist of love of his country; but such love—though it is "a noble passion"—like other such passions requires "regulation and direction." Price's stricture here reflects a separation between sensation and habit on the one hand, and understanding and conscience on the other, which runs through his earlier works of moral philosophy. In his *Review of the Principal Questions and Difficulties in Morals* (1757), he had argued that "right and wrong are more than mere names"; that such words denote "*a real character of actions*, or something true of them, something necessary and immutable, and independent of our perceptions"; and that human beings possess a power, "the *Understanding*," which is able to perceive right and wrong. His argument three decades later for universal benevolence relies on a similar trust in the sovereignty of a faculty of comparison, abstraction, and judgment. Only conscience, looking abroad, knows how to abstract "our country" from a spot of soil so as to encompass the "community of which we are members," or a government "bound together by the same civil polity." Our country, after all, is an artificial term, which acquires reality through repetition and habit. Its very familiarity strengthens the "common delusion" of the "superior value of it to other countries."

This is the error that Price would warn us against. At the same time he acknowledges the priority, in the order in which we acquire and exhibit social affections, of family, friends, and country over so vast an abstraction as humanity. However widely our affections may reach, "our obligation to love our own families, friends, and country, and to seek, in the first place, their good, will remain the same." So he grants the premise of common sense and common feeling. Yet Price deplores the fact that the love of our country has, thus far in the history of mankind, largely signified "a love of domination." Historically, national loyalty has meant a hardening of the principle of selfish interest as opposed to universal benevolence. To counter that habitual sense and convey a Christian idea of what unselfish love ought to be, he invokes the parable of the Good Samaritan.

Price stresses at the outset that the Jews and Samaritans were rival nations, which "entertained a hatred of one another the most inveterate." The duty of the honest patriot is to enlighten his country by teaching the law of conscience against intolerance and persecution; and the same duty requires that one's own actions serve as an example of "rational and manly worship." What, then, was the teaching of Jesus on the love of our country? He surely did not preach the good of patriotism. Price, however, interprets the gospels to affirm that Jesus, by his example if not his precepts, meant to include our smaller loyalties within the category of benevolence. "He taught the obligation to love all mankind and recommended universal benevolence as (next to the love of God) our first duty. . . . But we must not infer from hence that he did not include the love of our country in the number of our duties." I do not think that Price was seeking to make the judgments of Jesus appear innocuous, pliable, or appeasable; and his reading of the gospels affirms the priority of general benevolence over patriotic sentiment and parochial piety. The rungs of the ladder that begin with daily habit and loyalty ascend at last much higher than that. The ambition of Price's argument is unmistakable at its close: "Tremble all ye oppressors of the world! Take warning all ye supporters of slavish governments and slavish hierarchies!" He believed, as did many others in 1789, that a millennial change was at hand and that human nature was on his side. This was the assurance that Burke meant to shake.

Burke scored against Price in the *Reflections* by claiming for familiar attachments a reality Price had seemed to deny. On the contrary, Burke takes the felt strength of natural sentiments—"wisdom without reflection" and local loyalties—to suggest that a perverse psychology must underlie any attachment I profess to an entity greater than my country. To reject the very loyalties one was born to cherish and taught to share is an act imaginable only to a peculiar subset of the human race, of whom Burke offers various descriptions: "political men of letters," "turbulent, discontented men of quality," "smugglers of adulterated metaphysics," and so on. In opposition to such cabals, he says, "the people of England well know, that the idea of inheritance furnishes a sure principle of conservation, and a sure principle of transmission; without at all excluding a principle of improvement." Further: "I almost venture to affirm, that not one in a hundred amongst us participates in the 'triumph' of the Revolution Society." The cause of the popular coolness toward radical politics, as Burke presents it, lies deep in the English character: "Thanks to our sullen resistance to innovation, thanks to the cold sluggishness of our national character, we still bear the stamp of our forefathers." So much for the people of England, who in Burke's estimation stand with himself and with human nature. Who, then, could oppose them? The answer is, defectors from the English national character and from human nature itself. Burke denies—and denies so completely as not even to mention the possibility—that there may be a special value in the quality of judgment that *breaks* from inherited patterns of loyalty.

The trustworthiness of parochial virtues is proved, for Burke, by the commonness of their exercise: "To be attached to the subdivision, to love the little platoon we belong to in society, is the first principle (the germ as it were) of public affections. It is the first link in the series by which we proceed towards a love to our country and to mankind." In this celebrated passage, Burke is not describing a neighborhood or a civil association, as is now widely supposed, but rather a class or an affiliation within a class—say educated men of the middle station who owe their status to their talents and intellectual energy. Burke adopts the old word *order* from the seventeenth-century French theologian Jacques-Bénigne Bossuet, and his appeal for attachment is a defense against the passions of men who have detached themselves from their order in society. Only toward the end of the book does Burke finally recast the passage about "little platoons" to suggest he has in mind neighborhoods and associations: "We begin our public affections in our families. No cold relation is a zealous citizen. We pass on to our neighborhoods, and our habitual provincial connections. These are inns and resting-places." Even in the later passage, the little platoon we grew up in is not taken to be our destination.

In Burke's understanding as much as Price's, the passage from local to public affections, from national self-love to a concern with humanity as a whole, is pictured as a progression. To act with regard to and for the sake of mankind is the ultimate aim of moral conduct. The originality of Burke's attack lies only in his suspicion that those who imagine themselves to be citizens of the world have mistaken their reasons for motives. We ought to measure conduct by the highest standard, Burke agrees, and that standard is indeed universal; but to suppose men and women can be *moved to action* by an apprehension of something so vast and remote is to fancy they can identify with others while having no identity of their own to support them. Burke's surmise is not about the proper range of moral consciousness but about the particular or abstract character of our motives of action.

Burke never suggests that our original loyalties are primal, God-given, and untouched by human artifice. Though the social arrangements of our country may seem so familiar that we regard them as second nature, it is we who have made them so: "We have given to our frame of polity the image of a relation in blood; binding up the constitution of our country with our dearest domestic ties; adopting our fundamental laws into the bosom of our family affections; keeping inseparable, and cherishing with the warmth of all their combined and mutually reflected charities, our state, our hearths, our sepulchers, and our altars." The illusion that a meaning we have given to ourselves is a meaning we have received is brought out here by the image of an act of binding, which overlays an image of already existing bonds. The Constitution (in Britain a fictive unity and not a readable document) comes to be bound up with the "ties" of domestic life; and the sense of "mutually reflected" feelings contributes to a mutually reinforcing strength. The virtues of political life, as Burke will show later in the *Reflections*, depend on our forgetting the human handiwork of the artifice. "The very idea of the fabrication of a new government, is enough to fill us with disgust and horror." Was Richard Price guilty of seeking to fabricate a new morality (a thing as strange and repellent as a new government) when he spoke of universal duties?

He would not have said so. Recall that Price had urged as a necessary burden "our obligation to love our own families, friends, and country, and to seek, *in the first place*, their good" [italics added]. The Roman imagery that Burke deployed in his answer, which speaks of hearths, sepulchers, and altars, may actually prove more than it should. The piety Burke thinks essential to the Constitution appears to be non-moral for the same reason that it is non-Christian. The community he invokes of the dead and the living—the dead before the living—has priority for Burke in shaping our ideas of society and the state. This community is a self-sufficient good, which interests us not because of its rightness but because of its grandeur. The mere morality of the choices it supports is beside the point.

Let us turn to the biblical text both Price and Burke had in mind. The parable of the Good Samaritan (Luke 10:25–37) holds a radical doctrine on the treatment of strangers, and a doctrine that seems to support Price's view of the universal character of moral duties. Jesus has sent the seventy disciples away from their homes or places of rest to prepare for his coming "into every city and place" where his word will be sown. To the man who would first bury his father, he says, "Let the dead bury their dead" (all quotations here are from William Tyndale's translation). To him who would bid farewell to his family, Jesus says that no man that "looketh back, is apt to the kingdom of heaven." The teachers are asked to adopt the ways of each city they enter; the cities that deny them are to be warned their fate will be worse than that of Sodom.

When the disciples return, having subdued the very devils "through thy name," Jesus shows his delight; but a "certain lawyer," on hearing the injunction to love thy neighbor as thyself, asks, "Who is then my neighbor?" In answer, Jesus relates the parable:

> A certain man descended from Jerusalem into Jericho and fell into the hands of thieves, which robbed him of his raiment and wounded him, and departed leaving him half dead. And by chance there came a certain priest that same way, and when he saw him, he passed by. And likewise a Levite, when he was come nigh to the place, went and

looked on him, and passed by. Then a certain Samaritan, as he journeyed, came nigh unto him, and when he saw him, had compassion on him, and went to and bound up his wounds, and poured in oil and wine, and put him on his own beast, and brought him to a common inn, and made provision for him. And on the morrow when he departed, he took out two pence and gave them to the host, and said unto him, Take care of him, and whatsoever thou spendest more, when I come again, I will recompense thee. Which now of these three, thinkest thou, was neighbor unto him that fell into the thieves' hands? And he said: he that showed mercy on him. Then said Jesus unto him, Go and do thou likewise.

The story is intuitively appealing, but also deeply counterintuitive, for it passes far beyond the instant impulse of charity to strangers. That impulse would command relief of some sort; "compassion," in its usual sense, might also suggest the warmth of friendly help; but the literal Christian meaning of "love thy neighbor as thyself" goes beyond either of those expectations. For the act of the Samaritan is more than momentary. It deters him from his journey for part of a day and all of a night, and he pays out money that will not be returned by the victim. He passes out of himself and into the stranger, as if the stranger were himself; he has to exist, for the purpose of succor, in two identities at once, until the man is decently cared for.

And yet to the sufferer, the Samaritan remains a stranger all the while that he performs a benefaction normally reserved for friends or relations. He, or his resources, are completely given to the man, up to the time of his repair; yet he is detached from any connection of expressed and

mutual feeling. The sympathy thus portrayed is deliberately made to appear *distant*, by our usual canons of
parochial attachment. The Samaritan does the sufferer
an unsentimental good, and this is felt to be surprising,
baffling, as well as generous. It is beyond the service any
but the most available friend or family member would be
expected to offer. The stress of the parable has everything
to do with the negation of familiar sentiments at the end
of Luke 9: "Let the dead bury their dead." Generalize the
sanctity of familial ties that Jesus has demoted and you
are left with the conventional and pardonable indifference
of the priest and the Levite who pass by the sufferer. He
is simply not one of theirs. Yet the same priest and Levite
would have taken the trouble to bury their dead, just as
they would have looked back and said farewell before
departing to preach the word of God.

The moral of this parable, in fact, goes much further
than Richard Price's exhortation to benevolence. In his
early treatise on morality, Price had allowed that other
things being equal, "it is right, friends, relations, and
benefactors should be preferred to strangers; and, whoever does otherwise, acts contrary to his duty." The gospel
text is more radical here: the claims of the family and the
native community to which Price paid tribute by demot-
ing strangers, both here and in his sermon "On the Love
of our Country," belong nowhere in the frame of thinking
of the Good Samaritan. Price's ideal of the citizen of the
world does confirm the promise of the parable—but only
as an end that humanity may finally reach. We will act in
keeping with the truth of the parable when we have ceased
to barter conscience for the safety and piety of the city-
state. Burke, however, departs much further from the core
of Christian precept. His analysis of the motives of moral

action seems to forbid that politics should ever aim at such an elevation of sympathy: "We know that *we* have made no discoveries; and we think that no discoveries are to be made, in morality." In practice this means: no widening of the list of strangers whom we treat as neighbors. It was not for nothing that Joseph Priestley (the keenest-witted of the anti-Burke pamphleteers of the 1790s) inferred that the author of the *Reflections* had he lived at the time of Jesus would have sided with the Roman governors.

Burke, it must be added, in order to make Price's views appear derisory, abridged what he knew of his public character. It was true Price had defended the American resistance to British rule a decade earlier, but so had Burke. As for the passage about the king and queen being "led in triumph," did Price there mean to justify any violence by the crowd against the nobility? In the fourth edition of his sermon, he denied the imputation and replied indignantly to what he called "this horrid misrepresentation and menace." He had in mind, he said, not the events of the Sixth of October but of the Fourteenth of July. I suspect that Price's reference was more ambiguous than he liked to remember, but no doubt Burke put the harshest possible construction on his words.

Still, in their attitudes toward the revolution itself the two commentators may not have been so divergent as first appeared. Richard Price died in April 1791, after the confiscation of church lands by the revolutionary assembly of France, but before the massacres of September 1792; and we may guess his likely response to subsequent events from the views expressed by his close friend and follower Mary Wollstonecraft. She defended the revolution in her *Vindication of the Rights of Men* (1790), the first published reply to Burke's *Reflections*, but in *An Historical and Moral View of the French Revolution* (1794) she gave a carefully qualified endorsement. Wollstonecraft deplored the use of violence and the dependence of the national assembly on the Paris crowd: two portents of disaster on which Burke had laid particular emphasis. Ultimately the difference between Burke on one side, and Price and Wollstonecraft on the other, may be traced to the widely different degrees of suspicion with which they approached the idea of equality. Social equality, Burke thought, and the discovery of political rights to support equality were a catastrophic error that could lead to nothing but violence. For Price and Wollstonecraft, democratic equality was a natural effect of our coming to know that inequality, and institutions such as primogeniture that sanctified inequality, were a human invention that produced more misery than happiness. None of these writers was without ambivalence about democracy, but Price and Wollstonecraft were contingent allies of democratic reform and showed it in their own time; while Burke was a resolute opponent of democracy, and did his best to slow down the progress under way in Britain toward a reform of representation in parliament.

We are apt to regard Burke today as having had a subtler insight into political morality than Price. Perhaps we mean by that a surer psychological grasp of the motives of action. Or is it rather that our moral and political education has continued on Burkean lines, taking our own pieties, time by time and place by place, to be "wisdom without reflection" so that we approve of what we already knew? But there is a modern development that ought to give us pause. The state, as we know it, is an institution of mass society, and this fact would seem to render invalid at least one all-important premise of the loyalty to the subdivision and the little platoon that Burke evoked so tellingly. The possible significance of the change of view was captured by a critic and essayist, William Hazlitt, who seems to have learned a great deal from the contest between Price and Burke.

Hazlitt wrote "On Patriotism—A Fragment" in 1814 to exhibit a contradiction that had not yet caught up with the followers of Burke. "In modern times," said Hazlitt, patriotism is "the creature of reason and reflection, rather than the offspring of physical or local attachment." For all who live in settings less coherent and circumscribed than, for example, the cantons of Switzerland, "our country is a complex, abstract existence, recognized only by the understanding." What are the consequences of our country being known to our minds but not felt intimately by sight and touch? "It is not possible that we should have an individual attachment to sixteen millions of men, any more than to sixty millions. We cannot be habitually attached to places we never saw, and people we never heard of. Is not the name of Englishman a general term, as well as that of man?" Just as much as our feelings toward "general humanity," therefore, the love of our country must be ranked among the "general affections." The older idea of patriotism came out of the city-states of Greece and Rome, "where the country of the citizen was the town in which he was born"; but as Hazlitt concludes, "where our country is no longer contained within the narrow circle of the same walls—where we can no longer behold its glimmering horizon from the top of our native mountains— beyond these limits, it is not a natural but an artificial idea, and our love of it either a deliberate dictate of reason, or a cant term." Thus, love of our country, if it is to be justified by reason, can be "little more than another name for the love of liberty, of independence, of peace, and social happiness." Other circumstances besides the judgment of awakened conscience, Hazlitt admits, may go to form the "superstructure" of the patriotic sentiment, and the accidents of language are among those circumstances. Yet to observe that fact is to mark limits that observation is destined to exceed. "He," writes Hazlitt, "who speaks two languages has no country."

To overcome parochial prejudice, to recognize that it *is* prejudice, may be the easier half of enlightenment. Every age has found it harder to pass from the surrender of unreal pieties to a renunciation of imposed enmities. But why? An answer may come from the recognition of how much is entailed by the acknowledgment that "an Englishman" is a general term. It stays general so long as we have no individual in mind. By the same logic, the idea of this or that German or Frenchman ought to individuate the image of an "enemy," and place us in the position of the Samaritan whose conscience obliges him to treat persons as neighbors. What is difficult is to bring to mind that individual image and to keep it there against the unremitting and obstinate pressure of loyalties.

Hazlitt offers his analysis of patriotism as a philosophical discovery, but it is also an ordinary one. Etty Hillesum wrote in her diary, in Amsterdam, March 15, 1941, "It is the problem of our age: hatred of Germans poisons everyone's mind" (quoted by Nicholson Baker, in his documentary chronicle of the Second World War, *Human Smoke*). She thought: suppose there were one decent German in all of Germany—that person should be cherished, and should suffice to discredit the hatred. "Because of that one decent German it is wrong to pour our hatred over an entire people. Indiscriminate hatred is the worst thing there is. It is a sickness of the soul." Had Richard Price chosen to draw out the parable of the Good Samaritan in order to make a considered reply to Burke's defense of patriotism, he might have gone further on the lines suggested by that diary entry. The cure for the indiscriminate hatred of a community that is not one's own can never come from the feeling of community itself. The answer springs rather from the individual case that acquires a general authority—-an authority which by metaphysical conviction eventually extends to any person and all persons.

2011

TWO

LINCOLN AND WHITMAN AS REPRESENTATIVE AMERICANS

A WAY OF LIFE LIKE AMERICAN DEMOCRACY HAS NO PREDES-
tined shape, and when we call historical persons representative, because they helped to make us what we are, we
generally mean that in their time they were exceptional.
Abraham Lincoln, a lawyer, state legislator in Illinois, and
one-term congressman who became president, and Walter
Whitman, a journeyman printer, newspaper editor, and
journalist who became a great poet, were extraordinary in
what they achieved. They were extraordinary, too, in the
marks of personality that they left on their smallest gestures. Yet the thing about both men that strikes an unprej-
udiced eye on first acquaintance is their ordinariness. This
is an impression that persists, and that affects our deeper
knowledge of both. By being visibly part of a common
world which they inherited, even as they were movers of a
change the world had only begun to imagine, they enlarged
our idea of the discipline and imagination of democracy.
But the accomplishment in all its intensity belongs to a
particular moment of American history. The great works of
Lincoln and Whitman begin in the 1850s—Lincoln's emergence as a national figure comes in the speech of 1854 on

the Kansas-Nebraska Act; Whitman's self-discovery comes in 1855 with the first edition of *Leaves of Grass*. What was special about those years?

In the 1850s in America, the feelings of citizens were turned back with a shock again and again, to one terrible, magnetic, and central issue. This was the national argument—already in places a violent struggle—over the possibility of the spread of slavery. The future of slavery and freedom had been an issue from the founding of the Republic, but it took on a new urgency in the 1840s, when people asked how to dispose of the lands taken in the war with Mexico: a debate in which Lincoln participated as a congressman, strongly and eloquently dissenting from the war policy of President James K. Polk. The same issue confronted the nation again and more starkly with the Kansas-Nebraska legislation of 1854, which repealed the Missouri Compromise and opened free territories to the owners of slaves. All through these years, the free citizens of the Union had felt the weight of the Fugitive Slave Law, which required law-abiding persons in the free states to return escaped slaves to their masters. The law raised a question for the accomplice as well as the master and the slave. Am *I* free in a country that uses the power of the state to compel me to assist in the capture of a human being who has risked his life for freedom? These things were sifted deeply in those years. There has not been another time when so searching an inquest drew so many ingenuous minds to discuss the basis in law and morality of the life we Americans share.

Both Lincoln and Whitman were part of a radical current of opinion that started out in dissent. In reading about their lives, you sometimes sense a peculiar self-confidence, as of people who know they have company in their beliefs.

You can feel it plainly when you read their writings, if you listen to the pitch of the words. Though the thunder comes when they need it, they are both of them, by practice and almost by temperament, soft-spoken writers. But they know that they are not alone; they know that someone is listening. A text from Whitman: "Whoever degrades another degrades me." And from Lincoln: "As I would not be a slave, so I would not be a master. This expresses my idea of democracy. Whatever differs from this, to the extent of the difference, is no democracy." The two statements have morally the same meaning. American slavery, they say, is a concomitant of American democracy and is its degradation and betrayal. The work of democracy in these years will be to resist that betrayal and save the constitutional system from destruction. In this contest the enemy is a selfishness so perfect that it would preserve a freedom to treat other persons as property. This then is the cause; but the motive of resistance is deeper. It comes from an idea of the self that—like the sense of property cherished by the Slave Power—could have arisen only in a democracy.

Both Lincoln and Whitman were familiar with an older and largely hostile tradition of response to the democratic character. Plato, who did not invent that tradition, gave it memorable formulation in book 8 of the *Republic* and elsewhere, and the echoes can be felt as late as Alexis de Tocqueville's strictures on the propensity of Americans for bargaining and mutual adaptation. The typical dweller in a democracy is gregarious, good-natured, conciliatory, socialized, enormously apt in the use of language (perhaps in a way that cheapens language by rendering it always negotiable), self-absorbed and yet commonly attuned to the pleasures and pains of others, full of seductiveness and a curious readiness to be seduced. This is a partial portrait, with enough truth to suggest a likeness in the personality of many Americans. And yet, whomever I call to mind as an example, I find on analysis that a part of me appreciates the very trait another part despises. The reason is that people in a democratic culture aspire to something besides democracy, something even beyond the fulfillment of the democratic character.

This is a paradox of manners that Whitman and Lincoln know well. All of the people want to be respected *as* the people, yet each wants not to be known merely as one of the people. Huey Long, the governor of Louisiana during the Great Depression and an instinctive and brilliant demagogue, captured the sentiment exuberantly in the campaign slogan "Every man a king." Do we in no way agree? And if you think that the phrase is sheer sloganeering, consider the satisfaction we take in the sort of democratic scene Whitman describes in his 1855 preface to *Leaves of Grass*. Speaking of "the common people," he praises "the fierceness of their roused resentment—their curiosity and welcome of novelty—their self-esteem and wonderful sympathy—their susceptibility to a slight—the air they have of persons who never knew how it felt to stand in the presence of superiors." Then, for illustration, he mentions a democratic custom: "the President's taking off his hat to them [to the people, that is] and not they to him." The people do not know what it is to stand in the presence of a superior; it seems to them a natural gesture when the president salutes them. Each of them is a gracious equal to whom he owes an unquestioned deference.

It is an ideal scene, "the President's taking off his hat to them and not they to him"—and no less ideal for its origin in actual experience. But notice that it exhibits a practice of virtue (chivalric virtue) as much as it does a performance of equality in manners. Readers of *Democratic Vistas*—the prose work of social criticism Whitman published in 1867 and 1868, in which on the whole he speaks as a friend of modernity—have sometimes wondered at the note of awe with which this modern author speaks of the Crusades. Maybe we have a clue in his appreciation of the president's taking off his hat to the people. The dignity, the generosity and sensitivity on points of honor, the sense of a grace of life that cannot be bought, all of which belong to chivalry, are to be transplanted into the New World as attributes of the people. The salute will be exchanged not between one exemplar and another of crusading valor, but between the representative of the people and the people themselves. The distance and deference and pride of station that went with the older virtues have all somehow been preserved. Whitman, who was a subtler psychologist than Huey Long, suggests that since kings are beneath us now, the ideal of democratic life may have become "Every man a gentle knight."

Two traits, says Whitman, essential to the practice of democracy are individuality and what he calls "adhesiveness." We might translate his terms as self-sufficiency and a comradely sympathy; and under those names they sound like modern qualities. But the pervading virtues that will always accompany them—again, if we can judge by Whitman's examples—are the older virtues of gentleness and courage. It is because our aspirations have been raised so high that we fear the conduct of the people may grow vicious and their judgments corrupt. For the ruin of the people brings a disgrace more terrible than the ruin of kings. Lincoln, in a letter of 1855, looked at the swelling constituency of the anti-immigrant party of his day and found his thoughts drifting to a gloomy speculation. "I am not a Know-Nothing," he begins:

> That is certain. How could I be? How can any one who abhors the oppression of negroes, be in favor of degrading classes of white people? Our progress in degeneracy appears to me to be pretty rapid. As a nation, we began by declaring that "*all men are created equal.*" We now practically read it "all men are created equal, *except negroes.*" When the Know-Nothings get control, it will read "all men are created equal, except negroes, *and foreigners, and Catholics.*" When it comes to this I should prefer emigrating to some country where they make no pretense of loving liberty—to Russia, for instance, where despotism can be taken pure, and without the base alloy of hypocrisy.

So the Old World distrust of the tyranny of democratic opinion can be shared even by so democratic a character as Abraham Lincoln. A democracy, he says, may be as slavish as a despotism, but it has the added evil of hypocrisy.

Much of Lincoln's writing and speaking between 1854 and 1859 will turn on the question whether the moral right and wrong of slavery can be decided by the will of a majority of voters. He was moved to an unusual show of anger when he thought about Stephen Douglas's saying that the question of slavery should be simply settled by the rules of popular sovereignty. Douglas liked to say, "I don't care if they vote slavery up or down," and as often as he said it, Lincoln would quote the words against him, with derision and a sense of baffled shame. *Can* the people do as they please in a matter of such interest to the conscience of human nature? Lincoln is compelled to admit that the majority can legally do so. But he thinks the constitutional founders were in principle opposed to slavery, and he finds his main evidence in the Declaration of Independence, in the words "All men are created equal." The will of the people at a given moment is not the standard of right and wrong. Whitman for his part shows the same readiness to criticize both the practices and the opinions of the majority. He writes in *Democratic Vistas:* "Never was there, perhaps, more hollowness at heart than at present, and here in the United States. Genuine belief seems to have left us." And again: "The depravity of the business classes of our country is not less than has been supposed, but infinitely greater." And: "The magician's serpent in the fable ate up all the other serpents; and money-making is our magician's serpent, remaining to-day sole master of the field." Lincoln and Whitman respect the people too much to want to flatter them. They agree that democracy—to remedy evils which it has itself brought into being—requires a self-respect more thoroughgoing than can be found in any other system of manners. The maintenance of democracy will be a task different in kind and harder than its founding.

Whitman traces the new democratic self-respect to "an image of completeness in separatism"; and he goes on, choosing his words awkwardly and vividly:

> of individual personal dignity, of a single person, either male or female, characterized in the main, not from extrinsic acquirements or position, but in the pride of himself or herself alone; and, as an eventual conclusion and summing up, (or else the entire scheme of things is aimless, a cheat, a crash) the simple idea that the last, best dependence is to be upon humanity itself, and its own inherent, normal, full-grown qualities, without any superstitious support whatever.

If the equality of individuals is for Whitman the self-evident truth of democracy, it is a truth we all of us confirm every day by the link between body and soul. What does "individual" mean if not undividable? One body, one soul. "I believe in you my soul," Whitman writes in *Song of Myself,* "the other I am must not abase itself to you, / And you must not be abased to the other." The range of possible reference in these words is wide. It is the body speaking to the soul—the body must not be pressed by the soul to ascetic torments, even as its sensualism must not tamper with the soul's integrity—but it is also a world of spontaneous impulse addressing a mind informed by high ideals.

In writing as he does about the integrity of body and soul, Whitman stands against a tendency that he calls realism. *Democratic Vistas,* in a surprising and memorable phrase, deplores "the growing excess and arrogance of realism." Evidently, Whitman has in mind the imperative to build a railroad and get rich fast, which has its correlatives in our own day. Realism is the voice that tells you to specialize your habits and feelings, to ride your personality in the current of things as they are, to do anything rather than stand and think and look at the world for the sake of looking. By contrast, the "unsophisticated conscience"—for it takes resolve to shed sophistication—is a result of prolonged and partly involuntary exposure to experience. Let me pause here to say a word for the kind of experience Whitman praises. It is the experience of a single person dwelling unseen among others—an experience, in fact, of anonymity. This condition ought to be a blessing in a democracy, where it need not go with material deprivation, yet we are apt to regard it as a curse. Anonymity is a vital condition of individuality—perhaps the only such condition that requires the existence of a mass society. When, in section 42 of *Song of Myself,* Whitman hears "A call in the midst of the crowd" and feels that he is being summoned by name, and that he must deliver his message with "my own voice, orotund sweeping and final," it is a profoundly welcome moment because he is being called from an interval of non-recognition and his speaking now will derive power from the time when he was alone in the crowd. Such intervals are not a kind of apprenticeship. They are supposed by Whitman to recur in the lives of the renowned as well as the obscure, and their continual return is to him an assurance of sanity.

The voice of *Song of Myself* rises from anonymity to the speech of "Walt Whitman, an American, one of the roughs, a kosmos," but this is not to be conceived as an ascent from a humble to an exalted station. It is an emergence of individuality that could happen only to someone nursed in anonymity, and the occasion prompts his speech only because he is sure of passing back to anonymity. During the Civil War, Whitman did not fraternize with the great, did not seek to interview and write up the sage and serious opinions of statesmen, generals, ambassadors. He visited the sick and wounded at New York Hospital and served as a wound-dresser in the military hospitals in Washington, D.C. He eked out a living in the years of war by clerical work in the army paymaster's office and clerkships in the Department of the Interior and the Office of the Attorney General.

As it happened, he lived on the route that President Lincoln took to and from his summer lodgings, and in his book *Specimen Days,* Whitman left a record of his impression of Lincoln. It stresses the commonness, almost anonymity, of the president as he passes by, but also his unsearchable depth.

The party makes no great show in uniform or horses. Mr. Lincoln on the saddle generally rides a good-sized, easygoing gray horse, is dress'd in plain black, somewhat rusty and dusty; wears a black stiff hat, and looks about as ordinary in attire, &c., as the commonest man . . . . I see very plainly ABRAHAM LINCOLN's dark brown face, with the deep-cut lines, the eyes, always to me with a deep latent sadness in the expression. We have got so that we exchange bows, and very cordial ones. . . . Earlier in the summer I occasionally saw the President and his wife, toward the latter part of the afternoon, out in a barouche, on a pleasure ride through the city. Mrs. Lincoln was dress'd in complete black, with a long crape veil. The equipage is of the plainest kind, only two horses, and they nothing extra. They pass'd me once very close, and I saw the President in the face fully, as they were moving slowly, and his look, though abstracted, happen'd to be directed steadily in my eye. He bow'd and smiled, but far beneath his smile I noticed well the expression I have alluded to. None of the artists or pictures has caught the deep, though subtle and indirect expression of this man's face. There is something else there.

The life that Whitman always went back to, even in the presence of great events and characters, was the life of an observer, an onlooker, with the patience to catch a subtle and indirect expression glimpsed by no one else.

His manner of looking at others has everything to do with his attitude toward himself. "Trippers and askers surround me," he says in section 4 of *Song of Myself,* "People I meet . . . . the effect upon me of my early life . . . . of the ward and city I live in . . . . of the nation"; and he says of all these environing facts and circumstances, "They come to me days and nights and go from me again, / But they are not the Me myself." There follows an unusual self-portrait:

Apart from the pulling and hauling stands what I am,
Stands amused, complacent, compassionating, idle,
    unitary,
Looks down, is erect, bends an arm on an impalpable
    certain rest,
Looks with its sidecurved head curious what will come
    next,
Both in and out of the game, and watching and
    wondering at it.

It is a self-portrait; but a portrait of what kind of self? Whitman has said that "the other I am" must not abase itself. But the person who lives as the crowd lives will always abase "what I am," which Whitman also calls "the Me myself," the self that stands apart from the trippers and askers, the pulling and hauling. Whitman's self therefore in this portrait stands apart from the work of pleasing others. He is, to repeat, a simple separate entity: *what I am.* The features of the portrait, which correspond to a pencil sketch that continues to appear in many editions of *Leaves of Grass,* have an expression of almost conscious aloofness. And yet his clothes are plain and the tilt of his head is inquisitive rather than rakish. He is wondering about himself as much as he is about those who are in the game full-time: the game of having things to do, titles to be known by, roles to be identified with. Being both in and out of it, he is sometimes able to stand and rest and watch.

Whitman has, and he encourages us to find in ourselves, the irony of the person who is not one thing—who, even to his own understanding, is composed of unseen parts—who can imagine that an event or experience may possibly alter what he is. The sequence of adjectives describing "what I am" is fascinating: "amused, complacent, compassionating, idle, unitary." *Amused* at what if not himself and at the likelihood, as he puts it elsewhere in the poem, that even now he discovers himself "on a verge of the usual mistake." But still, *complacent*, sufficiently pleased with his situation, not wanting to change it for another, and at this moment free of ambition as a true observer must be. The game he is in and out of is filled with other people, their pleasures and pains: he is *compassionating* as one made what he is partly by susceptibility to them. And *idle*—a great theme of Whitman's—for to act in the world and seek an effect would be to blunt his finer sense of mobility and alertness. By the way that all these words round off the portrait, they explain the choice of the climactic word *unitary*. The poet has a special endowment—which yet he shares potentially with any democratic citizen—and that is to be known by himself. One body, one soul.

His great book was called *Leaves of Grass* through all its editions. The title comes from a question early in *Song of Myself* about the meaning of life:

> A child said, What is the grass? fetching it to me with full
>   hands;
> How could I answer the child? . . . . I do not know what
>   it is any more than he.

As you know if you have ever watched children, the question is really (pointing to the grass), "This must mean something. (But what?)" The child assumes something that grownups also assume in their different ways. Because he plucked the grass, he is its owner; and an owner may create meaning; and the more meanings the better. And yet—we never stop being children—all of the meanings had better be specific. Whitman would like to cooperate and so he gives the child, gives us, a series of conjectures, which by their sheer variety confess that the truths they indicate will be partial. "I guess," Whitman says of the grass, "it must be the flag of my disposition"—whatever I feel is what I now make it be. Or the grass is itself a child, "the produced babe of the vegetation." Or it is an image and shadow of divine things, to be read as a message from the Lord. Or an emblem of democracy: "Growing among black folks as among white, / Kanuck, Tuckahoe, Congressman, Cuff, I give them the same, I receive them the same." This is a catechism strangely appropriate to the questionings of a child who, when asking *what,* also always wants to know *why* things are? For example, if they come to be, can they cease to be? Are some more important than others? And will this die, now that I have picked it?

Whitman begins to answer the last question with a haunting line, "And now it seems to me the beautiful uncut hair of graves." He continues in one of the greatest stretches of imaginative writing in our literature:

> This grass is very dark to be from the white heads of old mothers,
> Darker than the colorless beards of old men,
> Dark to come from under the faint red roofs of mouths.
>
> O I perceive after all so many uttering tongues!
> And I perceive they do not come from the roofs of mouths for nothing.
> I wish I could translate the hints about the dead young men and women,
> And the hints about old men and mothers, and the offspring taken soon out of their laps.

What do you think has become of the young and old men?
And what do you think has become of the women and
    children?

They are alive and well somewhere;
The smallest sprout shows there is really no death,
And if there ever was it led forward life, and does not wait
    at the end to arrest it,
And ceased the moment life appeared.

All goes onward and outward . . . . and nothing collapses,
And to die is different from what any one supposed, and
    luckier.

He says it is lucky to die and means it is lucky to live—to know that one *has* lived, without scheme or plan, restrained but not cautious, unobtrusive, uninhibited. The good of death, not that it happens to us, but that it happens and we are part of a world of things that happen, comes then only to this, that one sort of life makes room for another while life itself persists. All goes onward and outward, nothing collapses.

This is Whitman's ethic of "inception" or beginnings: "Urge and urge and urge, / Always the procreant urge of the world. / Out of the dimness opposite equals advance. . . . Always substance and increase, / Always a knit of identity . . . . always distinction . . . . always a breed of life." We would rather be part of something vital than part of something inert. In this light his creed seems one of entire and omnivorous acceptance. That is what it is, a free acceptance both ideal and physical among free persons, and Whitman connects it with a knowledge of identity that never can be fixed. He makes us feel all this in his address to the ocean:

You sea! I resign myself to you also. . . . I guess what you
    mean,
I behold from the beach your crooked inviting fingers,
I believe you refuse to go back without feeling of me;
We must have a turn together. . . . I undress. . . . hurry
    me out of sight of the land,
Cushion me soft. . . . rock me with billowy drowse,
Dash me with amorous wet. . . . I can repay you.

Sea of stretched ground-swells!
Sea of breathing broad and convulsive breaths!
Sea of the brine of life! Sea of unshovelled and always-
    ready graves!
Howler and scooper of storms! Capricious and dainty sea!
I am integral with you. . . . I too am of one phase and of
    all phases.

A similar current of ecstatic power belongs to many parts
of *Song of Myself.* The parts are almost self-contained, yet
the whole is different and is greater than the parts. How
often Whitman's ecstasy, his standing outside himself,
becomes a standing in some other kind of being, or an
inhabiting of a man or woman apparently far from him
in society. His originality is to insist that such changes
of feeling do not point to the inconsequence of a mind
adrift. They offer occasions for a sympathetic imagining
that is identical with self-invention.

Nobody would want to call Whitman a nationalist, in
any but the most loose-fitting sense, but in *Song of Myself*
he commemorates some heroic and singular deeds from
American history. He does it unforgettably in the sections
of the poem devoted to the Alamo and a frigate fight of the
revolutionary era; and again but more familiarly in domestic scenes like the one that shows him giving comfort to

a runaway slave. These narrative or historical parts of the poem turn out to have a feature in common, namely that they are about self-sacrifice, and their nameless heroes are individuals who know how much they are giving up. They know that nothing is better than life. There is accordingly no bombast, no triteness of assurance. Whitman sums up the losses in the sea battle, its deaths and amputations, in words of a simple finality: "These so. . . . these irretrievable." He admires great actions and thinks that physical courage is to be prized, but seems to feel that in the presence of readers who know the full worth of life, the words of an elegy ought to be calm and unarousing. A life of independence and self-respect: that is the good to be sacrificed for, and not the honor of a glorious death. By the manner of his words about death in battle, Whitman finds a way of persuading us that this is so. It is a grace he shares with Lincoln—something I hardly need to say.

Often in the course of *Song of Myself,* the poet seems in contact with the reader. (A scholar of American literature, Barbara Packer, said about Whitman with perfect truth: "You feel that he is in the room with you.") The alternation of his whispers and prayers and enticements, with the strenuous catalogues and shorter glimpses of rural and urban life, seen close-up or in a medium shot or montage, "The blab of the pave. . . . tires of carts and sluff of bootsoles and talk of the promenaders, / The heavy omnibus, the driver with his interrogating thumb, the clank of the shod horses on the granite floor"—these blendings of energy give the poem its sweep and poise and its miraculous air of inclusiveness. Then come the closing sections and we seem suddenly to have entered a different climate. Every reader has felt this. The poet turns and talks to us now in a daily voice, as a person might stop to exchange a few words with a passerby. He has said a moment earlier, "I concentrate toward them that are nigh" (meaning *us*)—"I wait on the door-slab"—and by the way, what an amazing and evocative word that is, "door-slab": the passage into a new home or into the grave. Both meanings fit Whitman's conception that every life is the leavings of many deaths. But now, in the last verses of the poem, it is as if his death and our life were different names for the same occurrence.

He says a gigantic farewell with no more ceremony than nature itself; he speaks to us as air, as breath:

> I depart as air. . . . I shake my white locks at the
>   runaway sun,
> I effuse my flesh in eddies and drift it in lacy jags.

> I bequeath myself to the dirt to grow from the grass I
>   love,
> If you want me again look for me under your bootsoles.

> You will hardly know who I am or what I mean,
> But I shall be good health to you nevertheless,
> And filter and fibre your blood.

> Failing to fetch me at first keep encouraged,
> Missing me one place search another,
> I stop some where waiting for you.

This stop is not really an ending. A pause, rather, that awaits resumption in another voice akin to his. The poem remains as an incitement, in our own lives, ever to be rebegun. Whitman is telling us also that the author of *Song of Myself* was never the Walter Whitman who took out the copyright, who has renamed himself Walt and appeared just once by that half-assumed name, at sections 24 and

25, in a tone that registers pride and mockery in equal parts. He has not said and did not mean to say, "This is *me*." The author becomes any of a multitude of people who learn what he means by asking, without external help or support, "What is the grass?"; fetching it to ask that question, as now we must fetch him from the knit of identity in which we know that we, too, have been woven. Different readers of a poem as long as this will choose different lines as their favorites, but a pretty irresistible candidate is line 577, which says in other words what Whitman's closing words have said: "Happiness. . . . which whoever hears me let him or her set out in search of this day." The leaves of grass that are Walt Whitman, the flag of his disposition, out of green stuff woven, are, he says, to be discovered under our feet and in our lives, indeed they were always there if only we had thought to look. So the poem keeps its modest and extraordinary promise: "what I assume you shall assume." The signers of the Declaration of Independence, who were also interested in what they called happiness, really meant no less than that when they subscribed the mutual pledge of their lives, their fortunes, and their sacred honor.

The rules or observances that cement society are largely implicit in a democracy, far more so than they are in any more hierarchical way of life, and so the tacit need for shared assumptions becomes correspondingly sharp. Lincoln, more conspicuously than Whitman, turned for moral guidance to the Declaration of Independence. He thought one could see the highest idealism of American democracy articulated in the words "All men are created equal." Throughout his early political career, he faced, in arguments by the slaveholders and their apologists in Congress, the counter-assertion that the founders meant by those words "all white men are created equal." As Stephen Douglas put it—a centrist by the standard of that time and by no means an abject apologist for slavery—the nation was "established by white men for the benefit of white men and their posterity forever." Now Lincoln is often and I think mistakenly described as a centrist or a moderate or a skillful pragmatist. Bear those words by Douglas in mind as you listen to Lincoln in 1857, in his Speech on the Dred Scott Decision, offering his interpretation of the well-known phrase. The signers of the Declaration of Independence, he says,

> defined with tolerable distinctness in what respects they did consider all men created equal—equal in "certain inalienable rights, among which are life, liberty, and the pursuit of happiness." This they said, and this they meant. . . . They meant to set up a standard maxim for free society, which should be familiar to all, and revered by all; constantly looked to, constantly labored for, and even though never perfectly attained, constantly approximated, and thereby constantly spreading and deepening its influence, and augmenting the happiness and value of life to all people of all colors everywhere. . . . They knew the proneness of prosperity to breed tyrants, and they meant when such should reappear in this fair land and commence their vocation they should find left for them at least one hard nut to crack.

The politician like the poet is a worker in words, though it seems fair to say they aim at widely different effects, the one to imagine, the other to persuade. Still, let us not exaggerate the difference. The imaginative work that persuasion implied for a man with Lincoln's aims was immense, and it required him to help his listeners discover what it was that created the value of life for them. Most of us probably now agree with him on the meaning of the words in the Declaration. Few of those whom he spoke to could have been sure that they agreed. Those who were sure they disagreed felt no compunction in calling his interpretation perverse and heaping abuse on Lincoln for having even dared to venture it.

Hatred of violence and love of liberty are the clues to Lincoln's political character. He believed that the history of slavery, in fact, was a history of violence under one name or another; that the only dangerous divisions in the United States ever since its founding had come from the contest over slavery; and that the forced return of Dred Scott to his master, and the sanctioning of it by the Supreme Court, were "an astonisher in legal history," a terrible extension of that violence. Nevertheless, Lincoln was for avoiding a war—the worst kind of violence because the most organized; a war whose result in any case could not be foreseen—so long as assurance was given that slavery would not expand and would be allowed to die a natural death. Until the firing on Fort Sumter by the guns of the Confederacy, he reiterated his purpose of standing firm without surrendering persuasion to violence. "Where the conduct of men is designed to be influenced," he said in an early speech to a temperance society, "*persuasion,* kind, unassuming persuasion, should ever be adopted." But Lincoln's opposition to slavery was founded on something deeper than his reading of the constitutional framers; it came from a settled belief about the constitution of human nature: "I hold if the Almighty had ever made a set of men that should do all the eating and none of the work, he would have made them with mouths only and no hands, and if he had ever made another class that he intended should do all the work and none of the eating; he would have made them without mouths and with all hands."

Persuasion, however, as Lincoln knew well, does not operate just through fable or example or the counting of short- and long-term benefits. It requires that we place ourselves in the situation of the people whom we would persuade—however disagreeable that may be when it obliges us to admit the irrational influence of custom and training. "I have no prejudice against the Southern people," says Lincoln in his Speech on the Kansas-Nebraska Act. "They are just what we would be in their situation. If slavery did not now exist amongst them, they would not introduce it. If it did now exist amongst us, we should not instantly give it up." When Lincoln speaks like this, he is engaged in a disagreeable and necessary act of sympathy. He is seeking to conciliate, and he is also telling the truth as he sees it.

And here we come to an uneasy fact—uneasy for people who like to divide the political world between saints and sinners—namely, that Abraham Lincoln was a politician. He was a man of strong beliefs, trying to change the thinking of people who began with very different strong beliefs, and his practical aim was to pull them to his side. He did not cherish a hope of converting them to all his opinions. The intensity of his dedication to this task at the peak of his powers is unimaginable. It had to happen for us to imagine it. In 1857 and 1858, even before the famous series of debates, Lincoln tramped up and down the state of Illinois in the footsteps of Stephen Douglas, arriving in a town sometimes a few hours and sometimes a few days after Douglas spoke. He would set the people right whose judgment Douglas was wheedling with. For he believed that by obtaining the passage of the Kansas-Nebraska

Act, Douglas had sold out the constitutional principle that slavery is the enemy of freedom. Yet Lincoln knew that many who agreed about this would not agree with the abolitionists that slavery was so intolerable an evil that it ought to be abolished at once. They would also disagree with him, and among themselves, about the appropriate policy to adopt toward the slaves once freed.

Some well-known words of his, taken in their full context, show as well as anything could what persuasion in politics means. Truly persuasive words always imply a kind of dialogue between our ideal views and the existing opinions of people whose starting point is quite unlike our own. Here, then, is Lincoln in the Speech on the Kansas-Nebraska Act, asking what will be the relation between black and white races once slavery has been abolished. He has begun by rejecting colonization for the time being as impracticable; and as he goes on, we can hear him thinking aloud—a practice in which he excelled every politician who ever lived. "What next?" he asks in this speech of 1854:

> Free them, and make them politically and socially, our equals? My own feelings will not admit of this; and if mine would, we well know that those of the great mass of white people will not. Whether this feeling accords with justice and sound judgment, is not the sole question, if indeed, it is any part of it. A universal feeling, whether well or ill founded, can not be safely disregarded.

So he leaves himself and his audience with a perplexity that is to be worked on. A profound central truth of democracy is that slavery is wrong—Lincoln once wrote, "If slavery is not wrong, nothing is wrong"—but when pressed to say what will follow once slavery is abolished, he confesses that he does not know.

His hope, before the war changed everything, was to put slavery "in the course of ultimate extinction"—a phrase he repeated again and again with little variation. It took the coming of the war, on terms that made the president appear a constitutional leader and not a fanatic, and it took the visible contribution on the Union side of Negro soldiers against the Slave Power, to move what he had called a "universal feeling" opposed to racial equality a long way toward the acceptance of former slaves as fellow citizens. The record of the extent of that change is eloquent in the thirteenth, fourteenth, and fifteenth amendments to the Constitution. But it would not be right to conclude that the war and its necessities alone changed the shape of the nation's self-understanding. When we look closely at Lincoln's speeches and writings of the 1850s, we are seeing the persuasive conduct of a man who is already a leader. Though out of office, he is already preparing the minds of his fellow citizens for a momentous change. And he contrives to do so even while serving as a publicist of the principles of his party.

This is the pattern of Lincoln's speeches, letters, and occasional and commemorative statements throughout the 1850s. He uses, for example, the occasion of a festival in Boston honoring the birthday of Thomas Jefferson, which he cannot attend, to compose a public letter in praise of Jefferson. He asserts in this letter of 1859 that the Republican Party of his day has become the true successor of the Democratic Party of earlier years; since the Democrats now hold the liberty of one man to be "nothing, when in conflict with another man's right of *property*. Republicans, on the contrary, are for both the *man* and the *dollar*; but in cases of conflict, the man *before* the dollar." It is a catchphrase and a good one, but it conceals a radicalism stronger than we may recognize at first. Really to put the man before the dollar would be to admit the wickedness not just of slavery but of the factory system and the ethic of moneymaking whose effects we have heard Whitman testify to a few years after the war.

There came a time before the war itself when Lincoln felt it necessary to speak of slavery from the point of view of the slave. He is at his firmest again in the Speech on the Dred Scott Decision, where, for the first time, he asks his white listeners to imagine the slave, not as an inferior creature but as another self—a "Me myself" or "what I am," to borrow Whitman's language—subject to a degradation without end, trapped by wheel within wheel of legal mystification and political compromise, a soul forever cut off from a body's experience of freedom. "One after another they have closed the heavy iron doors upon him, and now they have him, as it were, bolted in with a lock of a hundred keys, which can never be unlocked without the concurrence of every key; the keys in the hands of a hundred different men, and they scattered to a hundred different and distant places." In listening to these words, the free man or woman is asked to feel with the slave by virtue of nothing but a common humanity.

Look far ahead now to the middle year of the war—six years is not a long time as we normally reckon, but in 1863 the world had been turned upside down—and hear Lincoln as he utters the other half of the same appeal. The occasion is an open letter to a group of Union supporters who say they want peace but whose real objection is not to the war but to the Emancipation Proclamation. The abolitionist cause has now become an almost self-evident argument against white people who cannot admit a common humanity with the slave. "Peace," writes Lincoln in his letter to James C. Conkling, on August 26, 1863,

> does not appear so distant as it did. I hope it will come soon, and come to stay; and so come as to be worth the keeping in all future time. . . . And then, there will be some black men who can remember that, with silent tongue, and clinched teeth, and steady eye, and well-poised bayonet, they have helped mankind on to this great consummation; while, I fear, there will be some white ones, unable to forget that with malignant heart, and deceitful speech, they have strove to hinder it.

Lincoln describes the value of individuality and solidarity by showing what they are not. Yet the antislavery principle is not the central element of Lincoln's thought. More primary and more radical is the principle that was called in his time "free labor"—the name of a political movement and also of a commonsense demand, that every man and woman should be accorded the power of obtaining adequate pay for work of any kind. The end in view is a society where one moves from working for someone else to working for oneself and to employing others in turn. This is the promise of democratic activity—we might say of democratic energy—and Lincoln goes out of his way to associate it with education. A speech of 1859 about the ethics of labor directs itself against the so-called "mudsill" theory of the inevitability of a degraded workforce. Lincoln rejects the assumption that labor is not compatible with education. He was largely self-educated, and knew the value of genuine learning, as he did of energetic labor. He had worked his way from the humblest status to achieve the highest office in the land. The subject understandably provokes him to rewrite his fable of the body. With the slave and the master, the fable had told of the hands and the mouth. Now, with labor and education, it is the hands and the head: "Free labor argues that, as the Author of man makes every individual with one head and one pair of hands, it was probably intended that heads and hands should cooperate as friends; and that that particular head, should direct and control that particular pair of hands." The result of cultivating thought in the worker will be what Lincoln calls "*thorough* work." Every man and woman will become a virtuoso whose virtue is a particular kind of job well done. Word for word, perhaps, Lincoln's Second Inaugural Address is as great a work in writing as democracy has to show, but no piece of it is more characteristic than the phrase "Let us strive on to finish the work we are in." War, we know, presents a field of exertion that by forced collaboration may bring out the best in the energies of men and women. Peace offers a scene of labor more naturally suited to equal division. Command and performance in time of peace can be a thorough product of consultation and of free discussion.

Lincoln—it comes as a constant surprise in so melancholy a man—was a great believer in human progress. But he asks us to beware of our inventions and our inventiveness. As he noticed once in a speech on discoveries, slavery, too, was a human invention, a saver of time and maker of leisure for some, but not for that reason worth all the evil it brought. In every epoch we need distinctive moral helps to fortify us in the battle against the evils of that epoch. The mere belief in progress is not enough. "History," observes Whitman in *Democratic Vistas*, "is long, long, long. Shift and turn the combinations as we may, the problem of the future of America is in certain respects as dark as it is vast." This feels equally true if we read it today as a sentence about ourselves. And not to be tricked by any afterglow, we must not let the optimism of Lincoln and Whitman make us forget the despair that shadowed all their utterances, a despair that was the ground note of the time in which they lived. But as heroes go, persons distinctive of an age and yet beyond it, their peculiar quality is to give encouragement. There is a prejudice, still common among educated people, against the very idea of personal heroes, but it seems to me fundamentally mistaken. The unmasking of great men and women, true as a tactic, is false as a discipline. By proving you contingently superior to the most admirable examples from the past, it deprives you of a weapon of criticism and a wellspring of hope. It fosters not the love of perfection but moral snobbery and self-satisfaction, and only adds to the growing excess and arrogance of realism. Can we express the morality of true democracy better than Whitman and Lincoln did? "Whoever degrades another degrades me." "As I would not be a slave, so I would not be a master. This expresses my idea of democracy. Whatever differs from this, to the extent of the difference, is no democracy."

2002

CHAPTER 5

LINCOLN'S CONSTITUTIONAL NECESSITY

IN A TIME OF CRISIS A POLITICAL LEADER MAY SENSE THAT A change is going to happen and say to himself: "It needs someone to make it happen, and I am that person." The instruments of demography assume that this is a miraculous case, but, well into the twentieth century, it was the normal process by which the mind of a gifted leader worked upon the elusive medium of public life.

> And all sway forward on the dangerous flood
> Of history, that never sleeps or dies,
> And, held one moment, burns the hand.

When we look at political change in this light, the familiar oppositions melt away: events and actions, necessity and choice, determinism and free will. Necessity is not so inhumanly fixed as the metaphysicians suppose. Nor is human will so flexible. One way to think about the greatness of Lincoln—it was his usual way of reflecting on himself—is to see his career as a joining of necessity and personal resolve. The interest of the solitary figure becomes oddly more vivid with a recognition of the pressure of external circumstance. We see the relation between contingency and purpose as if things could not have gone otherwise, as if the logic of human causes and effects were self-evident.

What was Lincoln's starting point in his decision to lead? In a spread-out and mostly incoherent republic like the states of the 1830s, the task of citizenship, and so of leadership too, was to rehearse the good of certain approved sentiments: the good for example of obeying the laws in a country where the laws are made and can be changed by the people, and where they do not mainly assist or abet cruelty. Another such sentiment is agreement with the ideal that "All men are created equal" and a readiness to grant that the phrase is not a tissue of coded exclusions. Lincoln by 1858 will make it mean "all men," including Negroes, but as early as 1836, in a letter to the *Sangamon Journal,* he widened its sense unexpectedly: "I go for admitting all whites to the right of suffrage, who pay taxes or bear arms (by no means excluding women)." His recent biographer David Herbert Donald says that this was a joke, but why should it have been? Women's suffrage was in the air in the 1830s. The point is that agreement on approved sentiments may be a requirement for the deeper efforts of reform. The conservative basis is necessary for the radical deed, if only as an assurance of stability, a reminder. This is half of the meaning of Lincoln's first great speech, the Lyceum address of January 27, 1838. The remedy he proposes for the recent spate of lynchings and other evidence of "mobocracy" is to hold firmly to the memory of 1776.

Even in this youthful speech, Lincoln understands that loyalty comes more easily to people in time of war. For the older generation, the crisis was upon them, the alarm was given, and the imperative of action left no room for demurral. By contrast, Americans in the panic of 1837 had been living in a society at peace, and with the onset of disorder they naturally looked for someone to blame. It is at this revealing moment that Lincoln asks for an effort of memory and loyalty together: "Let every American pledge his life, his property, and his sacred honor; let every man remember that to violate the law, is to trample on the blood of his father, and to tear the character of his own and his children's liberty." But his interest in manners and habits—in the habit, especially, of following the rule of law as a good in itself—has not yet crossed in Lincoln's mind with the constitutional question, Who are the people by whom the laws are to be revered? He has not yet seen the question of slavery as central.

He will walk up to its brink a few years later, when considering the annexation of Texas, in a letter of October 3, 1845:

> It is possibly true, to some extent, that with annexation, some slaves may be sent to Texas and continued in slavery, that otherwise might have been liberated. To whatever extent this may be true, I think annexation an evil. I hold it to be a paramount duty of us in the free states, due to the Union of the states, and perhaps to liberty itself (paradox though it may seem) to let the slavery of the other states alone; while, on the other hand, I hold it to be equally clear, that we should never knowingly lend ourselves directly or indirectly, to prevent that slavery from dying a natural death—to find new places for it to live in, when it can no longer exist in the old. Of course I am not now considering what would be our duty, in cases of insurrection among the slaves.

It is curious how far the reservation leads him. For here is the germ of the platform Lincoln will help to make for the Republican Party a full decade later. Slavery is to be placed in a condition in which it can be allowed to die a natural death, a death it is bound for anyway since its manners and morals are inconsistent with democracy. What conduct ought to follow with respect to slave insurrections is already troubling to him. Or so one may suppose: he does not consider it here because the discussion would be intricate.

Sixteen years after the Lyceum speech, six years after the debate on the war with Mexico and annexation, it was the Kansas-Nebraska Act of 1854 that drew Lincoln onto the national stage. Such is his report of the matter—"I was losing interest in politics, when the repeal of the Missouri Compromise aroused me again"—and there is no reason to doubt it. To this moment can be traced the one steep change in Lincoln's understanding of America, and a change in the tenor of his speaking and writing about the future of the republic. Until then, he never felt himself to be living in an emergency, a crisis that must either widen or break the regime of freedom. But in his three-hour speech in Peoria on October 16, 1854—the greatest piece of political reasoning ever spoken by an American—he gave the first formulation, never substantially to be altered, of his revolutionary view that the framers of the Constitution did not approve of slavery, that the Missouri Compromise was meant to be an ultimate settler of the limit of its expansion, and that, consistent with the principles of liberty and equality, slavery was now to be placed on a course of extinction. Slavery and constitutional government are contradictory propositions. But the hidden evil of the slave system is that it engenders a tacit approval of servility, foreign to democratic manners, in order to produce the apologetics required by mutual cooperation:

This declared indifference, but as I must think, covert real zeal for the spread of slavery, I can not but hate. I hate it because of the monstrous injustice of slavery itself. I hate it because it deprives our republican example of its just influence in the world—enables the enemies of free institutions, with plausibility, to taunt us as hypocrites—causes the real friends of freedom to doubt our sincerity, and especially because it forces so many really good men amongst ourselves into an open war with the very fundamental principles of civil liberty—criticizing the Declaration of Independence, and insisting that there is no right principle of action but self-interest.

It is sometimes said that Lincoln was a pragmatist, appealing to the commonest ordinary motives and in tune with the supposed commercial realism of the founding fathers. His scorn here for self-interest as a principle of action shows how wrong that view of his politics has always been.

The moderation of the Peoria speech is a matter of stance not principle. Lincoln declines to speak as a prophetic denouncer of corrupt morals. He has a certain fatalism about the adaptation of morals to the customary life in which they find their soil: "I think I have no prejudice against the Southern people. They are just what we would be in their situation. If slavery did not exist amongst them, they would not introduce it. If it did now exist amongst us, we should not instantly give it up." Nevertheless, slavery is a monstrous human wrong. It is right to expect, even of those who would suffer from its abolition, that they be willing to give it up gradually. The sense of inevitability—so marked a trait of Lincoln's temper and almost of his idiom—is not to be confused with quietism. And yet in the Peoria speech he still evidently sees himself as a Whig, one who properly combines a disposition to preserve and an ability to improve; and he adopts a posture of legitimate compromise, even to the extent of attempting to strike a balance between abolitionism and the rights of the hunters of slaves: "Stand WITH the abolitionist in restoring the Missouri Compromise; and stand AGAINST him when he attempts to repeal the fugitive slave law. In the latter case you stand with the Southern disunionist. What of that? You are still in the right. In both cases you are right. In both cases you oppose the dangerous extremes."

This assured belief in expedience was nearly undone—if we consider the long-term consequences, it was virtually broken—by the Supreme Court's decision in the Dred Scott case. Lincoln responded as strongly again as he had to the Kansas-Nebraska Act. In looking at his reaction, what must be remembered is how unappeasably the case brought into view the need for enforcement of the Fugitive Slave Law. Taney's decision carved out an unlimited right for the slaveholder to reclaim his human property, and this in a free territory where, according to the previous and common-sense interpretation of the law, the slave had become a free man. So an emancipated Negro like Dred Scott could be retroactively defined out of his freedom. A constitutionalism opposed to Lincoln's enabled Taney to declare a Negro to be in his very nature *not* a citizen and to invoke the highest authority for that view. It was a matter Lincoln himself must have pondered in detail, and on which probably he decided that the Constitution did not offer guidance one way or the other, though he believed on strong evidence that the founders leaned away from explicitly refusing the rights of citizenship to Negroes. The result anyway was that the Fugitive Slave

Law—to which as late as 1854 Lincoln was urging faithful and resigned obedience—had now become an instrument for the extension of slavery. At the very least, since the decision curtailed the right of free men to confer freedom and affirmed the right of the slave hunter to reassert mastery, it is fair to say that the law had now been given a scope that worked against the circumvention of slavery.

Thinking of all that the founders did and refrained from doing to clarify their sentiments on slavery, Lincoln in the Peoria speech had concluded: "Necessity drove them so far, and further, they would not go." And how far had necessity driven *him* with the Dred Scott decision? The question is fair because Lincoln was a believer in necessity. This element of his intellectual character often gets explained away with a broad allowance for his belief in the force of circumstance. Lincoln did once say—what may pass for a token of the impersonal realism prized by historians and memoir-writers—that "I claim not to have controlled events, but confess plainly that events have controlled me." But we must hear his tone carefully. When he uses this language, in a letter to Albert G. Hodges on April 4, 1864, Lincoln is not invoking the blameless posture of the morally helpless. Nor is he confessing that events overbore his will. It is of some interest that in such remarks, for there are others scattered throughout his career, it is always things or tendencies that Lincoln says he obeyed. It is never people. Lincoln was not a vague thinker, and though a canny rhetorician, he had less of the mere virtuosity of persuasion, the pomp and sonority of dignified utterance, than may be found in rivals like Seward and Sumner and Stephen Douglas, or in predecessors like Webster and Clay and even Burke. Hardly a word or a phrase in Lincoln is there for its sound or the passing impression it may leave. What, then, are we to make of "necessity"?

In the late eighteenth century and through much of the nineteenth, the word and the idea signified an understanding of the system of nature that verged on atheism. It is pertinent that Lincoln himself was once charged with atheism, or "infidelity," as it was also called. The slander went out in the congressional campaign of 1846 and quickly became so current that he felt obliged to respond in a handbill to voters of the seventh district in Illinois. He says there about his own beliefs: that he is not a member of any Christian church but has never denied the truth of the Scripture; that he has never spoken with intentional disrespect of religion "in general, or of any denomination of Christians in particular"; that "in early life I was inclined to believe in what I understand is called the 'Doctrine of Necessity'—that is, that the human mind is impelled to action, or held in rest by some power, over which the mind itself has no control; and I have sometimes (with one, two or three, but never publicly) tried to maintain this opinion in argument." He says finally that he has not argued in this manner for more than five years. The explanation strikes me as too circumstantial, too interesting, and, even for the purpose of refuting a slander, too damaging to be anything but an honest account.

It was a feature of the mechanistic physics of Holbach and Helvetius that all thought is derived from and translatable into bodily impulse. Consciousness in this view, and the apparent work of conscience, become a result of a coalescence of forces beyond the control of a single human will. Joseph Priestley—a radical ally of Thomas Paine, whose *Age of Reason* (according to William Herndon) Lincoln read and "assimilated . . . into his own being"—had given popular form to the argument for the compatibility of necessity with freedom. Deterministic thinkers closer to our time have tended toward a distrust of imagination, but this was never a logical corollary of the view; nor did it favor either an optimistic or a pessimistic sense of the happiness of the human lot. Thomas Hardy was a believer in necessity, but so was Walt Whitman: "Immense have been the preparations for me, / Faithful and friendly the arms that have helped me." An idea of necessity may come from a perception, which has the force of a fact, about the total drift of events and tendencies. It is certain that Lincoln saw the holding of slaves as being opposed to the total drift of morality in an extended free republic. He thought the founders had always seen it thus. His difference from the abolitionists related to what a leader must do in the present circumstances. As he saw it, the abolition of slavery in the states where the institution already existed would cooperate with necessity, but would do so in a manner that required another revolution. This was a catastrophe, which, if possible, Lincoln meant to spare a country still young in its freedom.

In the Peoria speech, he made a chart of the probable intentions, in his view the *only* probable intentions, of the American founders toward slavery. The method was an explanatory catalogue of their actions. In 1798 they prohibited slaves from being brought into the Mississippi Territory, ten years before they had the authority to do so for the states existing at the time of the Constitution. In 1800 they "prohibited American citizens from trading in slaves between foreign countries"; in 1803 they passed laws restraining the internal slave trade; in 1807, a year ahead of the twenty-year termination point, they passed a law prohibiting African slave trade, with "heavy pecuniary and corporal penalties," to take effect the first day of 1808; in 1820 they passed another and an unusually stringent law, making this form of trade an act of piracy, and punishable by death. "Thus we see," comments Lincoln, "the plain unmistakable spirit of that age, toward slavery, was hostility to the PRINCIPLE, and toleration, ONLY BY NECESSITY."

The limits of necessity have widened between 1820 and 1854. The failure of human will on which Lincoln reflects is all the more peculiar considering the general advance of morals. Toleration of slavery as the letter, and suspension of concern with the spirit of the law, embodies a failure of the national will to concert itself against what has become a necessary development, namely the putting of slavery "in the course of ultimate extinction."

The speech concludes memorably by asserting that the doctrine that all men are created equal, and the idea of counting slavery as a "sacred right of self-government," are "as opposite as God and mammon."

When Pettit, in connection with his support of the Nebraska bill, called the Declaration of Independence "a self-evident lie," he only did what consistency and candor require all other Nebraska men to do. Of the forty-odd Nebraska Senators who sat present and heard him, no one rebuked him. Nor am I apprized that any Nebraska newspaper, or any Nebraska orator, in the whole nation, has ever yet rebuked him. If this had been said among Marion's men, Southerners though they were, what would have become of the man who said it? . . . If it had been said in old Independence Hall, seventy-eight years ago, the very door-keeper would have throttled the man, and thrust him into the street.

The observation is stirring, and yet perplexing too, when one bears in mind Lincoln's belief that moral necessity means a progress of sentiments. On the contrary the repeal of the Missouri Compromise seems nothing if not a moral regression. Lincoln in 1854 will say at last: "Let us turn slavery from its claims of 'moral right,' back upon its existing legal rights, and its arguments of 'necessity.'" Theirs, he means to say, is a false necessity, and we can prove it so by reducing the slaveholder to the maintenance of a defensive outpost. In that year, Lincoln was content to invite both sides to agree in such a tacit understanding. But what if the regression or depravation of sentiments should become more threatening? That is the eventuality Lincoln holds in view in his speech at Kalamazoo, Michigan, in August 1856. He explains how the toleration of slaves and masters, in a territory not yet given to slavery, would impede free choice in elections by the voters already there.

> Can men vote truly? We will suppose that there are ten men who go into Kansas to settle. Nine of these are opposed to slavery. One has ten slaves. The slaveholder is a good man in other respects; he is a good neighbor, and being a wealthy man, he is enabled to do the others many neighborly kindnesses. They like the man, though they don't like the system by which he holds his fellowmen in bondage. . . . These ten men of whom I was speaking, live together three or four years; they intermarry; their family ties are strengthened. And who wonders that in time, the people learn to look upon slavery with complacency?

So a misprision of the human will, the acceptance of the Kansas-Nebraska Act, because of the mix of manners it creates among settlers in the territories, naturally weakens the revulsion against ideas that taint the imagination of the person who holds them. The Kansas-Nebraska Act is sure to do moral damage to its adherents. For there are doctrines, belief in which degrades the believer, just as there are jokes that debase whoever laughs.

Lincoln asks his listeners in Kalamazoo to prevent this great harm to themselves:

> Now I make this appeal to the Democratic citizens here. Don't you find yourself making arguments in support of these measures, which you never would have made before? Did you ever do it before this Nebraska bill compelled you to do it? If you answer this in the affirmative, see how a whole party have been turned away from their love of liberty!

The questions lead to the same kind of exhortation that Lincoln would use to wind up the "House Divided" speech on June 16, 1858. It remains with us to *act* on what we are *compelled to believe;* and this is not a recondite procedure: our belief in principles makes us what we are. Thus the balance of choice and necessity recurs: "Wise *counsels* may *accelerate* or *mistakes delay* it, but, sooner or later the victory is *sure* to come." His italics emphasize the connection between probable means and an irresistible result.

Let us pass to a celebrated statement some months further on, only pausing to note that the "House Divided" speech was itself the most deliberate performance Lincoln ever devised for the drawing of a line, and that it was carried out against a good deal of prudential advice. The line in question ("I do not expect the Union to be *dissolved*—I do not expect the house to *fall*—but I *do* expect it will cease to be divided. It will become *all* one thing, or *all* the other") gave him a distinct position from which to launch his attack on slavery as a rooted system; and one can see the effects in the first debate with Stephen Douglas, where Lincoln accuses Douglas, by his unconcern with slavery, of "blowing out the moral lights" around us, "penetrating the human soul and eradicating the light of reason and the love of liberty." This is as much as to say that Douglas is acting against human nature, against the reason and feelings that alone serve to humanize us. How would Lincoln have described the difference between a nonhuman necessity and the victory he promises to those who now stand firm? This runs parallel to the difference between saying that something must happen and saying one sees the agency by which it will happen. It is the difference between, on the one hand, recognizing that a law expresses widely held sentiments and principles, and, on the other hand, assuring the enforcement of the law. This reduction of necessity to a practice will become Lincoln's absorbing concern in his effort to delegitimate, without suggesting disobedience to, the Dred Scott decision.

Chief Justice Taney had there argued that the subjection of negroes had always and appropriately been maintained by local "police regulations" enforced by white citizens. Stephen Douglas drew on this idea to assert that the decision did not encourage the spread of slavery in contradiction to the law of the land, because the people themselves could at any time frustrate the expansion of slavery by introducing hostile police regulations. Lincoln pounced on the shabby legalism in his third debate against Douglas: "I hold that the history of this country shows that the institution of slavery was originally planted *without* these 'police regulations' which [Douglas] now thinks necessary for the actual establishment of it." Further, when Dred Scott claimed his freedom because an act of Congress forbade his being held as a slave in the Minnesota Territory, he was returned to slavery "in the teeth of Congressional legislation supposed to be valid at the time." That is, they made him subject again to his master without any pretext drawn from police regulations. "This shows," says Lincoln, "that there is vigor enough in slavery to plant itself in a new country even against unfriendly legislation. It takes not only law but the *enforcement* of law to keep it out." And Taney and the Supreme Court, by suspending that enforcement, and even implicitly reversing the character of the law to be enforced, are now in the same position as John Pettit when he called the truths of the Declaration of Independence self-evident lies. From Lincoln's point of view, the right way to deal with Pettit was to oppose his sentiments articulately, to "throttle him" by the sting of a moral rebuke in some way compatible with outward decency. So, too, the right way to deal with Taney is to resist the Dred Scott decision, preferably by getting the law changed by a new Supreme Court, and getting the court changed by a new president. Meanwhile popular sentiment can show its disapproval of the new law by signals of discontent that do not add up to violation.

The speech given in Chicago on March 1, 1859, though its grammar of assertion is the same, presents a syntax so altered that the sense feels distinct from anything yet heard from Lincoln on the subject of slavery. He has said before that the Constitution permitted slavery where it already was, and not in states where it had not been; that the institution was to be disposed of in the territories as provided for in the Missouri Compromise; that it has long been understood that the founders meant slavery to disappear ultimately, and we cooperate with their evident purpose so long as we do nothing to assist its propagation. We do this best by acknowledging the principle that all men are created equal. But Lincoln now in the Chicago speech, after his debates with Douglas—still enunciating the principle above, which sounds like moderate republicanism, and still logically asserting no more than he was in the habit of asserting—seems to have arrived at a crossroads where his words meant more than he was used to seeing them mean. The propositions are now so ordered that the saying of them sounds a good deal less moderate. Once again, as in the "House Divided" speech, he is drawing a line and pointing to the place where, as a constitutional republican, he cannot think of compromise. Yet he seems to be fortifying himself for a larger battle of some sort:

> I wish now to add a word that has a bearing on the future. The Republican principle, the profound central truth that slavery is wrong and ought to be dealt with as a wrong, though we are always to remember the fact of its actual existence amongst us and faithfully observe all the constitutional guarantees—the unalterable principle never for a moment to be lost sight of that it is a wrong and ought to be dealt with as such, cannot advance at all upon Judge Douglas' ground—that there is a portion of the country in which slavery must always exist; that he does not care whether it is voted up or voted down, as it is simply a question of dollars and cents. Whenever, in any compromise or arrangement or combination that may promise some temporary advantage, we are led upon that ground, then and there the great living principle upon which we have organized as a party is surrendered.

The guarantees to the slaveholders written into the Constitution are still felt to be worthy of mention, but they have become a reminder in a subordinate clause. The *always* which might be supposed a duty of patriotic citizenship, "we are always to remember the fact of its actual existence among us"—this fact, never neglected in his previous statements, is brought forward dutifully again, but it is now frankly treated as a shameful fact, something eventually not to be countenanced. When Lincoln speaks of a *living* principle, the adjectival emphasis may be small, but it points to a burden that he now feels and wants his hearers to share. He wants to keep alive the probability of the extinction of slavery, and he knows that the result does depend on the will of men and women. That is why, near the end of this speech, one can detect a militancy not seen before. "All you have to do is to keep the faith, to remain steadfast to the right, to stand by your banner. Nothing should lead you to leave your guns. Stand together, ready, with match in hand."

The Cooper Institute Address of 1860 was, in effect, a preliminary campaign speech, to get Lincoln a hearing from the party grandees of the East by showing that he had a more than local grasp of national issues, and that he was therefore a stronger candidate than they had imagined. All this the speech accomplished. But it surprised the audience by being a work of scholarship in constitutional law. In arguing for the necessity of putting slavery on a course of ultimate extinction, Lincoln here cites the tradition of the constitutional founders as the best available support in the domain of political prudence. He proceeds to inculcate, precept by precept, what he takes to be the constitutional doctrine on slavery, but the emphasis of the argument turns from the wisdom of tradition to the force of necessity. "*As those fathers marked it, so let it again be marked, as an evil not to be extended, but to be tolerated and protected only because of and so far as its actual presence among us makes that toleration and protection a necessity."* The establishment of the right and wrong of slavery and the terms on which the Union can be preserved are a matter partly of the names we consent to give to things. What, asks Lincoln, will placate the South? "This, and this only: cease to call slavery *wrong,* and join them in calling it *right.* And this must be done thoroughly—done in *acts* as well as in *words.* Silence will not be tolerated—we must place ourselves avowedly with them. . . . . They will continue to accuse us of doing, until we cease saying."

But there is a point at which a choice of words and the staking of a fixed principle must coincide—where speaking well differs from speaking ill of slavery:

> Holding, as they do, that slavery is morally right, and socially elevating, they cannot cease to demand a full national recognition of it, as a legal right, and a social blessing.
>
> Nor can we justifiably withhold this, on any ground save our conviction that slavery is wrong. If it is right, we cannot justly object to its nationality—its universality; if it is wrong, they cannot justly insist upon its extension—its enlargement. All they ask, we could readily grant, if we thought slavery right; all we ask, they could as readily grant, if they thought it wrong. Their thinking it right, and our thinking it wrong, is the precise fact upon which depends the whole controversy. Thinking it right, as they do, they are not to blame for desiring its full recognition, as being right; but, thinking it wrong, as we do, can we yield to them?

What we will do is shown to be strictly derivative from what we must do. We cease to be who we are if we do otherwise. So necessity in the domain of nature converges with self-consistency in the domain of human nature.

"Morally right" and "socially elevating" are, of course, understatements of what the South says it is right to feel about slavery. At the same time, they are phrases which our understanding pronounces false even as our mouths are opening to form the words; and if, regarding the South and its manners, we cannot give their names to their things, no more can we turn their things into different things without force. There is not a touch of the entire description that deviates into sarcasm; not one word about which an advocate of slavery could say: "You avow of our beliefs but do not speak our language." Lincoln uses just their words for just their things. And yet one feels, after having read these sentences, that the morality of the South has been subjected to the most devastating assault it is possible to suffer, and that its only imaginable recovery will be through a war which it must lose.

The Cooper Institute Address is a speech preparatory to a war, even though it is marked by deliberate restraint. The abolitionists were right to feel that Lincoln was not temperamentally of their party. Yet the apologists for slavery were right to realize on his election that a war was inevitable. He, of all the candidates, was the one certain to make no further concessions. Lincoln was stronger on this point, more tough-minded with far less posturing, than his secretary of state William Seward—a radical Republican sympathizer, but eager enough to concoct a phony war against a European enemy, and thereby unite the North and South, if this would have prevented the shots at Fort Sumter. Not until the war had actually come did Lincoln offer a comprehensive view of the moral and political argument he had been working out since 1854. The Special Message to

Congress of July 4, 1861 gives his constitutional justification of the necessity of fighting the war.

The speech was a palpable success. It drew the uncertain in Congress to his side, and if one follows it step by step, one can still see why. In the game of maneuver and counter-maneuver, Lincoln's attempt to convey provisions to Fort Sumter was in part a stratagem intended to draw the South to strike the first blow. Certainly, that was the prudent strategy to have followed in beginning what its declarer believed a necessary war against the enemies of liberty, since war must appear to be decreed by necessity as by an external force. The leader who chooses to go to war must even convince himself of this, if he would have a solid footing in his own structure of motives, to resist the gross incitements of conquest, plunder, and revenge. So the intricate series of actions around Fort Sumter were necessary for Lincoln to test the good faith of both sides. He was determined to show that his trust in the South was not gone; even at the price, if they spurned the chance, of allowing them to gain an initial advantage. It would be a sacrifice, incident to their gaining that advantage, that in being the first openly to depart from mutual trust, they would have to fire the first shots. And as it happened, thousands volunteered to fight for the Union from an indignation planted in them because they knew the flag had been fired on. Lincoln first notified Major Anderson, in command at Fort Sumter, to take no unnecessary risks. He wrote to Governor Pickens that he was in fact sending provisions only, and "no effort to throw in men, arms, or ammunition, will be made, without further notice, or in the case of an attack upon the fort." *Or in the case of an attack* meant clearly that he intended to order a withdrawal from the fort, and allow the South to take it, if by doing so they chose to announce definitively their intention to go to war against the Union. This testing of the routine sustenance of a fort, the notification to the principals that it was just such a test, and the deliberate withdrawal that followed, were a piece of statecraft no doubt, but they were something more. The occasion of the war had been so proved that the South should be seen, and be correctly seen, as instigating the breakup of a political order that the Union was required to restore for its own preservation. In this way, a revolutionary change would go under the banner, which was not false, of a conservative restoration as well.

Already some months earlier, in the First Inaugural Address, Lincoln had said that "the central idea of secession is the essence of anarchy." The reason relates to the definition of majority rule in a democracy:

A majority, held in restraint by constitutional checks, and limitations, and always changing easily, with deliberate changes of popular opinions and sentiments, is the only true sovereign of a free people. Whoever rejects it, does, of necessity, fly to anarchy or to despotism. Unanimity is impossible; the rule of a minority, as a permanent arrangement, is wholly inadmissible; so that, rejecting the majority principle, anarchy, or despotism in some form, is all that is left.

Notice again the use of "necessity": never a casual matter with Lincoln. One may trace the logical steps by which it earns its placement here. A majority is prevented from becoming tyrannical only by constitutional checks and limitations and because it changes easily. When he speaks of rule by a minority, Lincoln has in mind the oligarchy of slaveholders. Theirs was the real control of the South, or so Lincoln believed. James McPherson in *Battle Cry of Freedom* confirmed the suspicion by tracing the votes on secession in counties of the South where slaveholding was a major and a minor enterprise: in the former, the sentiment for secession is plainly dominant; in the latter, recessive and often scarcely visible. On Lincoln's view, the South was not the harmonious society it affected to be, an old and dignified way of life, arming to protect itself by the noble spirit of rebellion. Rather it was a set of large property holders, in the market with ancient and disreputable wares that they could not easily unload, bossing the smaller property holders and erecting a government to defend their immediate self-interest. Lincoln thinks that such an arrangement cannot last for long. It will turn to anarchy or to despotism—though it is already, from the perspective of Lincoln's non-aristocratic republicanism, close to despotic in the way it places a class of the privileged over a class of the wretched.

The question to be answered four months later, in the Special Message to Congress of July 4, 1861, has become whether an extended free republic can survive against such a challenge—a government, as Lincoln now calls it, "of the people, by the same people." The subject and object of the government of the Union are identical, and the good it answers for, as he will add in the Gettysburg Address, is the good of the same people. This identity cannot obtain in the slave states—by necessity it cannot obtain. That is rather a government *over* some people, *by* quite different people, *for* an ideal and speculative good which improbably represents the interests of both. For such a government to emerge alongside the United States as a rival and offspring of these states would be to subvert the existence of the Union.

It was, as Garry Wills and others have remarked, a peculiar choice of Lincoln's in the Gettysburg Address to identify the American republic with a *proposition,* and to say that the proposition was being *tested* by a war. But this was for him a usual adaptation of the idiom of logical and historical necessity, another either-or. A leading clue to the language of the Gettysburg Address comes again from the Special Message of July 4, 1861:

> Our popular government has often been called an experiment. Two points in it, our people have already settled—the successful *establishing,* and the successful *administering* of it. One still remains—its successful *maintenance* against a formidable internal attempt to overthrow it.

Whether a nation so conceived and so dedicated can long endure is a question to be answered by history alone, with a resolve that the people must add for themselves. "There is nothing good or bad but thinking makes it so": the psychological truth of Hamlet's observation was well known to Lincoln. The guarantee in every state of the Union is made good person-by-person, with the carrying out of the resolve.

"If a state may lawfully go out of the Union," Lincoln adds in the Special Message, "having done so, it may also discard the republican form of government; so that to prevent its going out, is an indispensable *means,* to the end of maintaining the guaranty mentioned." This argument, which could have been prominent, is treated instead as subordinate, and the critical section of the Special Message concerns the omission from the Southern declarations of independence of any mention of the people. The point concerns the influence of words on people's feelings and hence on their conviction of what is necessary. "Why," asks Lincoln, do they substitute for "We the People" the pedantic and ungainly phrase "We the deputies of the sovereign and independent States?" And again, "Why? Why this deliberate pressing out of view, the rights of men, and the authority of the people?" The question answers itself:

> This is essentially a People's contest. On the side of the Union, it is a struggle for maintaining in the world, that form, and substance of government, whose leading object is, to elevate the condition of men—to lift artificial weights from all shoulders—to clear the paths of laudable pursuit for all—to afford all, an unfettered start, and a fair chance, in the race of life. Yielding to partial, and temporary departures, from necessity, this is the leading object of the government for whose existence we contend.

Lincoln believed that the honor already displayed by men and women in the Union cause would not desert them in the battle ahead. His belief in the constitution of the mind of the people is cognate with his belief in the goodness and worthiness of the political constitution.

Some way under the assertion of faith lies a distinct political principle, not divulged by Lincoln until now, but probably held in his mind half-formed throughout his thinking life. The Union preceded the states—preceded them theoretically and as a matter of executive potency and sovereignty. His understanding of the Union may be thought "mystical": an idea stressed by Edmund Wilson in an unsympathetic essay. It is also eminently practical, from Lincoln's point of view. As he explains in the Special Message, it is a sophism to suppose that any state may withdraw from the Union without the consent of the other states, thus making itself the sole judge of equity toward the Union. But Southern statesmen have come to credit the sophism; and like their attachment to slavery, the thought of the separate rights of states has become a habit, rendered familiar by reiteration, whose effects are visible only when it is too late: "With rebellion thus sugar-coated, they have been drugging the public mind of their section for more than thirty years." Lincoln observes on the contrary that the original colonies passed into the Union before casting off their dependence, and the new states each came into the Union from a state of dependence (except Texas, which had independence but not as a state). The identification is thus firmly established: independence goes with Union; statehood alone has always meant dependence. Yet Lincoln will not release the argument until he gives the Southern justification and on its own terms refutes it once and for all.

The defenders of secession presume that "there is some omnipotent, and sacred supremacy, pertaining to a *State*"; yet none of them was ever a state out of the Union; the description of the "United Colonies" as "Free and Independent States" never was ventured with a view to declaring the states independent "of *one another*, or of the *Union*; but directly the contrary, as their mutual pledge, and their mutual action, before, at the time, and afterward, abundantly show." As in the controversy over the founders and slavery, he shows himself more traditionalist than the upholders of tradition in the South. But a theoretical fallacy is of greater interest to Lincoln: "What is a 'sovereignty,' in the political sense of the term? Would it be far wrong to define it 'A political community, without a political superior'?" An extended free republic like the United States needs to feel the live importance of this definition, even more than other forms of government do, because its borders are long and because on all sides it is tested by those who would set up a dictatorship, or a slave republic, or some other system necessarily at odds with its own. The traditional and the theoretical discussion come together in a characteristic formulation: "The Union is older than any of the States; and, in fact, it created them as States"; and (Lincoln does not have to add) its dissolution would undo them. The revolting states are parasitic on an existing union, in the absence of which they would have nothing to part from except each other. Hence the anarchy which Lincoln has said is the only alternative to despotism. Meanwhile, there are practical matters to concern a president, which Lincoln picks up with a dry humor, as if the Union as the mature party must be responsible for such odds and ends. Notable obligations have been left undischarged by the states; what will be done about them in the event of secession? Such debts are recurrent if not continuous in political life, and that they are so makes another reason against secessions. "The nation purchased, with money, the countries out of which several of these States were formed. Is it just that they shall go off without leave, and without refunding?" He specifies the debts of Florida and Texas, to cover which the nation has gone into debt. If all the states secede, there will be no one left to pay the creditors, and in this way ordinary promise-keeping is for practical purposes terminated. The point is small, but the demonstration large: the keeping of promises is the very thing that slavery fails to teach because it renders less normal a contract between equal parties. We "purchased, with money," says Lincoln; and he has in mind not only money, but the nature of obligations over time. These grow rapidly perishable if someone who entered into them can always choose afterward to redefine his character from a changing estimate of his interest.

Society itself, and agreements between existing societies, cannot go forward unless self-interest is qualified by being merged in something larger; and that possibility is cut off whenever a nation-within-the-nation claims an indefeasible right to regroup and withdraw into itself.

What is opened up is an endless regress of exclusions; and Lincoln sounds characteristically terse when casting the fallacy into logical form. The right to secede must be either discarded or retained by the new-modeled entity in its constitution:

> If they have discarded it, they thereby admit that, on principle, it ought not to be in ours. If they have retained it, by their own construction of ours they show that to be consistent they must secede from one another, whenever they shall find it the easiest way of settling their debts, or effecting any other selfish, or unjust object. The principle itself is one of disintegration.

If a single principle guides the Union, it is the principle of being unified for the benefit of the freedom of separate persons. What militates against it must work toward disintegration, and the doctrine of secession defies it at every point.

The picture remains consistent when we turn from Lincoln's reasoning preliminary to war, to some representative documents written during the war itself, in which he defends his idea of constitutional necessity. The most rewarding may be the Annual Message to Congress on December 1, 1862; the letter to James C. Conkling on August 26, 1863; and the Second Inaugural Address. Of these, the first deserves particularly close attention because it deals head-on with the most radical decision of the war, the choice to issue the Emancipation Proclamation. The second is an attempt to bring into coherence the actions of emancipating Negroes and assuring the survival of the Union, so that, to the most bigoted and craven of doubters, the two will seem to exist in a necessary collaboration. The third looks back as far as the Kansas-Nebraska speech, but with the unfolded history of the war almost complete, and connects the fight directly with the abolition of slavery. All three are efforts, too, of self-persuasion, the last perhaps most of all.

On emancipation, Lincoln had made a canvass of his supporters before deciding on the appropriate timing. The abolitionists had wanted it since the start of the war; others had hoped its moment would never come. No doubt in the end the decision was Lincoln's alone. His message to Congress at the beginning of December 1862 was written chiefly to prepare the minds of the people, and of their representatives, for the new shape into which the conflict had cast their polity. It was, Lincoln believed, a reform toward some higher idealism of democracy, but also a reform many would hesitate to embrace, for they could not imagine, any more than he could, the kind of society that would result from black and white men and women living together equally free. He justifies it first of all as a step forced by necessity, which nevertheless ought to be accepted as a responsibility, and which, once understood, men will readily acknowledge as their own. Its effect, he thinks, will be to enlarge the liberty of all, but it will do so in a way that many, especially at first, are certain to find painful or estranging. So he asks whether it is possible to doubt that emancipation will shorten the war—by taking heart out of the Southern cause, by adding strength of numbers to the Union forces, and thereby lessening the expenditure of blood and money. If we would win, and win for the cause we say has driven our efforts all along, how can we do other than put our energy into the process of emancipation and help to assure its success?

This much is necessary to victory; but, says Lincoln, it lies with us to make what is necessary also real:

> The occasion is piled high with difficulty, and we must rise with the occasion. As our case is new, so we must think anew, and act anew. We must disenthrall ourselves, and then we shall save our country.
>
> Fellow-citizens, *we* cannot escape history. We of this Congress and this administration, will be remembered in spite of ourselves. No personal significance, or insignificance, can spare one or another of us. The fiery trial through which we pass, will light us down, in honor or dishonor, to the latest generation. We *say* we are for the Union. The world will not forget that we say this. We know how to save the Union. The world knows we do know how to save it. We—even *we here*—*hold* the power, and bear the responsibility. In *giving* freedom to the *slave,* we *assure* freedom to the *free*—honorable alike in what we give, and what we preserve. We shall nobly save, or meanly lose, the last best, hope of earth.

It may be the first time in American writing that *history* is used in quite this way, to denote a force outside human volition, and partly alien to it: not a question of mere heritage or the accretion of practices, and not the same, either, as a destiny projected from the past to the future. History is imagined rather as a force in the present that makes demands without parallel on those who would have any future at all.

A subtle workmanship of prose, here as in the Gettysburg Address, relentlessly narrows the moment of choosing until it is felt, by each citizen, as a consciousness of the necessity of acting now. Everything is at stake, in this individual action, for each who takes a part. Sincerity has been defined as saying things without any thought of self. It also implies a quality in public utterances that makes them the candid expression of innermost thoughts, and in these terms Lincoln is a sincere speaker and writer: one of the few, and apt to be valued most by those who know him best.

As we pass to the letter to James C. Conkling, we are moving from a public and ceremonial moment to a more particular occasion—an arranged meeting of Union men for peace, if those two descriptions can be said to coexist. Writing in the late summer of 1863, Lincoln's purpose was to persuade other readers of this open letter that Union and peace were not yet compatible propositions. The letter would be bound into an election pamphlet together with two others, of which the letter to Erastus Corning, which gives his defense of the suspension of habeas corpus, has become the most celebrated. But the letter to Conkling is one of Lincoln's most intense exertions of political mind, and in it we see not only a skilled writer but a great lawyer arguing. It has also the interest of affording a close view of his thoughts and feelings about the Union during the crucial year of the war. The work of making what was necessary to the Union entirely vivid to those required to defend it was never more troubling to him. But he drew steady support from his unshaken belief that the Constitution should always be read in the light of the Declaration of Independence. It is so radical a belief that it can still provoke incredulity: among originalist legal scholars, for example, who believe that equal rights are a late and dubious accretion rather than a constitutional promise.

Of these interpreters it is fair to say, not that they are making improbable claims, but that their thoughts are pre-Lincoln, for the war was fought to make such claims less credible. As, Lincoln supposed, the Constitution is to be realized only by being rendered consistent with the Declaration of Independence, so the Union must be made integral by being cemented as a body of citizens enjoying equal rights, a body free to expand without regard to any qualifications except loyalty and responsibility.

Lincoln begins the letter to Conkling by addressing the survival of the Union itself; and in order to avoid a perplexity that has obstructed the work of many commentators, it must be recalled that the preservation of the Union on the one hand, and the eventual extinction of slavery on the other, were defined by Lincoln in a circular manner. "Fulfillment" and "abolition" were different names for a single process; for the Union is, by definition, a contracted uniting of free citizens with equal rights. To remain a union in this sense it must be growing progressively more and not less free—lifting the weights from all shoulders, to adopt Lincoln's metaphor. So, to Lincoln, "Union" in its perfected sense always did mean abolition at some point. The extinction of slavery and the survival of the Union were mutually entailing propositions. As he saw it, this was a necessary truth of American history in the year 1863. In the rare moments when he leans on a possible ambiguity between the connotations of "Union" and "abolition," as in the public letter to Horace Greeley of August 22, 1862, he holds in reserve (but never inscrutably so) his understanding of the necessity of putting slavery in the course of ultimate extinction.

Are there larger ambiguities that should trouble us in the idea of necessity as applied to the Civil War? Interested skeptics like Greeley seem to have set the prevailing tone for later readers. If one's expectations have been shaped by modern philosophy and science, one is apt to find the word "necessity," as deployed by Lincoln, irresponsible or at least evasive. Yet a reader versed in the ways of nineteenth-century thought would have noticed a usual movement among a family of meanings. What most obstructs a common understanding here is the academic hypothesis that *belief* is constituted by *reasons* and that reasons are chosen by a deliberate act of the will. This moral psychology takes no account of the force of imagination, or of compelling sympathy—an element in the making of necessity for all but the strictest nineteenth-century utilitarians and positivists. A still wider gulf between our sense of fate, as it operates in politics, and the sense that could be shared by Lincoln's audience, comes from the waning of the belief that executive will, prudential care, and conscience may operate together in a single mind. The very word *conscience*—so vivid a constituent of American political language as recently as the civil rights movement—has passed from view and is now unheard in discussions of national affairs. Yet conscience, for the leader whom it possesses, is as potent a decider as circumstance. Its weight, when added to a chain of events all pointing one way, can be such as to leave no alternative. To read Lincoln with the energy of thought he provokes is to find oneself in the presence of an active mind for whom the logic of events and the verdict of conscience are ready to coalesce.

His intuition resembles that of the thinkers—close to the central idiom of the mid-Victorian generation—who gave no credence to an omniscient God but felt the moral order to be nonetheless immoveable. Their pattern of justification goes back to Joseph Butler's idea of an analogy between nature and morality. It appears again in Emerson's doctrine of compensation. In these ways of picturing human action, choice is seen as always voluntary, yet the result in the moral order is coercive and legible. Every injury to nature brings in its train an effect of corresponding dislocation, some way further on. "Right means straight, wrong means crooked," as the language of compensation says. To halt a war for preservation of the Union, a war whose moral claim has become larger once emancipation was a sure consequence—this, to Lincoln, would have been an unimaginable surrender of hope. It is true that as late as 1864 he entertained proposals that would somewhat have ameliorated the defeat of the South. But the condition of his attending to such proposals was that they compass the eventual abolition of slavery. None of them finally did meet that requirement.

Yet, on the occasion of his open letter to Conkling, Lincoln was confronted by a body of men who believed themselves loyal and free republicans, and who wanted the war to stop. They looked for some deference to be shown to the slave states, because they found the idea of emancipation repulsive. They thought this, but they did not say it. And within that reticence Lincoln finds his opening; to those who are dissatisfied with him, he says:

You desire peace; and you blame me that we do not have it. But how can we attain it? There are but three conceivable ways. First, to suppress the rebellion by force of arms. This, I am trying to do. Are you for it? If you are, so far we are agreed. If you are not for it, a second way is, to give up the Union. I am against this. Are you for it? If you are, you should say so plainly. If you are not for *force,* nor yet for *dissolution,* there only remains some imaginable *compromise*. I do not believe any compromise, embracing the maintenance of the Union, is now possible. All I learn, leads to a directly opposite belief.

He then discovers their real grievance: "You dislike the emancipation proclamation; and, perhaps, would have it retracted." Against the argument that supports the prejudice, namely that the proclamation is not constitutional, Lincoln says that he believes he is within the rights and duties of a commander-in-chief in time of war to take the property of the enemy; and since the slaves are a species of property, counted as such by the South and useful as such in defending the South, when he liberates them he is taking a common and prudent military step. The enemy must not be allowed the continued possession of militarily useful property.

On the treatment of Negroes as something called property, while they are also known to be not property because they are human and have a will and can make and keep promises—on this peculiar play of meaning Lincoln now makes his argument turn. There are two sentences of direct address in which his whole moral being seems present: "You say you will not fight to free negroes. Some of them seem willing to fight for you; but, no matter." It is as close as irony may press on the verge of contempt, but what it suggests is more subdued, a disapproval unwilling to show itself as disappointment. Notice that a perfect parallel construction would have said: "Some of them seem willing to fight *to free* you." This failure of the parallel, and of the moral reciprocity it ought to reflect, is itself a part of Lincoln's thought. What kind of free men will these white men be, once they have lowered their liberty to bargain for a settlement with the drivers of slaves? They will have

added their names to "the lousy combings and born freedom sellers of the earth," as Whitman called the nomina-
tors of Fillmore and Buchanan. Lincoln, however, does not
take the path of satire but elects to descend once more to
particulars: "Whenever you shall have conquered all resistance to the Union, if I shall urge you to continue fighting,
it will be an apt time, then, for you to declare you will not
fight to free negroes." To stop the fight, with some Negroes
still enslaved, of course would show that the moral understanding of "Union" was empty. But Lincoln is fighting a
tactical battle as well. This was a time when he still held
out a standing offer of compensated emancipation to the
owners of slaves who surrendered them voluntarily.

From moral challenge and exhortation, he passes on to
the character of the men for peace and Union as faithful
warriors. Why would they forgo any assistance that might
bring the war to a speedy end?

> I thought that in your struggle for the Union, to whatever
> extent the negroes should cease helping the enemy, to that
> extent it weakened the enemy in his resistance to you. Do
> you think differently? I thought that whatever negroes can
> be got to do as soldiers, leaves just so much less for white
> soldiers to do, in saving the Union. Does it appear other-
> wise to you?

Starting from an apparent divergence of interests
between races, he confronts his opponents with the identity of interests that they must favor if they would preserve
themselves free. It is an identity founded on the elemen-
tary human freedom to enter into agreements:

> But negroes, like other people, act upon motives. Why
> should they do any thing for us, if we will do nothing

for them? If they stake their lives for us, they must be prompted by the strongest motive—even the promise of freedom. And the promise being made, must be kept.

There is a tremendous satisfaction here in the transparency of the deduction from cause to consequence. The promise being made, must be kept. The South had converted the Negro from man to thing by regarding him as property. Now, Lincoln is saying, the Union men of peace will do the same, but by a more pusillanimous evasion, if they make a promise to him as a human being and default from the promise. In that case, it is their own humanity that they nullify. The severe simplicity of the moral challenge goes far to explain the unconditional cast of the phrase "must be kept." The promise must be kept though the world should end. It must be kept, even if as many white soldiers therefore desert the Union as Negro soldiers have joined. The promise must be kept because those Negroes who did fight to save the Union, by that choice and act, placed themselves among *us,* the free people Lincoln had in mind when on December 1, 1862 he delivered the words "we—even *we here.*" They have asked to be judged as defenders of liberty, under the eyes and in the memory of the world.

Memory, and the story that must be made of a war that has cost so much, and salvaged so much, is the subject of the Second Inaugural Address. Its words are well known. Yet two quite different sophistications in recent years have stolen upon the general understanding of the speech. It is said that the Second Inaugural Address shows the extent of Lincoln's personal feelings of guilt for having brought upon the nation the terrible sufferings of the war. It is also said that his invocations of God reveal the tightening grip on Lincoln during his final months of an almost uncontrolled prophetic fervor: a belief in his own election as a seer into the life and destiny of America. A compound of these views may be found in David Herbert Donald's *Lincoln,* where we are told, first, that to judge by the Second Inaugural the president lost no sleep over the tribulations of the Civil War and, second, that the address may nevertheless be read as his effort to expiate an unpardonable deed by putting it off on God. "If there was guilt," says Donald, "the burden had been shifted from his shoulders to those of a Higher Power." The tendency of such an interpretation is to diminish Lincoln from a heroic to an all-too-human scale, in a way congenial to modern historical study. Though Donald's biography has every strength compatible with deep learning, sound judgment, and a gracious narrative uncomplicated by much power of admiration, the result is to misread, and really to mishear, the Second Inaugural Address.

Much of the speech is a retelling of a history with which all in Lincoln's audience were familiar. But the story is told for a purpose: to remind them that the war was an event of necessity. "Both parties deprecated war; but one of them would *make* war rather than let the nation survive; and the other would *accept* war rather than let it perish. And the war came." Its necessity is established for the sake of exhibiting the justice that was exacted on both sides: "Neither party expected for the war, the magnitude, or the duration, which it has already attained. Neither anticipated that the *cause* of the conflict might cease with, or even before, the conflict itself should cease. Each looked for an easier triumph, and a result less fundamental and astounding." The result he speaks of is the abolition of slavery. Both sides, Lincoln goes on to say, read the same

Bible, and pray to the same God; and he has in mind the contest of irreconcilable opposites, so familiar to his way of thinking, when he now adds: "The prayers of both could not be answered; that of neither has been answered fully." But the God that Lincoln represents is not a listener to prayers: "The Almighty has His own purposes. 'Woe unto the world because of offenses! for it must needs be that offenses come; but woe to that man by whom the offense cometh!'" It is a moment of the gospels that stands out for all readers, whether or not they know about Lincoln's use of it, for the sentence expresses a radical and mysterious conviction shared by religious and nonreligious ethics: that the accidents of moral luck that went to make a crime in no way render the crime forgivable. To know an action to have been, in the largest of contexts, an accident may enforce charity but it cannot alleviate blame.

Here, one catches a glimpse of the motive of apology and vindication that underlies the speech as a whole; but for better or worse, it is a national and not a religious vindication; for Lincoln believes that slavery was a worse evil than white Americans have ever borne to realize.

> Fondly do we hope—fervently do we pray—that this mighty scourge of war may speedily pass away. Yet, if God wills that it continue, until all the wealth piled by the bond-man's two hundred and fifty years of unrequited toil shall be sunk, and until every drop of blood drawn with the lash, shall be paid by another drawn with the sword, as was said three thousand years ago, so still it must be said "the judgments of the Lord, are true and righteous altogether."

For two hundred and fifty years, white people thought little of their crime against the Negro. It was a matter of less than absorbing concern; and of this neglect, citizens of the North have been not less culpable than those of the South. As Lincoln now represents the war, it is not wrong that blood on both sides has been shed. And yet, he steps down from that height of justification to the unforgettable and conciliatory words: "With malice toward none; with charity for all; with firmness in the right, as God gives us to see the right, let us strive on to finish the work we are in." The allusions to the Bible that precede this sentence have been drawn from Matthew and the Psalms. "The judgments of the Lord are true and righteous altogether" comes from the end of Psalm 19, an interesting reminiscence for a great speaker, since that psalm also says "Day unto day uttereth speech, and night unto night sheweth knowledge." It was a favorite text with the Unitarian authors whom Lincoln seems to have known well, and, for him, it must have been especially resonant for its praise of "the law of the Lord" and "the statutes of the Lord." As for the quotation that opens the sentence of apparent deference to God—"Woe unto the world because of offenses!"—it is said by Jesus at Matthew 18:7, a chapter given to the duties of the prosperous toward the humble. The harsh morality of the verses is directed, with greater indignation than is customary even in Matthew, by the imperative of self-sacrifice. Complacent neglect and prudent self-interest are condemned here as vices not less reprehensible than the most unworthy of trespasses.

The Second Inaugural Address is in no sense an afterthought or a bewildered elegy on the casualties of the war. It is the sublime culmination of Lincoln's argument on necessity and the requirement of human choice in a moment of crisis. Because of its stature, one is interested to know what the speech may have meant to Lincoln himself; and there is a substantial clue in a letter he wrote to

Thurlow Weed on March 15, 1865. This is one of a very few personal communications in which Lincoln speaks with pride of something he has written. He tells Weed that he expects it "to wear as well as—perhaps better than—any thing I have produced." The speech has earned that esti-mate from him because it faithfully renders the springs of action in a train of events over which he himself had pre-sided. "But," he adds, "I believe it is not immediately pop-ular. Men are not flattered by being shown that there has been a difference of purpose between the Almighty and them." The second sentence is vulnerable; but the tone suggests to me endurance rather than arrogance. Lincoln is as impersonal in his ideas of the Almighty as he is impar-tial about himself. It is indeed an almost impersonal God that is evoked, a power, a "Spinner of the Years" or mere unknowable providence, not a God of the sort who would speak through a divinely chosen human vessel. Besides, the existence of suffering on both sides, which Lincoln has sought to vindicate in this speech, must mean that there has been a difference of purpose between God and every human agent in the war.

Yet Lincoln does believe the great purpose in question was the eradication of slavery. To deny that blame for the war should fall on slavery itself "is to deny that there is a God governing the world." The reality of the moral law was, for Lincoln, scarcely separable from the possibility of a just God. As he said in the same letter to Hodges in which he spoke of not having controlled events: "If slavery is not wrong, nothing is wrong." Yet the final words of the letter to Thurlow Weed give a more personal view of his reason for serving as the bearer of the "difference of purpose" between Americans and the God to whom they pray. "It is a truth," he concludes, "which I thought needed to be told; and as whatever of humiliation there is in it, falls most directly on myself, I thought others might afford for me to tell it." Students of Lincoln, on first encountering that sentence, often think that it betrays a touch of self-pity. Lincoln, it can seem, was accepting a blame he imagined himself to have deserved, but perhaps going further than he deserved. But how much guilt is too much for a leader who has sent many thousands to their deaths? How much is too much, even in a necessary cause? Lincoln, in fact, took a somber view of the battles that he oversaw. Yet the regret that he felt seems to have been neither exorbitant nor wholly personal.

His words in the letter to Weed suggest, instead, the vigilance of a man of conscience who cannot subsume his knowledge of particular evils under a general exemption on grounds of necessity. He is, in this respect, the opposite of Macbeth—the hero of his favorite play by Shakespeare, a man haunted by the consequences of power and ambition. In the record of Lincoln's conduct of the free election of 1864—the greatest glory of his presidency, for it was held in time of war and he believed until quite late that he would lose—one comes upon the "Memorandum of Probable Failure of Re-Election" (August 23, 1864). "This morning, as for some days past, it seems exceedingly probable that this Administration will not be re-elected. Then it will be my duty to so co-operate with the President elect, as to save the Union between the election and the inauguration; as he will have secured his election on such ground that he can not possibly save it afterwards." It is the message of a man who trusts the people unsentimentally and fears himself.

It seems wrong in any case to suppose that in speaking of a humiliation connected with the Second Inaugural

Address, Lincoln must have had in mind a guilt mainly associated with the fighting of the war. It is possible he was thinking rather of his own moderation, in the earlier days of his political career, and the results of that stance in delaying the fight. Every drop of blood drawn with the lash was vivid to him, but for much of the 1850s, he himself had spoken in justification of the Fugitive Slave Law. It cannot be proven, but when he spoke now of "the humiliation," would he not have been recalling, with cha-grin, the separate peace that his Republican Party made with that dubious enactment? This was a bad inheritance of a Whig compromise that had already broken down by the time Lincoln came back into politics. From 1854 through 1858, he was grim about it even while conceding this ground to the South. And as time went on, he came to feel not more tenacious of his politic vow but more stretched and troubled by the very idea of turning slaves back to their masters.

He had known the crookedness of the bargain, and yet he had gone along with it—devising against Stephen Douglas his paradoxes on the limits of popular sover-eignty, drawing his own line at the Missouri Compromise, and getting the nomination on sound Republican terms. Only a man of ostensibly moderate politics could have received the nomination, and only a relatively untried leader, denounced but also trusted for his dexterity, could have captured enough votes in enough regions to gain the presidency. The abolitionists had been right and the humiliation was not theirs. Yet none of their number could have done what Lincoln did, and not only because of their severity and the incapacity for common feeling that went with it. Hatred took them so far that it prevented their loving their country for what it might become.

Lincoln's humiliations, and the humility by which he worked to retain his constancy to an ideal object, made him a speaker for hopes that could change the look of necessity. He is a member of a party of resistance but so humanized, so general in his sympathies at last, that he can serve as the animating power for a triumph of charity over the human obstacles in its path.

2001

SHAKESPEARE, LINCOLN, AND AMBITION

To begin with the largest relevant facts: we know that Lincoln as president went often to theater, and we know, from the density of quotations and allusions in his speeches and from the testimony of others, that he had read deeply in the Bible. We might well suppose on similar evidence that his interest in Shakespeare had been strong for much of his life. Yet the only hard evidence of any depth about Lincoln and Shakespeare comes from a letter he wrote in the middle of the Civil War, about six weeks after Gettysburg.

Lincoln had received the gift of a book, *Notes and Comments upon Certain Plays and Actors of Shakespeare, with Criticism and Correspondence*, from its author, James H. Hackett. He wrote back from Executive Mansion, Washington, August 17, 1863:

> Months ago I should have acknowledged the receipt of your book and accompanying kind note; and I now have to beg your pardon for not having done so.
>
> For one of my age, I have seen very little of the drama. The first presentation of Falstaff I ever saw was yours here, last winter or spring. Perhaps the best compliment I can

pay is to say, as I truly can, I am very anxious to see it again. Some of Shakespeare's plays I have never read; while others I have gone over perhaps as frequently as any unprofessional reader. Among the latter are Lear, Richard Third, Henry Eighth, Hamlet, and especially Macbeth. I think nothing equals Macbeth. It is wonderful. Unlike you gentlemen of the profession, I think the soliloquy in Hamlet commencing "O, my offence is rank" surpasses that commencing "To be, or not to be." But pardon this small attempt at criticism. I should like to hear you pronounce the opening speech of Richard the Third. Will you not soon visit Washington again? If you do, please call and let me make your personal acquaintance. Yours truly . . .

There are several interesting details in this report—an unusually personal letter by Lincoln's standard. First, none of the plays that he mentions is a comedy. (Noah Brooks reports him as having said in conversation, "A farce, or comedy, is best played; a tragedy is best read.") Lincoln's choices also exclude the patriotic histories *Henry IV* and *Henry V*. Perhaps we could say—though this is to infer much from little—that Lincoln cared for tragedy, as a dramatic genre, more than he cared for history. But the most striking detail of the letter is Lincoln's preference for the short soliloquy in which Claudius confesses his guilt, over the meditation on will and action by Hamlet which was already among the best-known passages in all of Shakespeare. Lincoln recognizes that his view is heterodox but he stands by it. Finally, and this is another revelation, he confesses a superlative estimate of *Macbeth*. "I think nothing equals *Macbeth*." I will come back to some possible thoughts behind that remark and to a personal trait that perhaps underlies Lincoln's admiration for the soliloquy of Claudius in *Hamlet*. But let us grant this much: Lincoln was deeply touched by the portrait of the mind of a politician who had committed great wrongs. He was not equally moved by the thoughts of a hero who reproached himself for doing too little.

Turn, now, to a general statement by Lincoln on the hazards of political ambition. It comes in an early speech, the Address to the Young Men's Lyceum of Springfield, Illinois, on the Perpetuation of our Political Institutions, delivered in January 1838. The perpetuation of our institutions was a common topic of such lectures at the time; but Lincoln turned more particularly to the dangers of mob violence, of the "mobocratic" spirit (as he called it) that emerged in a spate of lynchings in St. Louis and Vicksburg. The victims were Negroes, and gamblers, and at last anyone who caught the ill-disposed eye of a crowd intoxicated with its own power. Lincoln takes these outbreaks to be a sign that Americans have never fully separated themselves from the excitable mood that was necessary for winning American independence. That excitable and distempered mood, he says, will no longer support the well-being of a country at peace. The right method of peaceable coexistence with our neighbors in a democracy is first of all to abide by the laws. The love of higher and wilder sorts of action may not be easily conjured away; yet we must live now by a different morale; we must learn the arts of self-restraint for the sake of different rewards than those that were sought and won by the heroes of 1776. The American founders succeeded in their experiment, says Lincoln, and by their success they have earned "deathless names":

> But the game is caught, and I believe it is true, that with the catching, end the pleasures of the chase. The field of

glory is harvested, and the crop is already appropriated. But new reapers will arise, and *they*, too, will seek a field. It is to deny, what the history of the world tells us is true, to suppose that men of ambition and talents will not continue to spring up amongst us. And, when they do, they will as naturally seek the gratification of their ruling passion, as others have *so* done before them. The question then, is, can that gratification be found in supporting and maintaining an edifice that has been erected by others? Most certainly it cannot. Many great and good men sufficiently qualified for any task they should undertake, may ever be found, whose ambition would aspire to nothing beyond a seat in Congress, a gubernatorial or a presidential chair; *but such belong not to the family of the lion, or the tribe of the eagle*. What! Think you these places would satisfy an Alexander, a Caesar, or a Napoleon? Never! Towering genius disdains a beaten path. It seeks regions hitherto unexplored. It sees *no distinction* in adding story to story, upon the monuments of fame, erected to the memory of others. It *denies* that it is glory enough to serve under any chief. It *scorns* to tread in the footsteps of *any* predecessor, however illustrious. It thirsts and burns for distinction; and, if possible, it will have it, whether at the expense of emancipating slaves, or enslaving freemen. Is it unreasonable then to expect, that some man possessed of the loftiest genius, coupled with ambition sufficient to push it to its utmost stretch, will at some time, spring up among us? And when such a one does, it will require the people to be united with each other, attached to the government and laws, and generally intelligent, to successfully frustrate his designs.

It has been argued—notably by Edmund Wilson in *Patriotic Gore* and by George Forgie in *Patricide in the House*

Divided—that Lincoln's portrait of a "towering genius" who disdains the level ground of equality and seeks domination really amounts to a confession of temptations that he recognized in himself but could not otherwise reveal. I doubt that this is true. Caesar and Napoleon and, closer to the present, Andrew Jackson, are more likely to have been the examples he had in mind. But it *is* true that Lincoln was aware of his own ambition as a necessary part of his energy for politics. His junior partner in legal practice and eventual biographer, William Herndon, said that Lincoln's ambition was "a little engine that knew no rest." We can call this, if we like, the remark of a junior partner more than of a gifted observer, but we cannot afford to neglect the depth of association that underlies it. Herndon had a daily exposure to Lincoln which few others could claim. But Lincoln in any case did speak consciously, on occasion, of the inward pressure of his love of fame. It is clear from his speeches, writings, and actions that he struggled against ambition in order not to let it prevail over his sense of justice. It *was* a struggle, and it never ended. And yet Lincoln did mostly succeed in confining ambition to a necessary motive and not a ruling passion in his exertions as a public servant. It is hard to name one instance in which ambition dictated his choice of a wrong over a right action.

From what familiar political sources might an American of Lincoln's generation have come to suppose that ambition poses a moral and political danger? The word occurs in the *Federalist Papers*, and for that matter throughout the debates on the Constitution, where it is largely but not exclusively employed in a pejorative sense. It denotes an extension of gregarious self-love, to the point of greed and self-aggrandizement, with a consequent loss of respect for

others and a weakening of the sense of reciprocal obligations. Yet the love of fame was a dominant motive among
the founders of the United States—it was indeed a motive
for the act of founding itself, as the opening and closing
words of the Declaration of Independence remind us—
and how far is ambition separable from the love of fame?
Let us say that ambition, as Lincoln came to know the
idea, was, if not a spotless, anyway a common and often a
necessary motive in politics.

A commanding statement on ambition, probably as
familiar to Lincoln's thoughts as any warning by an American, was the pair of speeches by Brutus and Marc Antony to the Roman crowd in act 3 of *Julius Caesar*. Brutus
speaks there of the assassination in a manner that seeks to
persuade by logical and pedantic steps, under strict emotional regulation:

> If there be any in this assembly, any dear friend of Cae-
> sar's, to him I say, that Brutus' love to Caesar was no less
> than his. If then that friend demand why Brutus rose
> against Caesar, this is my answer: not that I loved Caesar
> less, but that I loved Rome more. Had you rather Caesar
> were living, and die all slaves, than that Caesar were dead,
> to live all freemen? As Caesar loved me, I weep for him; as
> he was fortunate, I rejoice at it; as he was valiant, I honour
> him: but as he was ambitious, I slew him. There is tears,
> for his love; joy, for his fortune; honour, for his valour;
> and death, for his ambition.

The Roman crowd cheers for this apology, but their
approval turns out to be shallow and changeable.

By contrast, Marc Antony's great performance of dem-
agogy seeks to move the crowd against the conspirators
by crying up the popular virtues of Caesar's public life.

CHAPTER 6

Caesar gave luxurious parks to the people of Rome, and
he gave them what we would now call tax rebates; and
Antony recalls these gifts as if they had nothing to do with
the leader's hunger for popularity. Caesar of course was
bribing the loyalty of the populace for reasons of his own.
Seen in that light, Antony's denial of ambition in Caesar
is itself ambitious; he, for his part, wants to supplant Brutus in the affections of the Roman people; and so he turns
the crowd (by the force of words) into a violent mob. This
determination forms the basis of his mention of honor
as an aristocratic and republican virtue that is meant to
counteract ambition; the word "honorable" is repeated, in
his speech, with a menace and sarcasm that try to make us
sick of the very idea of honor:

> The evil that men do lives after them:
> The good is oft interred with their bones.
> So let it be with Caesar. The noble Brutus
> Hath told you Caesar was ambitious:
> If it were so, it was a grievous fault,
> And grievously hath Caesar answered it.
> Here, under leave of Brutus and the rest
> (For Brutus is an honourable man;
> So are they all, all honourable men)
> Come I to speak in Caesar's funeral.
> He was my friend, faithful and just to me;
> But Brutus says he was ambitious,
> And Brutus is an honourable man.
> He hath brought many captives home to Rome,
> Whose ransoms did the general coffers fill.
> Did this in Caesar seem ambitious?
> When that the poor have cried, Caesar hath wept:
> Ambition should be made of sterner stuff.

Yet Brutus says, he was ambitious,
And Brutus is an honourable man.
You all did see, that on the Lupercal
I thrice presented him a kingly crown,
Which he did thrice refuse. Was this ambition?
Yet Brutus says, he was ambitious;
And sure he is an honourable man.
I speak not to disprove what Brutus spoke,
But here I am to speak what I do know.
You all did love him once, not without cause:
What cause withholds you then to mourn for him?

It is a terrible accusation and causerie. The more stridently honor is devalued by Antony, the less credible seems any protest against selfish and overweening ambition. Antony tells the crowd, in effect: it is better to allow ambition, if it profits you the people at just this moment, than to be honorable if the only beneficiary of that honor is the constitution of the Roman republic.

Now Lincoln, to say it roughly, held sentiments for the American republic and constitution that were close to those declared by Brutus, but he took constant care not to allow any abstract argument to overcome the moral presumption against the good of killing. And that meant killing in the name of any cause whatever. There had been an outbreak of national and apparently lawful violence, within the span of Lincoln's own career, that aroused him to direct criticism of the ambition of a president. The event was the Mexican War, which began in 1846, whose progress overlapped with Lincoln's term in Congress from 1847 to 1849. On the floor of Congress, Lincoln posed several "Spot" Resolutions, as he called them; *spot* here referring to the disputation about the exact spot between the

Nueces River and the Rio Grande at which the first violence was said to have occurred. Was the war provoked by Mexico or by the United States, and did the lands between the rivers properly belong to Texas settlers or to the Mexicans living there?

Lincoln's Speech on the Mexican War of January 12, 1848 took up the challenge of his own resolutions. He addresses President Polk almost directly. "Let him answer," Lincoln says,

> fully, fairly, and candidly. Let him answer with *facts*, and not with arguments. Let him remember he sits where Washington sat, and so remembering, let him answer, as Washington would answer. As a nation *should* not, and the Almighty *will* not, be evaded, so let him attempt no evasion—no equivocation. And if, so answering, he can show that the soil was ours, where the first blood of the war was shed—that it was not within an inhabited country, or, if within such, that the inhabitants had submitted themselves to the civil authority of Texas, or of the United States, and that the same is true of the site of Fort Brown, then I am with him for his justification. . . . But if he *can* not, or *will* not do this—if on any pretense, or no pretense, he shall refuse or omit it, then I shall be fully convinced, of what I more than suspect already, that he is deeply conscious of being in the wrong—that he feels the blood of this war, like the blood of Abel, is crying to Heaven against him. That originally having some strong motive—what, I will not stop now to give my opinion concerning—to involve the two countries in a war, and trusting to escape scrutiny, by fixing the public gaze upon the exceeding brightness of military glory—that attractive rainbow, that rises in showers of blood—that serpent's eye, that charms

to destroy—he plunged into it, and has swept, *on* and *on*, till, disappointed in his calculation of the ease with which Mexico might be subdued, he now finds himself, he knows not where. How like the half insane mumbling of a fever-dream, is the whole war part of his late message! At one time telling us that Mexico has nothing whatever, that we can get, but territory; at another, showing us how we can support the war, by levying contributions on Mexico.

There are echoes, in this speech of 1848—echoes meant to be heard by Lincoln's audience—of the soliloquies in which the political assassin Macbeth conjures up images of his own guilt. Those images appear as a phantasmagoria of floating causes, yet, at the same time, they confess the concrete reality of his guilt. Macbeth has pursued an object of dangerous allure beyond the reach of self-understanding. The speech that opens act 2, which begins, "Is this a dagger which I see before me?"—that speech, for one, throws a shadow forward into actual history in the accusation by Lincoln against a president who seems to have become a usurper. Macbeth is referred to, elsewhere in the play, as an equivocator, and the same epithet by implication is extended by Lincoln to President Polk in his dealings with Mexico and his evasive explanations to the American people. Lincoln's description of such an adventurer having "swept, on and on," makes us aware, too, of the resonance in his mind of the words of Macbeth: "I am in blood, / Stepped in so far that, should I wade no more, / Returning were as tedious as go o'er."

Recent biographers of Lincoln, such as William Gienapp and Doris Kearns Goodwin, have treated his opposition to the Mexican War as a minor episode of his career. I am not sure on what grounds. It required unusual courage

for a first-term congressman to make the sustained accusation of which I have just quoted the climactic passage.
For this speech involved Lincoln early in the controversies
that would break out in the 1850s concerning the disposition of new territories conquered in the Mexican War.
He would say in his great Speech on the Kansas-Nebraska
Act, in 1854, that he must have voted for the Wilmot Pro-
viso at least forty times: that is, he voted again and again
for the congressional measure which would have prohibited slavery in any of the new territories. His Speech on
the Mexican War, then, already has in view a larger commitment. Its powerful allusion to *Macbeth* offers a clue to
his thinking that seems consonant with Lincoln's habits
of moral reflection generally. He gave full vent to his suspicion of high crimes and misdemeanors. And his judgment in this instance, as on so many later occasions, was
guided not by fascination with the glory of heroic virtue
but rather by a concern with the causes that may drive an
ordinary man to commit deep wrongs.

I have confined my argument thus far to an external
sense of ambition—the quality as it was exemplified for
Lincoln in domestic scenes of disorder, or in his knowledge of state power gravitating toward war. Can we come
any closer to the intuition shared by Herndon and other
witnesses that Lincoln knew the workings of ambition
in himself? There is fascinating evidence on this point in
one of the unexpected fragments of Lincoln's notebook—
those miscellaneous paragraphs in which he worked out
problems about the meaning of democracy or the logic of
slavery or the perplexities of determinism and free will.
The entry concerns his rivalry with Stephen Douglas. It is
dated circa December 1856, twenty months before the first
of their famous debates, but at a time when Lincoln was

already following Douglas around Illinois and opposing his arguments wherever he went. Stephen Douglas was then engaged in a campaign to open the new territories to slavery, provided that the people of the territories voted for slavery as their majority preference. For Lincoln, to decide the right or wrong of slavery by majority vote was to nullify the moral law implied in the words of the Declaration of Independence, "All men are created equal." That was an imperative that should trump any imaginable majority.

Now in the notebook entry we are looking at, in 1856—two years after Douglas opened the door to the extension of slavery by securing passage of the Kansas-Nebraska Act and the repeal of the Missouri Compromise—Lincoln reflects:

> Twenty-two years ago Judge Douglas and I first became acquainted. We were both young then; he a trifle younger than I. Even then, we were both ambitious; I, perhaps, quite as much so as he. With me, the race of ambition has been a failure—a flat failure; with *him* it has been one of splendid success. His name fills the nation; and is not unknown, even, in foreign lands. I affect no contempt for the high eminence he has reached. So reached, that the oppressed of my species, might have shared with me in the elevation, I would rather stand on that eminence, than wear the richest crown that ever pressed a monarch's brow

If Lincoln's Speech on the Mexican War seemed to say that the love of power has an inward drive, an energy that feeds on itself, this note on Stephen Douglas eight years later indicates the origin of that momentum in *political* ambition. And there is something strangely impersonal, maybe we should say something de-personifying, about ambition. It takes you out of yourself. By its dynamism, you become a name, and the sound of that name may fill the nation and be known in foreign lands: but who is the person under the name? Where ambition takes its full swing, it is as if a break in oneself had occurred, out of the need to acquire fame or power from a force outside oneself, a force that reaches in and pulls without letup or allowance for thought. The person who has become a prey to that force is "swept on and on."

Ambition then has this peculiarity, that it begins from an egotistical motive, the wish to leave a deep impression on the world; yet the effects of ambition, its momentum and pressure for external aggrandizement and its instrumental use of available objects and other people, all lead away from any proper self or individuality. The lips of the office mumble the words for an act of state no person could ever vouch for. By the changes wrought by ambition, the person disappears into the force-field of the act. For the person captured by ambition, the power of agency increases vastly, while the identity of the actor dwindles to the sum of his effects. The mask becomes the face; and it is a quality of ambition that the person whom it seizes is half aware that this *will* happen, sees it start to happen, and wants it to go on happening. He wants it even as he may feel that the mask weighs heavily, and even as he regrets that the expression on the face of the actions is no longer his own. The ambitious politician was once a person, but a person with this peculiar germ in his constitution, that he was willing to be changed utterly by the necessities of power. Achieved ambition is success at undergoing that change.

Lincoln seems to have held in view from 1858 the strong possibility of a war over slavery. And, close as he was to abolitionist opinion (though not an abolitionist himself), he must have recognized emancipation as a possible result or consequence of a civil war. To do good for his country, however, meant to avoid war if possible. Yet it may be a thin line that separates conscious prudence from corrupt manipulation—a line that a character like Macbeth or Caesar must cross many times, and that most politicians, if offered the rewards of violent action, will do what they can to erase. A politician strongly tempted has no trouble picturing himself as "a principal actor," to quote the formulation of Edmund Burke, "weighing as it were in a scale hung in a shop of horrors,—so much actual crime against so much contingent advantage." Lincoln practiced a more rigorous restraint: there were things he would not do. Still, he came to know the allure of calculations that must present themselves as preliminary to an *unjust* political action. He had to come face-to-face with such moments if only to reject the temptation.

A clear example was the strategy he chose to follow in March 1861, by which he declared that Fort Sumter would be provisioned—as was required to support the troops who worked on that federal property—but added that it would be done without aggressive intent or any supply of arms. Or again, consider the choice that faced him after a massacre of settlers in Minnesota, when the regional commander, General Pope, urged the wisdom of hanging all 303 of the Sioux Indians implicated in the attacks. Lincoln knew that some had to die, but he asked for the native names of each of the condemned, and pored over each case to find exceptions where applicable, below the threshold of wanton actions or participation in killings. In the end, of the 303 condemned to death, thirty-nine were hanged by order of the president. The rest were spared. This act of mass clemency toward an obnoxious group did not add to his popularity, and Lincoln knew that it would not.

As a final example, I think one can hear the uneasy voice of ambition, pressing forward yet held at bay, in a short note by Lincoln to Andrew Johnson (then a senator from Tennessee) dated March 26, 1863. "The colored population," Lincoln writes, "is the great *available* and yet *unavailed* of, force for restoring the Union. The bare sight of fifty thousand armed, and drilled black soldiers, on the banks of the Mississippi, would end the rebellion at once." The sight, unaccompanied by words, would end the war. Lincoln means to say that it would do so by the immediate operation of a salutary fear. To come to such a recognition involves impersonal calculations of force and a specific weight of responsibility on the person who is to decide: a burden which may threaten to overwhelm the acknowledgment of personal responsibility.

Why did Lincoln so seldom jump from such a perception to a sudden decision by fiat? When one searches his principles of action, one sees lines of explanation that lead away from a policy of dictatorial command or deliberate expedience; the pattern, in Lincoln, instead leads back to a radical aversion from injustice. Among the sources of that aversion, I believe, was his reading of *Macbeth*. Recall his words: "Nothing is equal to *Macbeth*."

One speech must have been at the heart of the play, for Lincoln. It is a speech about action, like "To be or not to be," but from a man who *will* act with disturbing force. I abridge the quotation here to bring out the close relationship between ambition, action, and justice:

If it were done, when 'tis done, then 'twere well
It were done quickly: if the assassination

Could trammel up the consequence, and catch
With his surcease success; that but this blow
Might be the be-all and the end-all—here,
But here, upon this bank and shoal of time,
We'd jump the life to come.—But in these cases,
We still have judgment here; that we but teach
Bloody instructions, which, being taught, return
To plague th'inventor; this even-handed justice
Commends th'ingredience of our poison'd chalice
To our own lips. . . .
                              —I have no spur
To prick the sides of my intent, but only
Vaulting ambition, which o'erleaps itself
And falls on th'other.

Surely when Lincoln thought of this speech, he took
it as a warning. Ambition, by its nature, moves from a
thought of something that might happen—something one
might do and enlarge one's own power by doing—to the
idea of actually improving the odds by creating for oneself
the relevant favoring circumstances. So one might ban-
ish all second thoughts and commit the wicked deed, and
make sure of being so placed as to gather in the benefits
to oneself. An accompanying fantasy is that moral effects
will cease with the end of the action itself: to "catch /
With his surcease success"—the victim's death and the
killer's triumph seem almost a pun on each other. Death
will crown the bringer of death because the two words
sound so close. Thus, in the logic of the passions, a con-
necting channel is carved out from "I can do this" to "I
will do it," with no intervening prohibition of conscience,
no thought of the actual good or harm that will come to
others far from the scene. Self-deception also comes in to

do its usual work. I say: "This was forced on me—I merely used an opening in the circumstances that anyone would have filled." Or, alternatively: "How could I know all the terrible consequences at the time of action?" Both of these excuses lie adjacent to the claim concerning a voluntary action, "I did not mean it," which comes close to saying that I am not I.

Ambition, in this way, makes of the individual agent a person who is no longer coherent over time. Often enough, the temptation and the thought "I can do it" forge a link so rapidly that the agent is scarcely conscious of a motive: consciousness is blotted out. And this, to repeat, is a marked quality of ambition: it reduces or empties consciousness, because it sends the person out of himself.

In the great speech I have quoted from the end of act 1, Macbeth has gone far already on the path of self-deception, but he finds the path blocked by his thought of judgment in an afterlife, and then by the thought of a judgment in this life. What we do to others will return on ourselves; justice is done somehow by the mere fact that injustice always has witnesses. "We but teach / Bloody instructions, which, being taught, return / To plague th'inventor." The extremely elliptical character of the thought in Shakespeare comes out most impressively in the final words: "Vaulting ambition, which o'erleaps itself / And falls on th'other." On the other *side*, this seems almost to say—but the other side of what? The other bank of the river suggested by the metaphor "this bank and shoal of time"? Or the other person, as opposed to myself? Or perhaps, more allegorically, the other end of a calculus of acts and effects by which real wrongs would be magically vindicated. But the word *falls* takes away the consolation that appeared ready to greet the agent. This is not a successful leap, after all, but a collapse. And so we are back to costs that must be reckoned here on earth. Our acts stay with us.

Macbeth, and this lies at the heart of his drama, gives up self-sufficiency in exchange for self-aggrandizement. His self-possession is never stable thereafter; the possession of other persons and other things becomes the substitute. (There lies a residual meaning, perhaps, of the dreamlike phrase "falls on th'other.") The category of sincerity no longer applies to persons overtaken by ambition. Their words and their thoughts cannot afford to agree. Admittedly, Lincoln might seem to have been explaining away the personal element of his political choices when he said, in a famous and elusive remark about the Emancipation Proclamation, "I claim not to have controlled events, but confess plainly that events have controlled me." This is, by the sound of it, an evasion in Lincoln, somewhat like the evasions of self-ascription by Macbeth. But let us not understand him too quickly. His sentence denying control of events, as I read it, is a tactical statement, but it is far from putting off responsibility for the actions of the war. Its sense ultimately is not that he did what history forced him to do, and that anybody in his position would have done the same, because he had no choice. It is rather that he could not have issued the Emancipation Proclamation any time he pleased; he had to wait for the victory at Antietam to gauge a moment when the continued rise of Union fortunes depended on the addition of new recruits; and a moment when, of such recruits, only emancipated slaves offered a large and conspicuous source. So Lincoln is saying: events did play a part in the timing of my judgment, but they did not constitute my conscience. I am I. And I would have wanted to do this at any time when the conjunction of events made the action plausible. I would always have done it, as in fact I did, under the highest visibility.

Let us conclude by taking up a hint implied by Lincoln's fascination with the soliloquy of Claudius in *Hamlet*. Did he interpret that speech as another warning? I suspect that it was, for him, an actual judgment on himself, as it is a judgment on any person whose conscience is heavy from the knowledge that power has come to him through the sacrifice of others.

> Pray can I not,
> Though inclination be as sharp as will,
> My stronger guilt defeats my strong intent,
> And, like a man to double business bound,
> I stand in pause where I shall first begin,
> And both neglect. . . .
> My fault is past—but O, what form of prayer
> Can serve my turn? "Forgive me my foul murder"?
> That cannot be; since I am still possess'd
> Of those effects for which I did the murder,
> My crown, mine own ambition and my queen.
> May one be pardon'd and retain th'offence?
> In the corrupted currents of this world
> Offence's gilded hand may shove by justice,
> And oft 'tis seen the wicked prize itself
> Buys out the law. But 'tis not so above:
> There is no shuffling, there the action lies
> In his true nature, and we ourselves compell'd
> Even to the teeth and forehead of our faults,
> To give in evidence.

Claudius's speech is a despairing appeal to heaven by means of a prayer that is not answered. Or rather, the prayer is answered by foreknowledge of the faults that will count as evidence at a tribunal on our deeds—a trial that occurs in this world and not in the life to come. This speech marks a pause in the plot of *Hamlet*. It is the only clear showing of a person of wicked intent, in a play whose moral bearings otherwise are extraordinarily elusive. None of Hamlet's own soliloquies addresses conscience in the plain and conventional sense of the idea evoked by Claudius. Of course, Lincoln, for many reasons, would hardly have associated himself or his political conduct with the character of Claudius—a weak and sensual man who seems to have committed murder for the usual rewards.

Yet it would be characteristic of Lincoln not to want to deny his kinship with Claudius. His interest in the neglected soliloquy in *Hamlet* belongs to the same honesty of thought that we feel when he admits the resemblance between himself and Stephen Douglas. "We were both ambitious; I, perhaps, quite as much so as he." Lincoln's whole political life, most of all his time as president, was directed at avoiding the imposition of his will on others whenever that would involve injustice. Conscience, often if not always, stopped him short of the grand assertions of arbitrary power that the ambitious have no second thoughts about.

2012

THREE

CHAPTER 7

THE AMERICAN PSYCHOSIS

IF YOU HAVE EVER LOOKED INTO THE PSYCHOLOGISTS WHO wrote a generation before Freud, you will know that psychosis did not always mean a state of clinical derangement. In the writings of William James and others, it often denoted an intense or crystallized mood, a mental state that defines a character or that just takes hold of the mind for a time. The quality of this mood or state or moral cocoon is to be impervious and self-contained. That is the connection with our later meaning. I found the phrase "the American psychosis" in Hart Crane's essay "Modern Poetry": "The most typical and valid expression of the American *psychosis*," wrote Crane, "seems to me still to be found in Whitman." He had in mind the polar tendencies of self-isolation and an expansive disposition that knows no limit. As my examples will show, I mean to address only the first of those tendencies: an idealism at once primitive and incorrigible. But D. H. Lawrence spoke with precision of the broader phenomenon when he observed that the hero of Cooper's frontier novels was "hard, isolate, stoic, and a killer." This judgment, from *Studies in Classic American Literature* (1923), is famous now and is usually read with a narrower sense than Lawrence intended. But he had another shot at the analysis of Americans in his short novel *St. Mawr,* and another in the essay that appears as his introduction to Edward Dahlberg's novel *Bottom Dogs*. It is the last of these pieces that interests me. Other people must have seen what he saw there, but nobody else has put it into words.

What Lawrence finds ingrained in Americans is something life-hardened, yet untouchable by life. Their experience does not finally get to them. This is true not only of people who have had the luck to know the rewards of ego; it is also true in America, most surprisingly, of the very young and the very poor. Go a little under the surface, says Lawrence, and "you begin to see how terrible and brutal is the mass of failure that nourishes the roots of the gigantic tree of dollars." America has produced a sparse and almost totally neglected pioneer literature that is a chronicle of failures. It tells of "hard first-comers" who "fought like devils against their difficulties" but who have been defeated, broken, their efforts and their amazing hard work lost, as it were, on the face of the wilderness." Americans, says Lawrence, will only hear these reports in small and sentimental doses, because "they know too well the grimness of it, the savage fight and the savage failure which broke the back of the country but also broke something in the human soul. The spirit and the will survived: but something in the soul perished: the softness, the floweriness, the natural tenderness." This breaking of the heart of a generation, in every pioneer generation, brought a peculiar and detached result. "The will-to-success and the will-to-produce became clean and indomitable once the sympathetic heart was broken." Thus was secreted in the American mind a belief so profound it need never be articulated. "It is not God's business to be good and kind. . . . God's business is to be indomitable. And man's business is essentially the same."

Familiarity with people and "friendliness"—an American word for an American idea—are encouraged and grow easier in the after years of the frontier. But Lawrence thinks that these are surface effects.

Of course the white American believes that man should behave in a kind and benevolent manner. But this is a social belief and a social gesture, rather than an individual flow. The flow from the heart, the warmth of fellow-feeling which has animated Europe and been the best of her humanity, individual, spontaneous, flowing in thousands of little passionate currents often conflicting, this seems unable to persist on the American soil. Instead you get the social creed of benevolence and uniformity, a mass *will*, and an inward individual retraction, an isolation, an amorphous separateness like grains of sand, each grain isolated upon its own will, its own indomitableness, its own implacability, its own unyielding, yet heaped together with all the other grains.

The mass of individuals that Lawrence is talking about have the property of being each finished, each constructed to shut things out and reduce consciousness to a necessary minimum beyond the needs of the self.

This imperviousness is a human possibility that first took root in America. It has not flourished anywhere else; maybe it cannot be exported—though the global market presumes it is the form of morale that people would choose, if they could choose, everywhere. Anyway the people who live in the antinomian way I am speaking of, the larger and the smaller grains of sand, agree in supposing that the self is real and society a bondage. Jonathan Swift could think he was describing an admirable social capacity when he devoted a sermon to "mutual subjection."

None of these American believers would grasp his point. The only relevant mutual subjection, for them, is between consciousness and itself or between an isolated man and God. This assertion and this negation mark a normal self-imagining only for Americans. Still, how can it seem warped or perverse when it thrives so heartily? Self-subjection and mutual resistance are the native turn given to the older virtues of self-sufficiency and fortitude.

Like Lawrence, I am talking mainly about white people. Or, rather, initially them. But the ways in which the mood was transmitted to European immigrants will be plain to anyone who has observed the American *drive* toward improvement as a thing distinct from its official and managerial surface. Many later immigrants and many black Americans have absorbed it through the theology of money. I have a word to say at the end about money. I have nothing to say about the "ideology of the nation," which the field of American Studies, for a generation now, has treated as the master clue to the American idea of the self. This seems to me an intellectualist fallacy, but it is pointless to look for a knockdown argument on either side, and where you come out probably depends on intuition and prejudice. Scholars like Sacvan Bercovitch, who find traces everywhere in American thought and writing of a national ideology, aim to convey a sentiment of deep futility about the American project. They have it sewn up; and the sense of a finished interpretation leaves very little room for wonder, for admiration, or even for salutary fear. The state of mind I am speaking of has the quality of accident not design, and there is reason to believe that it made the nation far more than the nation made it.

The leading exhibit of course is Emerson's "Self-Reliance"—a work so definitive of the psychosis that it hardly matters who read the essay, who heard reports of it, and who assimilated the doctrine through its lay-apostles among popular lecturers and the authors of self-help tracts. But to realize the strange compactness of Emerson's teaching, you have to go back before him to the thinkers who acted as his ultimate sponsors. These were, as Perry Miller saw, the radical Separatists who broke away from the Congregationalism of Massachusetts Bay Colony in the early seventeenth century. The church of those first New Englanders was non-separating: that is, it chose not to defy the Church of England openly, and aimed otherwise to hold itself together in a wilderness, where unity of some sort was a condition of survival. For the sake of survival too, members of the colony would eventually relax the demand for a conversion in each believer, and would adopt the expedient custom of baptizing every adult who merely assented to the faith. Yet these non-separating Congregationalists had all but nominally separated from the Church of England. Those in England who most nearly correspond to them would come to be called Independents: a name that cannot mislead. Meanwhile, those destined to be the peculiar heroes of the colony, the purifiers of conscience who threw the community back upon first principles, were themselves, once more, separatists.

Everyone has a rough idea of this atmosphere of belief. Let me sharpen the impression by quoting some lines from a modern poet, John Brooks Wheelwright. Politically, Wheelwright was a Trotskyist of the thirties, and aesthetically a separatist of the invisible avant-garde. "Bread-Word Giver" (dedicated to "John, Unborn") is meant to be chanted as a prayer for strength and sustenance; and it begins by invoking the poet's ancestor John Wheelwright, one of the most contentious, eloquent, and disturbing preachers in the colony's first generation.

> John, founder of towns,—dweller in none;
> Wheelwright, schismatic,—schismatic from schismatics;
> friend of great men whom those great feared greatly;
> Saint, whose name and business I bear with me;
> rebel New England's rebel against dominion;
> who made bread-giving words for bread makers;
> whose blood floods me with purgatorial fire;
> I, and my unliving son, adjure you:
> keep us alive with your ghostly disputation
> make our renunciation of dominion
> mark not the escape, but the permanent of rebellion.

John Wheelwright, the ancestor, was the brother-in-law of Anne Hutchinson, who would be tried as an Antinomian by the General Court of the colony and expelled when she claimed as the source of her doctrine *immediate revelation from God*. John Wheelwright was one of only two preachers whom Mrs. Hutchinson acknowledged to be "under a covenant of grace," that is, justified to God, as distinct from the mass of His servants "under a covenant of works," who were sanctified by men only and preoccupied with the forms of worldly preparation. The small band of separatists was fractious, and their influence worked against the perpetuation of the society. Some men in Boston, for example, had refused to fight against the Pequods because their chaplain, John Wilson, was declared to be under a covenant of works. To be thus preoccupied by works, to hope illicitly by a record of positive deeds to improve one's odds at heaven, was a version of an older heresy that the Puritans knew as Arminianism; and nobody ever denounced that heresy more stirringly than

Wheelwright, who rose once at the end of another minister's sermon to warn against the seeming goodness of those who trusted their standing in the church as evidence of justification. "The more holy they are," said Wheelwright, "the greater enemies they are to Christ."

Edmund Morgan, whose history of the colony, *The Puritan Dilemma,* I have been drawing on, says that Wheelwright meant those words figuratively. But Morgan's book shows that to refuse such testimony from the inspired among the community of saints always looked like defending the lukewarm, while to follow the schismatic inspiration of Wheelwright and Hutchinson would have been fatal to the colony as a political entity. This was the constant though hidden version of the Puritan dilemma experienced by such believers: not only the necessity of both living for God and living in the world, but the impossibility of rejecting those who reject the world without thereby endangering the germ of what is most godlike in yourself. The leading doctrine of Anne Hutchinson, namely that "the person of the Holy Ghost dwells in a justified person," meant that the outward sanctification of the church member offered no clue whatever to his or her state of inward justification. It also meant that any interposition of ministerial helps, or any other external guide to conduct, was potentially a trespass against the indwelling spirit of God in those who were truly saved. Hutchinson crossed the line that separated the doctrinally controversial from the politically intolerable—and thereby forsook command of a strong countertendency within the colony—only when she asserted under questioning by the court that she knew it was God who urged her to act as she did. She knew this not, she said, by a personal interpretation of the Bible, which would have been allowed, but rather as Abraham had known that it was God who urged him to offer his son—"By an immediate revelation . . . . By the voice of his own spirit to my soul."

Mrs. Hutchinson's excommunication in March 1637 was not the first and would not be the last such result of the contest between Puritan expedience regarding the world and the soul's imperative of justification. Scarcely a year before, the greatest of the separatists, Roger Williams, had passed from Salem and Plymouth to Narragansett Bay, where he would found the new colony of Rhode Island. An entirely coherent progress of convictions led Williams to declare his break. Soon after arriving in Boston in 1631, he avowed that he could not join in worship with those who, having founded a new Congregational church, would not repent their former impurity in having had communion with the churches in England. Unless they would change and repent, he could never foresee joining them. Williams declined to officiate during the absence of another minister in Boston ("I durst not officiate to an unseparated people, as upon examination and conference I found them to be"), and he went on to Salem, where again a certain native sweetness of temper won him a following, so that he was offered a ministry. The offer was withdrawn after reconsideration of his doctrines, and he moved once more to Plymouth, where it is reported that he objected to the application to the unregenerate of the name "Goodman"; and where, as Morgan impartially says, he "raised the question whether the colonists had any right to the land they occupied." Williams thought the land belonged to the Indians. The accepted legal understanding, namely that the Massachusetts Bay Company had acquired the land by a patent from the king, did not impress him. The presumption that the king had the power to make such a grant Williams called "a solemn public lie."

And so his fortunes turned, as he wished them to turn, against the worldly success that his attainments and character had made available to him. In April 1635 he was brought before the colony's court of assistants for his refusal to take an oath of loyalty against the enemies of the colony. The very word *oath,* like the ceremony itself, betokened a mixing of the act of worship with affairs of state, and it was Williams's firm conviction that government had no authority to encroach on matters of belief, any more than believers could with impunity transfer the objects of their interest from conscience to dominion. In the end he took the advice of his friend John Winthrop, and fled before he could be arrested; he would write soon after to Winthrop, in the hope of gaining his companionship: "Abstract yourself with a holy violence from the Dung Heape of this Earth."

The followers who came with him to Providence were soon rebaptized, but Williams was already losing his assurance that there could be, in Morgan's words again, "a proper church at all until God raised up some new apostolic power." He felt at last that he could have communion only with his wife, and passed to the final implications of his own position when, denying the state all authority over private belief, he recognized that churches themselves, being placed in the world, were by that fact rendered irremediably impure.

Obedient to this logic, as John Winthrop observed of Williams drily, "having, a little before, refused communion with all, save his own wife, now he would preach and pray with all comers." Yet Winthrop's comment speaks in the voice of a worldly irony and from a point of view informed by the necessity of worldly compromise, whereas the ideals of Puritanism had been unworldly from the first. The question, even before departure from England, had been whether one could somehow reduce to a practice a principled refusal of accommodation. How far, given the need of political as well as ecclesiastical authority, should one "render unto Caesar the things which are Caesar's"? There is no single answer to this question that both preserves the integrity of conscience and can serve as an earnest of social stability among neighbors. Read in this light, Williams's stance and his transformation have a consistency denied to Winthrop. Of the two great men, the preserver of a society and the discoverer of a conscience to which all society is an encroachment, it is the latter who vividly exemplifies the American psychosis. Winthrop helped America to become a live option. He helped indeed to preserve it against dangers like Williams himself. But America did not have to be invented for his sake.

The conversion of private experience to general amenability comes always in America at the cost of an original vigor of separatism. On the other hand, the germ of separatism is compelled again and again, in order to refresh and prove its faith, to withdraw from a deep to a still deeper solitude. As for the tolerance that the separatist may concede by a tactical submission to authority, this seems a way of saying that in pragmatic terms the claims of all are equally real because they are equally unreal. What could be the grounds for Williams's refusing to worship with anyone, once he had seen that he could only worship in himself? This would be the advice of Emerson too, in his great essay "Experience": "Let us treat the men and women well; treat them as if they were real; perhaps they are." But is that all? To the ear of a secular observer of morals, say a reader familiar with Jane Austen, Elizabeth Gaskell, and other nineteenth-century writers famous for treating the men and women well, the equability of Emerson's statement is wild, wild to the point of hilarity, and not least for the air of unassuming kindliness with which the injunction is uttered. Can it be so hedged a bet that the men and women *will* turn out to be real? But Emerson is speaking the sober truth of a "schismatic from schismatics." More than this, in sincerity, he cannot say.

There is little difference between what Anne Hutchinson meant by *soul* and what Emerson will come to mean by *self.* The latter word is charged with similar implications in a changed climate of belief; one needs to bear this in mind in order to avoid some common mistakes about Emerson's essay "Self-Reliance." If you fail to see, at the bottom of this "self," the spirit of God addressing the enraptured soul, you are liable to exaggerate his kinship with an optimistic and property-loving individualist like Henry Ford. The puzzle about the great essay is that it does initially seem addressed to healthy young democratic citizens, as a recipe for getting along without too much chafing insincerity. Yet the self that Emerson describes is not in the smallest degree a social creature. Its abiding sense of identity comes from awareness of its difference from others. But that is too mild a paraphrase: the self portrayed in "Self-Reliance" subsists by virtue of its defection from society. I am permitted to assume obligations as the lightest of burdens only after I have recognized that they can do nothing for me. They cannot even do much harm.

Emerson has a word for the process of becoming certain that society does not participate in conscience. He calls it "absolution." The self is the entity that gives and receives absolution.

Absolve you to yourself, and you shall have the suffrage of the world. I remember an answer which when quite young I was prompted to make to a valued adviser, who was wont to importune me with the dear old doctrines of the church. On my saying, "What have I to do with the sacredness of traditions, if I live wholly from within?" my friend suggested, "But these impulses may be from below, not from above." I replied, "They do not seem to me to be such; but if I am the Devil's child, I will live then from the Devil." No law can be sacred to me but that of my nature. Good and bad are but names very readily transferable to that or this; the only right is what is after my constitution; the only wrong what is against it. A man is to carry himself in the presence of all opposition, as if every thing were titular and ephemeral but he.

The doctrine is religious in one important sense. It is concerned with, and wants to change our minds about, the nature of first and final things. That the phrase *absolve you to yourself* is no casual paradox may be judged by the antinomian sentiment that Emerson soon after candidly affirms. "If I am the Devil's child, I will live then from the Devil."

Enlightenment polemicists against institutional religion would never have ventured such an assertion. The rational doubts they did express, they would shelter rhetorically by placing them in the mouth of a friend, a professed skeptic, or an "infidel." Emerson, by contrast, claims the words for himself as a child or as a young man. It will be part of the teaching of "Self-Reliance" that the child is wiser and stronger than the man precisely because he is more self-willed. About the child in general, and especially the boy-child, Emerson says admiringly "you must court him; he does not court you. But the man is as it were clapped into jail by his consciousness. As soon as he has once acted or spoken with éclat he is a committed man, watched by the sympathy or the hatred of hundreds, whose affections must now enter into his account." Evidently, the sympathy of others is as much to be shunned as their hatred. It, too, becomes an accessory to yourself, which you may easily and falsely reckon part of yourself; and by thus falling in with other people's opinion, unavoidably you enter those people into your "account"—a kind of moral bookkeeping that is death to conscience. In this way you commence to treat yourself as property and yourself as the proprietor: the sort of inert property that Emerson deplored as a dead weight on society. But there follows a sharper provocation. Emerson goes on to deride philanthropy—that benign and regular expression of a covenant of works, the pride of New England's seventh generation—as nothing but canting hypocrisy. The cheat of philanthropy is that it cements a passive relationship between oneself and one's acts. It corrupts all the more spontaneous affections.

Not only in this essay but in his Divinity School Address and elsewhere, Emerson goes out of his way to associate his own teaching with that of Jesus. "I shun father and mother," he says, "and wife and brother when my genius calls me." The relevant text is Matthew 10:34–38, after Jesus raises the dead and cures the blind: "Think not that I am come to send peace on earth; I came not to send peace, but a sword. For I am come to set a man at variance against his father, and the daughter against her mother, and the daughter in law against her mother in law. And a man's foes shall be they of his own household. He that loveth father or mother more than me is not worthy of me: and he that loveth son or daughter more than me is not worthy of me.

And he that taketh not his cross, and followeth after me, is not worthy of me." This is meant to shape our response to the apparently trite and unremarkable statement that "the only right is what is after my constitution; the only wrong what is against it." Emerson means the constitution of his own nature, of which his physical illness and health are a fair index. But he also means the constitution of his faith, which has its own communion of one, with a reflex understanding of absolution. May not the same test then be applied to state and society? One always has the right to appeal from a political to a personal constitution. History and politics, Emerson says, are merely extensions of this singular and exclusive principle of the self. "An institution is the lengthened shadow of one man . . . and all history resolves itself very easily into the biography of a few stout and earnest persons."

Where Roger Williams and Anne Hutchinson had set themselves against all acquiescence in other people's doctrines, Emerson makes it clear that his enemy is fashion, and perhaps above all the currency of political and moral *opinions*. In this, he speaks as a man of genius of the nineteenth century. At the same time he is translating to a later idiom an inveterate motive of suspicion. The danger once lay in a servile obedience to theological precepts, a docility not easily to be distinguished from fear of one's neighbors; now, the menace comes instead from a timid identification with the mass of people, which may extend to a craving for uniformity. By means of such unconscious and external identification, people are encouraged actually to feel better about themselves from knowing that a great many others feel the way they do. Against the tranquilizing faith of this settlement, Emerson directs all the eloquence of his power of hatred ("the doctrine of hatred must be preached, as the counteraction of the doctrine of love, when that pules and whines"). So he urges the upright man's "conviction that envy is ignorance; that imitation is suicide; that he must take himself for better or worse as his portion. . . . We but half express ourselves, and are ashamed of that divine idea which each of us represents." He regrets even the necessity of using language—a medium of expression that, just because it is shared, conforms one person's meaning with another's simply as the price of being understood. We but half express ourselves, but we do in this way, at least, impress some meaning on our hearers. Emerson's sorrow at the pervasiveness of half-expression has something of the programmatic inutility of all consistent idealism.

Yet a psychological perception informs his judgment. We come to be wrongly ashamed of something unexpressed in ourselves when we are taught to value in ourselves chiefly the part that is well understood. The self-reliance of Emerson hates the very idea of utility, as it repels every demand on behalf of the common good. Accordingly, the essay concentrates some of its energy into an attack on the realist premise that society is prior to the individual. "Society is a wave," begins a passage in a mock-clinical idiom that Emerson could not always keep under control. "Its unity is only phenomenal. The persons who make up a nation today, next year die, and their experience dies with them." These neutral-sounding axioms carry the afterglow of a blast earlier in the essay, where Emerson has deployed a paradox to invert the usual defense of compromise for the public good.

Society everywhere is in conspiracy against the manhood of every one of its members. Society is a joint-stock company, in which the members agree, for the better securing of his bread to each shareholder, to surrender the liberty and culture of the eater.

This reverses the fable (related by a patrician to the Roman mob in *Coriolanus*) of the rebellion of the body's "members" against the belly. The members are wrong, thinks Emerson, not because the belly feeds the other parts and so they owe it obedience, but because there should be no such thing as parts.

"The virtue most in request is conformity." Well, but society only exists (it might be said) to achieve a decent conformity of parts in a total design. This much would not have been denied by republican theorists like Milton and Harrington, whose stock among American readers was always high. Emerson, however, is denying that there can ever be a gain for the soul in the barter of mutual advantage that is the reason-for-being of organized society. He will say unforgettably about those who define themselves by this working of an artful prudence against the ends of character, "Their every truth is not quite true. Their two is not the real two, their four is not the real four; so that every word they say chagrins us and we know not where to begin to set them right." *Chagrins us,* because we see in ourselves the traces of a conformity that, if we did not feel the shame of it acutely enough, would land us in the position of those weak and wasted souls; and how plausibly then we might arrive at arguments explaining our two which is not the real two. The subject of this essay on self-reliance has turned out to be the dignity of separatism.

It is worth pausing a moment longer at the anti-Whig undercurrent of "Self-Reliance," not only because its details are clearly accented and yet easy to miss the drift of, but also because the whole performance says something about Emerson's broader attitude toward politics. At least until 1850, when Daniel Webster threw his weight behind the sectional compromise that contained the Fugitive Slave Act, Emerson was himself a sympathizer with the Whig party and a strong admirer of Webster in particular. Webster was a pure Whig, if such a thing is possible, Emerson a very impure one, but both would have traced their lineage to Burke, and one may gauge how far Emerson's morality runs ahead of his politics by comparing some well-known sentences from Burke's *Reflections on the Revolution in France* with the answers to them in "Self-Reliance." Emerson's words appear below in italics:

> Our political system is placed in a just correspondence and symmetry with the order of the world, and with the mode of existence decreed to a permanent body composed of transitory parts; wherein, by the disposition of a stupendous wisdom, moulding together the great mysterious incorporation of the human race, the whole, at one time, is never old, or middle-aged, or young, but in a condition of unchangeable constancy, moves on through the varied tenour of perpetual decay, fall, renovation, and progression. *Society is a wave. . . . Its unity is only phenomenal. The persons who make up a nation today, next year die, and their experience dies with them.*
>
> One of the first motives to civil society, and which becomes one of its fundamental rules, is that no man should be judge in his own cause. *Absolve you to yourself, and you shall have the suffrage of the world.* He abdicates all right to be his own governor. He inclusively, in a great measure, abandons the right of self-defense, the first law of nature. Man cannot enjoy the rights of an uncivil and of

a civil state together. That he may obtain justice, he gives up his right of determining what it is in points the most essential to him. That he may secure some liberty, he makes a surrender in trust of the whole of it. *Society is a joint-stock company, in which the members agree, for the better securing of his bread to each shareholder, to surrender the liberty and culture of the eater.*

Notice that Emerson point by point confronts the case for a liberty founded on restraint and a nature given plasticity by the slow accretions of habit. If the public trust is to be replaced by self-trust, then man must become his own governor. He *ought* to be the judge in his own cause and will rightly view any proposed surrender of his liberty as a conspiracy against body and soul.

In order to recover an idea of self-reliance severe enough to have pleased the first-generation Separatists, it was necessary for Emerson to establish not just the lesser reality but the unreality of society. In front of every advantage of the social state, which Burke had greeted as a softening of manners and an amelioration of life, Emerson therefore simply puts a minus sign. He transfers the sociable virtues to the column of vices. The real test of his argument comes in what he has to say about the calculable benefits to be derived from common enterprises. These may be thought of broadly as the benefits of promise-keeping, also a familiar topic in political thought. Locke, who did what he could to solidify the uncertain correspondence between words and things, treated the good word of the promise-maker as a uniquely apt index of personal eligibility for citizenship. Promises are secured by conscience—a judge, according to Locke, incapable of acting selfishly. Indeed, it is partly for the sake of assuring sincere promises that one must refrain from tampering with the privacy of conscience. It followed for Locke that a regime of liberty and toleration was practically suitable to a race of reasonable and promise-keeping beings. It likewise followed that people such as Catholics, unable to secure their promises with a conscience separate from the church hierarchy, were properly to be excluded from religious toleration. Emerson was well aware of this history of disputation, which laid the groundwork for the creation of the political rights of individuals under the American Constitution. And yet, speaking again for *"my* constitution," he elects to give up the game of promise-making and promise-keeping. "Suppose you should contradict yourself; what then? It seems to be a rule of wisdom never to rely on your memory alone, scarcely even in acts of pure memory, but to bring the past for judgment into the thousand-eyed present, and live for ever in a new day."

In this way the individual promise is summoned before the tribunal of the present self, to be kept or broken according to its value at the present moment. A more regular and binding procedure may be "adored by little statesmen and philosophers and divines"; but "with consistency a great soul simply has nothing to do. He may as well concern himself with his shadow on the wall." On the face of things, it would seem that the genius of self-trust who attempted to follow this advice could not be easily discriminated from the opportunist, the dandy, or the slave of caprice. But this challenge is anticipated by Emerson's words about the integrity of the speaker who dares to contradict himself. "Speak what you think now in hard words and tomorrow speak what tomorrow thinks in hard words again, though it contradict every word you said today." Of course, not everyone has hard words to speak, or will venture to speak them even once. It is not clear what to make of the endorsement of contradiction as applied to feebler spirits.

Rhetorically, Emerson knew that with consistency denied as a value, something else was needed to give miraculous justification to a self whose reliance is revealed with every new posture. Though he says the relying matters more than what is relied on, he does also seek to offer one substantial point of anchorage. He calls it by other names in other places—"principle" is one such name, perhaps the most available one. But here he asks, "Who is the Trustee?" and the answer is "the aboriginal Self." This "shoots a ray of beauty even into trivial and impure actions, if the least mark of independence appear." The power of self-reliance, then, is such as to transform any act or word, or any contradiction between acts or words, into an occasion of beauty, provided it show some mark of independence. Emerson probably knew and certainly suspected that John Brown was a murderous enthusiast, but the least ray of independence had shone in his actions at Harper's Ferry and in the speech he made at his trial. It is entirely in keeping with the plan of "Self-Reliance" that its author should later have treated Brown as a prophetic hero worthy of the company of Copernicus, Galileo, Newton, Luther, and Jesus. We read the signs of independence in the self-trusting person just as we read the glories of nature. After all, we are mainly in the world for the sake of these. "It is only in isolate flecks," as William Carlos Williams would write, "that something is given off."

I have read Emerson for many years, and have never been sure how to describe the effect he carried into the work of later writers. Plainly, his individualism conferred a self-recognition on American literature, to the extent that our literature is anything but an epithet to augment the dignity of a geographic entity or a mixed ethnic constitution. Maybe rightly a literature *should* be no more than those things; but ours does sometimes seem to be more or other; and Emerson is the reason why it seems so. One hesitates to call his usual subject psychological, because psychology, as the word is commonly used, involves the mind's operations and an interest in the reciprocal relations of the self and a world of other people. One of the odd things about the Emersonian self is how it floats free of such concerns. His subject matter is inward but not in any ordinary sense psychological. Yet I agree with many the recent commentators who tell us that Emerson is to be read as a moral psychologist. The appropriateness of seeing him that way is justified in his descriptions of such feelings as pride, shame, chagrin, and exhilaration.

The moral relation that counts for Emerson, the only one, is set in motion when, by accident, something in me responds to something in the world as if it were part of me already, a part I needed to come to know again. He took what he liked from Romantic and Puritan writers to assert "that matter is the shadow and spirit the substance—that man acts by an influx of power" (the paraphrase is Perry Miller's). Emerson in this sense shared with minds as diverse as Wordsworth and Jonathan Edwards an intimation of a distance that separates the visible from the invisible. But though in "Self-Reliance" he might speak of "the sense of being which in calm hours rises" in the soul, the source of his sentiment had become, more strictly than in any earlier writer, the soul's peculiar testimony of being steeped in its own ecstasy. The space that seems to widen from such self-discoveries is often described by Emerson as if it were the physical space of a landscape. He knew of course and mainly spoke about the soul's testimony from pleasure. Yet his aesthetic was always inclusive. In such a place and gifted with such freedom, why should the soul not testify also of its pain?

Here is a characteristic landscape by Emily Dickinson:

> There's a certain Slant of light
> Winter Afternoons —
> That oppresses, like the Heft
> Of Cathedral Tunes —
>
> Heavenly Hurt, it gives us —
> We can find no scar,
> But internal difference,
> Where the Meanings, are —
>
> None may teach it — Any
> 'Tis the Seal Despair —
> An imperial affliction
> Sent us of the Air —
>
> When it comes, the Landscape listens —
> Shadows—hold their breath —
> When it goes, 'tis like the Distance
> On the look of Death —

The poem, notwithstanding the mention of death, despair, affliction, and hurt, is not particularly elegiac. I do not think it is about the death of anyone. Nor does it show us the poet saying an unwilling farewell to a hidden aspect of herself. The mood it embodies and means to evoke in the reader is, instead, a mood of attention, the prayer of a soul. The emotion for which the outward correlatives are all picked out with sublime accuracy is the emotion that Dickinson calls despair, but she gives the word its neutral sense of hopelessness, or an absence of hope. This was a mood encouraged by Emerson: "There is somewhat low even in hope" (ambition is as much of a drag as "this corpse of your memory"), but despair may be imperial. As it took Dickinson to see, the tuning of the soul's attention to a pitch of clarity not burdened by any earthly desire calls for a preternatural suspense of habit, a suspense even of nature itself. So her poem dwells in a moment when "Shadows—hold their breath"—a line that by itself would declare the presence of a great poet. An implication of the metaphor is that the physical world has turned ghostly, in sympathy with a poet who is neither one of the living nor one of the dead. A ghost may walk without casting a shadow, which is like speaking while holding your breath.

The critics of poetry, by now a majority, who think it is shallow and needless to connect poetry with the natural world, are taking away our rights. There is a certain slant of light you find peculiarly in New England on autumn and winter afternoons. It deepens the red of brick and stone, and darkens the green of lawns. It brings every blue closer to purple and sharpens the edges of shadows. Church and Inness and Martin Johnson Heade all painted it, this light that feels as if it came after something, a light before a sunset that will come on quickly and unremarkably. It is made by Dickinson the clue to a certain quality of the poet's soul. Maybe the light would take on a different enchantment if it were glimpsed streaming through the high window of a cathedral; but though it is tempting to link "Cathedral Tunes" to funeral music, "affliction" to a fatal disease, and "the look of Death" to a corpse turned face up in a coffin, these suggestions are muted because the figure is meant to stay figurative. The poet speaks of "the Distance / On the look of Death"—nothing is more fixed and endless than that look. Searchers after types in old New England looked for images and shadows of divine things, and Dickinson finds here in actual things images and shadows of herself. It is true the metaphysical poets also did this, especially Vaughan and Herbert, who from traits of idiom and sensuous texture have some affinity with Dickinson. But the metaphors of self and world explored by these poets connect the self and the world more firmly by means of their resemblances to God. The metaphors of Dickinson do not work like that. They yield a record of herself alone, and her difference from herself, "internal difference / Where the Meanings, are." For Dickinson, this mood of estrangement is a gift and is to be cherished.

I do not find in her work, what many readers say they have found, the presence of a character whom I can know. "Success is counted sweetest" does not do it—does not carry the note of interested invitation—much less "Because I could not stop for Death" or "I'm Nobody! Who are you?" or any of the obvious candidates. She is not, like Whitman, "Both in and out of the game, and watching and wondering at it." She is out and out. Her great subject is the affliction, or exhilaration, of continuing the game within herself. She sets any possible companion at a distance, often with stock effects of deliberate absurdity, as in the ingenious metaphysical anti-erotic courtship poem that begins "I cannot live with You." Nevertheless, there are a few poems in which Dickinson allows us to watch her as she looks at herself, the way a novelist may regard a created character.

A loss of something ever felt I—
The first that I could recollect

Bereft I was—of what I knew not
Too young that any should suspect

A Mourner walked among the children
I notwithstanding went about
As one bemoaning a Dominion
Itself the only Prince cast out—

Elder, Today, a session wiser
And fainter, too, as Wiseness is—
I find myself still softly searching
For my Delinquent Palaces—

And a Suspicion, like a Finger
Touches my Forehead now and then
That I am looking oppositely
For the site of the Kingdom of Heaven—

The last stanza confesses that though once she was punished for living as the devil's child, today she continues still to live from the devil. This is said without Emerson's boyish assurance of maintaining his credit with upright natures. It is more like a sigh of self-exasperation—I still have not got it right. She is restless for satisfactions not of this world, which she has known in herself since childhood, when she was a solitary mourner among the children. She looks on these postures now with a sense of their comedy, but without condescension toward her earlier self. To grow older is to become what they call wise, but this maturity is a weakening of the soul's thirst, a kind of faintness. And so her search has continued. The speaker might be Cathy in *Wuthering Heights,* grown old, except that Dickinson sees herself from outside, and what she looks to recover is not another person. That is one sense in which her palaces are "delinquent." Nature, taken as an end, is as opposite as can be to the kingdom of heaven. But Dickinson abides by her nature without complaint. The poem affords a sociable imagining of the aboriginal self, and it shows that self as gregarious as it ever becomes. How many of the heroes of American fiction are, like the speaker of this poem, day-dreamers? Or, if not dreamers, people who, when they avoid thinking of themselves, commence to see spectral characters, animated shadows, ghosts?

Goodman Brown is a young and susceptible and credulous member of the church in Salem, who goes walking in the woods one night, away from his wife Faith, to meet a gentleman who has lured him on this errand with a vague promise of a spectacle of unsanctified doings. The gentleman, who is the devil, performs what he promised. Several members of the congregation are disclosed to Brown in the commission of lust and other sins. Finally, he is given to witness them gathered in a clearing, in rapt attention at a devil's mass. The consequence, for the rest of his life, as Hawthorne tells us, is Goodman Brown's withdrawal into a profound melancholy. We may understand it as cynicism or disillusionment, but, to him, it is something darker, a loss of faith that can barely be concealed. Brown was a man of the crowd left suddenly alone with his knowledge of the crowd. His self-distrust is unspeakable—figuratively so in the course of the story, literally so by the end.

"Young Goodman Brown" has been interpreted as an ironic record of a delusion, or as a drab commentary, in Hawthorne's plain historical mode, on the fanaticism of Puritan belief. Yet there are clues planted in the story that indicate a quite different intent. The names that pass in review in Brown's consciousness, Sarah Cloyse, Martha Cory, and others, members of the congregation about whom he may or may not be learning the truth on his unseemly errand, include among them actual persons caught up in the witchcraft trials of 1692. Historically, what clinched the cases against those sentenced to death was evidence of a new and dubious kind, "spectral evidence." This meant eyewitness reports of the doings of the spectral shapes of actual people. Such evidence, when admitted to a court of law, as the Salem judges soon determined that it should be admitted, would count against the persons whom a witness could testify to having spectrally seen. It was hearsay evidence raised to a supernatural power. That an accused person had been observed to act in a way that suspended the laws of nature, even though one admitted the laws of nature could never be suspended—this, in Salem, long after the witch-craze had died out in Europe, was permitted to contribute to a proof that the accused was performing acts of wickedness. The process of secularization was far advanced in the laws of Massachusetts in the 1600s, but it made this stop on its way. One of the hanging judges was Judge Hawthorne, the ancestor of Nathaniel.

Of the story's commentators, Michael Colacurcio, in *The Province of Piety*, has done justice to the psychological realism of Hawthorne's portrait, and to the relevance of spectral evidence to Brown's real or imagined terrors. But what happens if we read it as a story about the fate of the self in the nineteenth century as much as the fate of the soul in the seventeenth? I believe the writing of "Young Goodman Brown" served Hawthorne as a delayed penitential exercise, but it was also in its time an ironic work of social commentary. We are invited to treat Brown as typical of the pathology of civic life at Salem, a life that allowed the accusations to go forward because self-trust and social trust had been vexed against each other beyond the breaking point. On the one hand, it is understood by those who seek justification that all social intercourse is a secondary fact of experience; one who judges by such evidence is exposing his crooked assurance regarding the authority of a covenant of works. On the other hand, how shall we judge our experience otherwise? How, given that we are judging in society? A covenant of grace, by definition, is inscrutable to any eye but God's. The covenant of works brings anyway the amenity that it can be known by visible goods. The crudeness and ingenuity of Salem had been to ask whether corruption, wickedness, a secret turning of the heart, could not also be known by visible signs. The trouble is that to believe this requires a translation of grace into a palpable and calculable good. Faith does naturally crave some token of reward. Yet once allow the proof of faith to rest in sensible form and you have confessed your faithlessness.

Goodman Brown is caught in this trap. A conformist to the core, a citizen and member-in-good-standing, it does not occur to him to question how sincere his faith can be if it depends on his knowledge of the constancy of his neighbors. So he becomes an unhappy doubter for life, under cover in his place in church. The story dramatizes an unspoken dialogue that must have passed in the minds of many believers.

Q: What holds you back from sin?

A: Nothing in myself.

QED: This knowledge is so dreadful that you will do anything to evade it. Thus you will put off on your neighbors the terror of your own disobedience.

The more Goodman Brown loses his faith—literally, according to the allegory, the farther he walks from home—the thicker grow the spectral terrors that crowd upon his consciousness. By the end of the story he is ready to testify against them or to withdraw into melancholy. It is a matter of whim or chance which of these endings will befall an individual like Brown. But the whole story is cast as a contrary-to-fact experiment of thought: this apparently is a Salem in which the trials did not happen. No mention is made of them in the denouement recounting the rest of Brown's life; and, to give point to Hawthorne's fable, the trials did not have to happen. They have taken place with sufficient finality in one haunted mind.

Like much of Hawthorne's fiction, "Young Goodman Brown" embodies a thought. It is a diagnosis of why radical Protestantism, with its idea of an aboriginal soul, was destined to be extinguished. Any man whose faith is constituted by his *fear of the eyes of other men*, and whose sense of their faith is constituted by an intuition of *their fear of seeing him*—such a man will take this journey in his mind, if not in the physical world, and the result will always be the same. To be inquisitive about other people's faith is already to have lost your own. Note that though Hawthorne is not an Emersonian, he accepts the Emersonian *either/or* regarding the self and society. An incorrigibility that may look like indifference lies at the heart of Protestant justification. Yet an eager interest in the condition of other people's faith is necessary to the regulative function of all religion. How then can a mind dwell separately in its neighborhood—sufficiently attentive to others, but still living in the light of conscience? The ideal citizen, in this way of life, was supposed to resemble Anne Hutchinson and Roger Williams in independence of spirit, and yet to resemble Young Goodman Brown in anxiety of concern with the actions of others. The society chose Brown as its model; how could it have done otherwise? Society was the chooser, and the person is a social creature. And so the faith died out. Or perhaps, Hawthorne seems to say, it changed its identity without a change of name. He knows because he is living among the wreckage.

Two centuries later, in the New York society that Henry James describes in "The Jolly Corner," the conflict between the private and the social self has moved to a field of action where commerce calls the tune. It does so without embarrassment, in every walk of life. The question asked by the novice has ceased to be, Shall I be known under a covenant of grace or a covenant of works? It is now, rather, Shall I be free to study myself or shall I make a lot of money? A choice like this, between spiritual and financial profit, has determined the mature life of the hero of James's story. The action turns on a visit he makes to the scene of his departure for that life, to look back and wonder whether his imaginable other self (who devoted a career to money-making) could have had as strong a claim as the self he became instead. About the previous actions of this hero, Spencer Brydon, there hovers the faintest hint of scandal and immoralism: this is the part of his life that he cannot speak of to his confidante, Alice Staverton; we are told it has had to do with "the freedom of a wanderer, overlaid by pleasure, by infidelity." Yet Brydon's has been on the whole a passive life, given to the generous fetching of impressions—a life, in short, a good deal like that of Henry James and not much like that of the grandfather who gave the James family its tremendous fortune. One might say that Brydon has chosen a path of grace; but grace is defined now entirely in aesthetic terms.

He plots and at last achieves an encounter with the ghostly version of himself. And the ghost is terrifying. It has a hunted look: the face appears damaged somehow beyond re-entry into humanity; the creature seems to know this and to feel a speechless chagrin. It says nothing at all when discovered, its only gesture being to shield the face from view. The double trick of the revelation is that Brydon, as we gradually come to know him, seems himself to have had an unsatisfactory life, in his withdrawal from the active and commercial world. Now it appears the self he would have turned into, in the course of enterprise and assimilation, was to have suffered a far worse deformity, to be physically and spiritually maimed, an object equally of horror and pity. We are meant to take the ghost simply as a given. But to take it that way means not to credit the eulogistic self-deception by which Brydon allows himself to believe that it was not really the ghost of his own other life. This is the comfort that he coaxes at last from Alice Staverton: "He isn't—no, he *isn't—you!*" Yet the ghost has been memorable enough to show what the story wants it to show.

The salvation or the fall of a self cannot be decided by a right choice of withdrawal from the world of action. That is what Brydon's hunt and his discovery and his self-deception prove, if they prove anything. He has indeed withdrawn, yet he is among the fallen; and, as the presence of the ghost suggests by indirection, he was always secretly among the fallen. It is this that the ghost has come to tell him. He was fit to live under a covenant of works, instead of which he became a collector of works, and the result has left him bewildered. What he thinks of the new face of the city, which has changed so ominously in his absence, is also what he detects about himself on the track of the ghost: ". . . he missed what he would have been sure of finding, he found what he would never have imagined." His other self has had a prosperous career as a monster in the business of building "monstrosities." This is one of several such floating expressions in the story, which test with startling results the power of near puns to construct more than verbal ambiguities. "The ghost of a reason" is another; much play is made with what life may have "made of me"; and James lavishes all his skill of echo and suggestion at the edges of the word "value." This last the story has caught on the point of a larger change of signification, and James uses Brydon's predicament to comment on the traces of cash value in the general theory of value.

On the most optimistic reading, one can take the allegory to suggest that the good man buys a façade of goodness at the price of paralysis and inhibition. Yet it may be a price worth paying. Behind that façade lies a world of action that turns people into ruins, or at best "a tall mass of flats," like the buildings that the new-money men of the city thoughtlessly make and unmake. As an account of the utter contrariety of grace and works, or beauty and utility, "The Jolly Corner" has a companion nearby in James's oeuvre, "The Beast in the Jungle."

There the hero is a man waiting for the romantic action or passion that will give his life a meaning, or rather fill it with the one meaning that was to have been its glory. He recognizes too late that this life of waiting has only assured that experience itself should pass him by; the thing, if anything, that was to have happened was a love with the woman beside whom he has stood apprehensively watching. Both of these heroes exemplify an *aporia* (as T. W. Adorno calls it): an insoluble complication that reveals a thing at once central and unspeakable about a society and its language. The standoff between will and thought that confronts Brydon—that they should be mutually definitive and mutually exclusive—is a necessary effect of his acceptance of an "aboriginal self." Yet grace, if that is the name for the election Brydon seeks for himself—grace that does not aim to produce its own reflection in works or buildings—now more than ever stands in need of external justification. By contrast, in an America frankly dominated by a commercial morality, works are seen as carrying their justification with themselves.

"The Jolly Corner" is written from the conviction that life is a progress or a regress from myself to something deeper in myself. If this lower layer should turn out to disclose another and alien self—an "*alter ego*," as James puts it in an early use of that phrase—I have a preternatural duty to confront it and return with news of the meaning this *alter ego* discerns in me. When James describes the shiver of pleasure with which his hero bathes in the first glory of his hunt for the ghost, Brydon's sensations uncannily share the emotional pitch of "Self-Reliance," of "a sense of things which rises, we know not how, in the soul," a sense that is "not diverse from things . . . but one with them and proceeds obviously from the same source." What Emerson asserted of the self's relation to the phenomena of life, James will say rather of the self's relation to a ghost that has lived its other life in an unknown possible world. The knowledge that this was therefore a possibility in oneself, that it perhaps remains a part of oneself, has been so forgotten or repressed that it can only be encountered in this shadowy form. "We first share the life by which things exist and afterwards see them as appearances in nature and forget that we have shared their cause." This sentiment, from Emerson on the self's surprise at finding evidence in nature of its own alienated majesty, might well have come from James instead, writing about Spencer Brydon.

CHAPTER 7

So, too, James on Brydon's intuition of the ghost sounds
very like Emerson on the self:

He was a dim secondary social success—and all with people who had truly not an idea of him. It was all mere surface sound, this murmur of their welcome, this popping of
their corks, just as his gestures of response were the extravagant shadows, emphatic in proportion as they meant little, of some game of *ombres chinoises.* He projected himself
all day, in thought, straight over the bristling line of hard
unconscious heads and into the other, the real, the waiting
life; the life that, as soon as he had heard behind him the
click of his great house-door, began for him, on the jolly
corner, as beguilingly as the slow opening bars of some
rich music follows the tap of the conductor's wand.

He always caught the first effect of the steel point of his
stick on the old marble of the hall pavement, large black-
and-white squares that he remembered as the admiration
of his childhood and that had then made in him, as he
now saw, for the growth of an early conception of style.
This effect was the dim reverberating tinkle as of some far-
off bell hung who should say where?—in the depths of the
house, of the past, of that mystical other world that might
have flourished for him had he not, for weal or woe, aban-
doned it. On this impression he did ever the same thing;
he put his stick noiselessly away in a corner—feeling the
place once more in the likeness of some great glass bowl,
all precious concave crystal, set delicately humming by
the play of a moist finger round its edge. The concave
crystal held, as it were, this mystical other world, and the
indescribably fine murmur of its rim was the sigh there,
the scarce audible pathetic wail to his strained ear, of all
the old baffled foresworn possibilities.

216

This is the incitement to the hunt—a motive entirely aesthetic, a "hum" audible only to himself. "You don't care
for anything but yourself," Alice Staverton says to Brydon. Whether one takes her judgment as praise, or a signal of benign complicity, or an accusation, depends on
one's reading of James's complex relationship to Protestant antinomianism. At any rate this is not an innocent
remark, in the tradition I have been sketching. Brydon for
his part might reply—there are Jamesian characters who
do almost reply—"How could I care for anything else?"
To the extent that this is so, it follows that the object he
has been caring for, the ghost, must in some way be himself. That is the hardest vein of irony in the happy ending
of the story.

If one asks why Brydon should carry his quest to so
absurd a length, for he faints and nearly dies at the encounter, the reason can only be that he is hoping to learn definitively that he is absolved. Most of all, perhaps, absolved
for not having worked at business, for having had his
inconclusive life of freedom and of pleasure touched by
infidelity. Whom can he rely on to absolve him, if not himself? Nietzsche in *Beyond Good and Evil* has an aphorism
in the form of a dialogue: "'I have done that,' says my
memory. 'I cannot have done that,' says my pride, and
remains inexorable. Eventually—memory yields." James's
story is this aphorism, with the interest shifted from action
to identity: "I am that"; "I could not be that." Eventually, self-knowledge yields. Further under, it is one of the
unhappiest endings in all of fiction. No hero's marriage to
a spouse in whose company he or she is bound to prosper
and suffocate has ever produced so despondent a feeling
as Brydon's supposed certainty of his innocence. We are
left to speculate what the ghost, were the story told from

its point of view, would contrive to make of this hero—passive, self-pitying, comfortable, bloodthirsty in his pursuit of curiosities. It could hardly be less terrified by Brydon than he by it.

"For example," it has been said, "is not an argument." But in criticism sometimes it is the least false thing we can offer. If proof were wanted of the ascendancy of an intractable Protestant spirit centered in the self, the control for the experiment would have to come from witnessing the same principle at work in a religious writer of an apparently opposite sort. Say a Catholic writer, in the line of Mauriac and the Graham Greene of *Brighton Rock,* for whom God's justice is absolute and separate from man and the patterns resembling faith in the soul are never what they seem. Flannery O'Connor's story "A Good Man Is Hard to Find" is a drama of recognition between two unbelievers. A normally disagreeable family, husband and wife and excitable children and a baby, are on a car trip with the husband's mother and the cat Pitty Sing. They hear of The Misfit and his gang along the way, and the meddling grandmother, sure of herself and very wrong, leads them on a picturesque side trip down an unfamiliar country road. They go off the road into a ditch, and The Misfit is the one who finds them. He has a theory that Christian revelation only matters if it was divulged to him directly, a theory in which there are strange echoes of the high-minded Antinomians.

"Jesus was the only One that ever raised the dead," The Misfit continued, "and He shouldn't have done it. He thown everything off balance. If He did what He said, then it's nothing for you to do but thow away everything and follow Him, and if He didn't, then it's nothing for you to do but enjoy the few minutes you got left the best way you can—by killing somebody or burning down his house or doing some other meanness to him. No pleasure but meanness," he said and his voice had become almost a snarl. "Maybe He didn't raise the dead," the old lady mumbled, not knowing what she was saying and feeling so dizzy that she sank down in the ditch with her legs twisted under her. "I wasn't there so I can't say He didn't," The Misfit said. "I wisht I had of been there," he said, hitting the ground with his fist. "It ain't right I wasn't there because if l had of been there I would of known."

A grotesque flicker of charity comes through the grandmother's answering gesture of extending her arms to embrace the man: "You're one of my own children!" That is when he shoots her.

"She would of been a good woman," The Misfit will say later, "if it had been somebody there to shoot her every minute of her life." This is a boisterous joke but it also speaks the literal truth of his relation to the grandmother. The menace of violent death alone could precipitate the freely given act of love by which at last we know that she is prepared. "The least ray of independence" came to be visible in the most impure and confused of her moments. Flannery O'Connor, when she commented on this story, was at pains to stress an orthodox reading of the moment when the grandmother beckons in a Christ-like posture. In the same lecture, O'Connor directed some well-chosen words of derision against the sophisticates who made The Misfit into a kind of hero. But though her portrait of The Misfit is indeed penetrable as that of a "prophet gone wrong," to use O'Connor's description of him outside the story, his actions are so stark in their self-reliance as to eclipse the grandmother's change of heart among the motives inside the story. The Misfit has performed a gratuitous act obedient to the law of his constitution. The obstacle that all institutions are to the Emersonian believer, Jesus Christ and the reports of His divinity are to him. The only way to right the things that Jesus set wrong—the only way not to shrivel and wither in His shadow—is to act regardless of any previous law or custom. In O'Connor's novel *The Violent Bear It Away,* and in other characteristic stories such as "The Life You Save May Be Your Own," no alternative ever arises to counter the dominant type she aimed to satirize, the misfit who can absolve himself. These stories are one of the great things in American literature of the twentieth century: impartial, fearless, disciplined yet utterly wild. O'Connor believed that her work was misunderstood, but did she not also misunderstand herself? She returns again and again to characters like The Misfit, not to damn them, since that would be redundant, but chiefly to watch and listen. She was a Catholic in the grace she asserted, but her particular subject, and the knowledge of America it reflects, are antinomian with a ferocity the author may judge but cannot shed.

These pages have sketched a tendency that is not exhausted. The American psychosis has not yet come to anything like a provisional end. One sign of its prevalence is the way the myth is assumed as a challenge even by gifted writers who are not quite possessed by it—Mailer in *An American Dream,* Bellow in *Henderson the Rain King.* Through all the testimony, one fact anyway stands out with distinctness. This is the growing importance of money as a dissolvent of manners and customs, money as an image of something deeper than experience, money as a power that converts every rival symbolism to a language of its own. In every period of our history, but never more so than today, money has been the leveler by which self-engrossment is made to adapt to a surface ideal of gregarious practicality. Money has taken increasingly to itself the obscure and compelling charge that Emerson assigned to the hidden self. It has the right kind of abstraction, and the right kind of opacity. It is at once an embodiment and a creator of value: the further from any produced object, the better. It is the thing, more convenient than a person, that absolves you to yourself. By comparison with money, the soul has lapsed to the inferior reality of an entity that cannot be modified or exchanged. It would take a novelist of James's powers to focus "the thousand-eyed present" on a communion so purified of people that even the self has become a name for a thing.

2002

CHAPTER 8

HOW PUBLICITY MAKES PEOPLE REAL

WHAT FOLLOWS IS A REMINDER OF THE VALUE OF CERTAIN experiences, or rather a way of regarding experience. The value sometimes went by the name of privacy, and the destruction of privacy is the great collective project of our time. All the dominant tendencies of mind and society abet this project: the general and unquenchable optimism of American life; the promise that technologies of the self can render us transparent to each other (with the unspoken assumption that this is to be desired); the intuition that the one thing more precious than human thoughts and feelings is the acquired ability to engineer small differences in ourselves and in those whom we love or buy. Penetrating all these tendencies, and invisibly assisting them, is the belief that *choice* is the metaphor that should govern free action. *Consumer* is the word, in turn, that naturally goes with choice; and for the emancipated consumer the locus of choice is the *market*—if not the stock market, then a market of some other kind; and further back, to prepare for the decisions of the market, an institution that contour-builds the best minds for the best choices: what would that be if not *the marketplace of ideas*? Narcissism has a long future. An expected child of an aspiring consumer couple, whose plan of life has gone through a rigorous first draft long before birth, the shape of whose probable character, temperament, and prospects can be read out from the arc of elective traits on the human genome map—this creature will be knowable from age zero by medical, state, and market authorities with a clarity, distinctness, and intimacy of oversight that could not have accrued to a member of an earlier generation before middle age.

I aim to describe a mood all Americans have lived with for some time: the mood of broadcast intimacy. I heard a non-celebrity guest on *Oprah* once confide to Oprah that she had never told her best friends what she was about to say, but: the real truth was that her marriage broke up almost totally because of the mayhem her daughter created at home. A typical revelation of broadcast intimacy. The guest from ordinary life did not want to say it to her closest friends or even her family; but to say it to millions of viewers was a comfort. Anyone who has ever watched a talk show is familiar with the syndrome. The woman never told her neighbors because that would have been gross. Why then was she telling the camera now? At this point the usual instruments of moral psychology are at a loss. The mass media represent life, through an intervening layer, or so we had supposed. We have yet to reckon with the novel fact that the media have been so naturalized in the lives of many that they are now widely understood *to intercede for us.* They confer on experience a reality it would otherwise lack.

All this occurs in a haze of euphoria that is the very element of the media and that only an artist informed by unpleasant irony can hope to convey. In the remarks that follow, I will rely on the testimony of artists who have been close observers of American mass culture. But it should be plain from the first that publicity, as I use the term, does not refer narrowly to the mass media of exposure— advertisements, scandal sheets, the radio call-in and television talk shows. I have in mind a more generalized process, a rite of passage now conducted by American society in a great many venues, by which we are solicited to recognize ourselves and to know ourselves most alive as an image. It is essential to the procedure that the new self-image be identical with a broadcast image identifiable to people who never heard of us until it came into public view. The achievement of publicity—not the decision to "go public" or the process of being forced into public view, but the deliberate making-public of oneself—is to merge the private with the general conception of who one is. Its success depends on the puzzling fact that the irrevocable passage from depth to surface can be experienced as a relief.

Another anecdote. I was at a friend's house watching him cook dinner, leafing through a newspaper, half attentive the way one can be in such settings, when the phone rang and across the kitchen I heard my friend's voice rise. "Who? You *what?* Wait a minute. *Are you trying to sell me something?*" A pause. "Yes, that is my name, that's the right spelling. Now listen. I want you to underline this number and *never* call it again." At which he resumed the conversation where we had left off. My friend is in his mid-fifties, an aesthete, a religious believer, and an anarchist. I mention these facts because nobody younger, and nobody rendered docile by profession and prejudice, would have handled the moment quite as he did. He was breaching a decorum of the commercial culture of democracy; to do so did not particularly strain his resources. The same decorum has been adopted in national politics. At the

Democratic Party convention of 2000, Al Gore's daughter introduced him with these closing words: "He's a really cool person, and I know you'd like him." It helps, if you want to avoid encounters like this, to shun politics as well as market surveys. My friend has boycotted the last six presidential elections.

Politics and market research today share with the media the assumption that anyone's life may have to be *coaxed* into publicity. Naturally, it is done for the target's own good. This was the thought of the legislative assistants working under Senator Howard Metzenbaum when they dragged Anita Hill in front of the footlights to rehearse some pent-up grievances against her friend and mentor Clarence Thomas. Under publicity, they had reason to believe, the extracurricular and lurid details would be alchemically transformed and would yield a conversion of the past and present understandings of both personalities. As things fell out, however, Thomas was not hip to the publicity cure. This, as much as the offense of harassing monologues recollected in the distress of Anita Hill's afterthoughts a decade later—this culpable immunity to the logic of public confession was the real scandal of the Thomas confirmation hearings. The usual nameless dramaturge had lined up the action, all the levers of penitence were in place, but the protagonist-scapegoat failed to carry through. Hill had herself been reluctant to appear before the Senate until the suasive energy of the publicity culture, and the moralized gloss it was able to promise, showed their ascendancy at last and brought her over. Some way in back of the dream of the publicity cure lies a belief that all withdrawal from publicity is suspect. One can deduce this belief from the rage exhibited by the practitioners of the cure when they are disappointed. It is as if such a withdrawal were really a breach of a new kind of public trust.

To be content with anonymity, with a recessive position and its noncelebrity, when the opposite is once offered, is, in modern American society, anomalous and almost perverse. Better, under the benign gaze of camera and cassette, to admit to any transgression than to imply a contentment with thc habits and manners of invisibility. A person who resists the gaze of the mass culture, to the extent that he or she is the desired object of its gaze, will, for that sufficient reason, be classified as opaque, unreliable, even (in some hard-to-capture sense) potentially hurtful to the normal people. Someone who acts like that has opted out of a common faith. It follows that he or she is to be treated as one would treat a member of a very small cult. The younger you are, and the more democratic your milieu, the more unmistakable the prejudice becomes. The generality of these attitudes may help to explain some recent attempts to coax into publicity an American artist conspicuously associated with an idea of privacy.

The history of J. D. Salinger's reputation in the past decade has been one of coercive exposure to the point of torment (if one could imagine a private person feeling anything). The appetite for information seems to have grown with every satisfaction it was denied. The first well-known effort to open up Salinger's privacy came from the British literary journalist Ian Hamilton. Having written an authorized biography of Robert Lowell, Hamilton soon after conceived the ambition to write a biography of Salinger. Eventually he found his way blocked by a refusal of permission to quote from letters. Not wanting to be done out of a project, he chose to publish a first-person narrative, *In Search of J. D. Salinger*, about the obstacles placed by modern life in the way of an earnest biographer and an inquisitive public. Then a net of a finer mesh was spread and dropped. Another journalist, once known for her ruminations on family life and the importance of the genuinely personal, broke into full publicity after a muffled decade of waning renown, with a memoir of her youthful love affair with Salinger. The author was Salinger's admirer, protégée, and, as she now divulged, his former lover, Joyce Maynard.

Maynard had enrolled at Yale in the 1970s, and in her freshman year wrote a cover story about herself for the *New York Times Magazine,* under the title "An 18-Year-Old Looks Back." It was the first piece of confessional journalism by someone who claimed to represent the post-Sixties generation. Because the posture was new—that of the novice to experience, already disenchanted, yet innocent and uncertain how to enter the world—the essay was talked about and brought its young author hundreds of letters. One of these came from Salinger. He expressed admiration for the poise of the writing, and offered some words of advice against too much early exposure. Maynard wrote a winsome reply, asking, in effect, if he could somehow teach her the meaning of his advice. This brought an invitation to pay him a visit; the meeting went well; and Maynard dropped out of college to spend several months with the celebrated author and private man. Salinger threw her out when he discovered that, thanks to Maynard's pressing need for promotion to sell her book-length memoir, *Looking Back,* his phone number was now in the hands of her literary agent and *Time* magazine. For the next twenty-five years, Maynard said nothing. Then, in her forties, with children to send to school and no bigger game in prospect than an Internet fanzine dedicated to herself, she decided it was time to be made real again. Salinger was now seventy-eight: it was perhaps better to have the reality conferred while he was alive. Around the time that her book, *At Home in the World,* appeared, Maynard announced a plan to sell at auction her correspondence with Salinger. The pair of moves was sufficient to provoke a number of journalistic profiles, and though a good deal of the attention was unfavorable to her, it also led to a new wave of speculation about Salinger and his seclusion. It is as if the public mind—of which Maynard's writings and choices in life have been at various times so sensitive a barometer—it is as if the mind of publicity itself had discovered, in the second character in this story, an irritant beyond words and beyond explanation. Salinger stands for the person who *might* be made real by publicity but who, given chance after chance, unaccountably does not elect to be remade.

There is a postscript. Last year, J. D. Salinger's daughter Margaret published a memoir of growing up in her family. The contents of the book are unremarkable. It is the story of a girl who admired her father in spite of many tensions and peculiarities. In retrospect, she finds him exorbitant, and, as she comes of age and begins to see her family from the outside, she gradually realizes that he is one of those people the world agrees to call eccentric. Her book, though to a lesser degree than Maynard's, professes to have been written partly to heal or expunge a long-buried trauma. Yet it soon becomes clear to a reader of both books that the confessing women, in ways they are not fully aware of, have grown up anxious—and anxious in ways that, if obliquely traceable to, cannot be easily or confidently blamed on their experience of J. D. Salinger. It likewise becomes clear that one thing inhibiting that plain perception has been a heavy exposure to advice informed by trauma theory. Margaret Salinger has come to think, as most of us finally do, that her parents made mistakes she herself would rather not make with her children. This resolution would not appear to require for its confirmation the publishing of an intimate memoir. But on the premise that we are made real by publicity, it does of course require that, since a resolution in private life is insubstantial until its grounds are worked up in public. "Ms. Salinger," reported Dinitia Smith in the *New York Times* on August 31, 2000, "said she wrote *Dream Catcher* because 'I was absolutely determined not to repeat with my son what had been done with me.'" That is to say, the examined life has not been fully examined if no record is disseminated to prove it. "Does [her father] know about her book? 'He does now,' said Ms. Salinger." Margaret Salinger refused to give the interviewer her husband's name, or that of her son, or her son's age. She did say that she hopes to write more books. If Joyce Maynard's confessional trespass seems a peculiar and at last an aberrant case, Margaret Salinger's suggests the normal American state of mind about publicity. That state of mind is often self-contradictory, it is capable of self-doubt, and it tends toward the resolving of doubt through self-exposure.

The assaults on Salinger are an inverted homage to an actual quality of the book that has kept his name alive. *The Catcher in the Rye* is an exuberant and delicate monologue by a quiet character whom we overhear talking to himself. He stands in a predicament that many readers, and especially adolescent readers, have taken to heart with a fondness of self-recognition. The book showed us the unburdening of a self that by its freedom offered a kind of invitation. This was a message that was meant to pass from the character to the reader, not from the person of the author to the person of the reader; and yet Salinger's achievement is not quite unconnected with the possibility of that confusion. Holden Caulfield, the hero and narrator, has an idiosyncratic code of conscience that serves him as rigorously as a code of honor—a word he does not use any more than he would use other words of the same family. "*Grand.* If there's one word I hate, it's grand. It's so phony." Holden despises the phonies who have internalized an accepted public manner from the first of any encounter you have with them. These include potentially most people, but grownups more than children. The one unquestionable non-phony, a party of the elect in herself, is Holden's younger sister, Phoebe. His favorite partners in dialogue are mostly in his mind; some of them in fact are writers of books. "What really knocks me out is a book that, when you're all done reading it, you wish the author that wrote it was a terrific friend of yours and you could call him up on the phone whenever you felt like it." Which author would you call up on the phone? It is a characteristic private game of Holden's. He likes *Out of Africa* by Isak Dinesen more then he thought he would. Maybe she is one. Probably Fitzgerald is another, for *The Great Gatsby.* "Old Gatsby. Old Sport. That killed me." Anyway, the authors you would play the game about are either dead or safely remote by virtue of their distance or their worldliness. The game of "call up the author" was meant to suggest an inward freedom—an example of Holden's candor with himself, of an entirely impractical curiosity, like his anxiety about what happens in winter to the ducks in Central Park. What shall we conclude? Fifty years ago an American wrote a wonderful book about the endlessness of privacy. He had the fate to publish his book in America.

It was inevitable that numbers of readers would take the gesture as an invitation to call up the author.

While I was writing the last few paragraphs on a train, two voices rose distinctly above the murmur of conversations. Were they talking to me? Actually, they were talking into their cell phones, with a nattering authority proper to a phone call in one's home or office. Let these voices stand for the mature and uncoerced publication of privacy. There was an audible shifting in some seats, but the veteran passengers felt no stir of irritation, having come symbiotically prepared with CD or radio Walkman. The situation would have been immediately comprehensible to Rupert Pupkin, the hero of Martin Scorsese's film *The King of Comedy*. Rupert calls the receptionist's desk at a talk show he wants to book an appearance on, from another receptionist's desk to which he has just delivered a package; and, asking after the star of the show and being told that the star is at a meeting, he says without an air of absurdity: "I'm at a meeting myself." The many people who contrive to be heard using cell phones in public places, by that very fact can feel themselves to rise in importance. They are audibly present at two meetings.

It is hard to speak in the older manner of nineteenth-century fiction, or of twentieth-century psychology, about the motives that drive people to consent to be made real by publicity. Certainly they know that careers can get a jump this way; and that there is cash value in the revelations. But one has to take into account a curious shade of moral approval or fellow-feeling that is elicited now by self-exposure of any but the most rancid and debasing kind. Besides, the euphoria of the mass culture itself is a keener incentive than any countable reward. This mood is its own reward. How many people have come to realize, with a queasy cheerfulness, that by vandalizing their own lives and emptying out the contents of their usable relationships, they were entering into the company of the absolved. But the bridge of excuses runs both ways. The public person through an exposure of privacy steps into the accessible lower reaches of a knowing and sharing audience. The private person through a painful and maybe accidental ascent to publicity is enabled to shed the infinitesimal but crushing burden of anonymity. Both, equally, gain access to the universal drama of mass culture by which one becomes a fixed quantity for other people. How to measure the incidental sacrifice—the surrender of the freedom to live a life that people do not have a name for? Andy Warhol said that in the future everybody would be famous for fifteen minutes. He did not say those were bound to be pleasant minutes. The compulsion that drives the assault on privacy, like the compulsion that Freud believed to underlie the pleasure principle, is beyond any rational calculus of pleasure and pain.

The portrayal of conversions from private to public life has a long history in the American arts; and some of the most enigmatic of our fictions revolve around the paradox of a reality brought into being by publicity. Once having been made real by publicity, the transposed man or woman may want to be rescued from public reality after all, and privacy may become the name of that paradoxical hope. The heroine of Henry James's novel *The Bostonians* has spent her youth preparing to exert her mature powers as a charismatic speaker for the philanthropic religious, moral, and political forces of Boston society. Verena Tarrant is expected, for her destined years of fame on stage, to breathe fresh life into the transcendental embers of the last of the Peabodies and Alcotts. Yet there has flickered about her a suggestion of the counterfeit or bogus: her father, Selah, before all her speeches, winds her up to get her started with a hocus-pocus vaguely reminiscent of Mesmerism. Her admirers know this, they take it in, but do not care. She is their private public star. The crisis of the plot occurs at the intervention in her life of a Southern gentleman, Basil Ransom, who falls in love with Verena and decides to rob her patrons of their prodigy, to remove her forever from the glare of recognition. His passion and the excitement of the theft are, for Ransom, a single compound emotion, while from her point of view he has a mysterious power as the deliverer of a gift her patrons could not promise: a life of private devotions and feelings.

The Bostonians ends somewhere between irony and tragedy. An intimation is there, for us to make of what we will, that Verena Tarrant's life in the shadow of Basil Ransom will not be happy. By his resolution and her consent, we are assured only that their life will be private to the core. James understood that in America, the very thought of such a reversal is charged with melodrama; and he pronounces the last words of the novel with a full sense of their strangeness as well as their ambiguity:

> "Ah, now I am glad!" said Verena, when they reached the street. But though she was glad, he presently discovered that, beneath her hood, she was in tears. It is to be feared that with the union, so far from brilliant, into which she was about to enter, these were not the last she was destined to shed.

The reserve in the closing phrase has to do not only with the dimness of the match Verena has made, but also with the muffled pleasure of privacy itself, in contrast with the brilliant rewards of a public renown. There is a mingling of self-pity in her tears of sorrow and joy. The author of the words, who at the time was dreaming of public success for himself as a dramatist, would have entered fully into the complex feelings of his heroine.

James's novel came out in 1886. Let us look ahead 50 years to an American book that compels us to think disagreeable thoughts about the way publicity makes people real. But a separate problem confronts us in Nathanael West's *Miss Lonelyhearts:* an odd complicity between the satirical treatment and the misanthropy of the author. Where James writes sympathetically of the capacity of a public role to carve up human agents to its ends, West is decisive and hard-hearted and impartially bitter about the crowd's appetite for a suitable martyr. The hero of the novel, the columnist Miss Lonelyhearts, is denied even an individual name, and he comes to know by violence what his creator already knows, namely that for the tear-soaked and the traumatized who write to ask his advice, the public working-through of their misery from a low to a lower depth is its own reward. It is more real to them than the life to which they would return if their letters ever had to stop. So they bring the hero closer to themselves than mere confidence implies. They include him in their lives, and, though he is by temperament a cynic and an immoralist, with a remnant only of a baffled idealism that appears in his very fascination with the letters, they nevertheless treat him according to his title as their own personal Jesus Christ. (A parody letter in the novel addresses the Jesus of the Bible as "Dear Miss Lonelyhearts of Miss Lonelyhearts.")

West's novel deals by counterpoint with the feeble efforts of the hero to care for a woman he thinks he loves, and his automatic attempts to seduce the wife of the features editor at his newspaper. The editor, Shrike, is a satanic figure actually much farther gone in unbelief than the hero—one for whom the publicity world denotes the whole of that created life whose end is to crush the human will. Shrike has given up and he has the courage of utter bankruptcy. By contrast, Miss Lonelyhearts needs others to give him up by proxy. The moral disintegration the story traces is expertly summarized by the hero when he tells his lover why he has felt himself going dead to personal experience:

> Let's start from the beginning. A man is hired to give advice to the readers of a newspaper. The job is a circulation stunt and the whole staff considers it a joke. He welcomes the job, for it might lead to a gossip column, and anyway he's tired of being a leg man. He too considers the job a joke, but after several months at it, the joke begins to escape him. He sees that the majority of the letters are profoundly humble pleas for moral and spiritual advice, that they are inarticulate expressions of genuine suffering. He also discovers that his correspondents take him seriously. For the first time in his life, he is forced to examine the values by which he lives. This examination shows him that he is the victim of the joke and not its perpetrator.

Miss Lonelyhearts is killed on the last page by the impotent husband of a fervid reader who has come to cherish adulterous feelings for "Miss Lonelyhearts." To this man in his trance of grief, the part of the wronged husband is the best he will ever have to play. So the hero is crucified in the same action that consummates his mission as an evangelist of the publicity cure. Earlier, Shrike, on discovering a desperate letter from the killer, has delivered the only possible moral. The letter writer, he says, is a physical cripple and Miss Lonelyhearts a spiritual cripple: "Let each hindrance be thy ladder." The gap is impassable in this novel between those who know the publicity world to be unreal and those who are sure it contains all the life they can possibly care for.

I have already alluded to *The King of Comedy*. This movie belongs to the early 1980s—a period when the image culture of the present first showed the full reach of its appetite, its glibness, its compulsive mobility, and its assurance that alongside a well-wrought simulacrum, the real thing is lucky to break even. The peculiar vehemence of the film owes much to the genius of its director Martin Scorsese. It owes just as much to a screenplay by Paul Zimmerman alert to the chatter of bars, restaurants, streets, and waiting rooms; and to a daring performance by Robert De Niro, a nervous dance of public faces that renders credibly human a person whose life is all on the surface. One might describe *The King of Comedy* as a comic version of a better-known film by Scorsese, *Taxi Driver*, where the notion of publicity as intoxicant was a notable secondary theme. The earlier and more conventional film was about an urban cowboy who, by perfecting his psychosis and emulating every cliché of revenge in the mass culture, finally succeeds in becoming a mass killer and a tabloid hero. Like the protagonist of *Taxi Driver*, Rupert Pupkin in *The King of Comedy* encroaches on the lives of people who do not belong to him. He tries to solve his life by solving theirs. But though not a shot is fired, *The King of Comedy* is emotionally the more violent of the two films. It presses to a terrible limit the irony that James and West were already exploring in their meditations on American privacy and publicity. No genuine life is here to be glimpsed as an index of morale beyond the image. Not only Rupert's aims and aspirations but his very demeanor suggests an erasure of the difference between the celebrity and the private self.

Three scenes from the film bring out with uncanny vividness the merging of inner with outer and private with public. In the first, Rupert is practicing for a visit to the late-night talk show hosted by his idol, Jerry Langford. He stages his fantasy on an upholstered armchair in the basement of his mother's home—his version of the talk-show armchair where the guest relaxes and unwinds. He greets with a kiss a life-sized cardboard Liza Minnelli and tells her that she looks wonderful. He kisses Jerry and tells the audience "I love this guy." Jerry's imagined questions go unheard, but Rupert, conducting his side of the interview at nicely spaced intervals, can be heard bragging sheepishly in the talk-show manner. "Oh boy, I'll tell you. Every time you come back from a tour, I don't know what it is, but there must be something in the air on the tour, it really becomes you, it's like you become rejuvenated, I don't know what it is. Isn't that so, everybody?" The scene ends on a shout from his mother upstairs. The bus has come early. This full-scale homemade simulacrum of redemption-by-publicity tells a truth about the character that could not be conveyed otherwise. Rupert has arrived at a sublime readiness for celebrity. The smugness, the strut of the show-biz elect, the patina of suavity, and most of all the first-naming—which oils every conversation with an ever-adjustable intimacy—all of the traits of the character that Rupert puts on, cribbed from top to bottom out of Jerry Langford's television manner, come to seem part of a predicament larger than the character itself.

A later scene shows him cooling his heels at the office of *The Jerry Langford Show*. He has turned in audition tapes to showcase his talent and is waiting for Jerry to listen to them. A sleek-haired personal assistant who handles the bookings for the show has told him plainly that he needs to be seen in nightclubs first and to come back when his material has sharpened. Rupert does not get the hint, and sits down for a long wait, and as he sits he thinks of the moment when the crooked will be straight. Another fantasy: he has now advanced to full celebrity guest on Jerry's show, and, on the pattern of *This Is Your Life*, Jerry says they have brought in someone to surprise him. Enter an ineffectual-looking older man with glasses and a mustache—a face like many others. Do you know who this is? Jerry asks. Rupert, by now too important to be embarrassed, grins and says no. It is the principal of Rupert's high school and he has come to perform Rupert's wedding ceremony on TV. The talk-show partitions swing back to reveal a television chapel and the piano on which the principal is next heard playing the wedding march. Before he performs the service, much moved, he delivers a public testimonial to Rupert:

> When Rupert here was a student at Clifton High School, none of us, myself, his teachers, his classmates, dreamt that he would amount to a hill of beans. But we were wrong. And you, Rupert, you were right. And that's why tonight, before the entire nation, we'd like to apologize to you personally, and to beg your forgiveness for all the things we did to you. And we'd like to thank you personally, all of us, for—for the meaning you've given to our lives.

We are present at a miracle akin to transubstantiation. Rupert, in the glow of these abject words, passes from defeat to triumph forever, and as that happens the talk-show audience is made to feel that by applauding his success, it can legitimately admire and absolve itself. Privacy, such as may belong uniquely to one's own victories and defeats, has here been transformed into a medium of unlimited sharing.

If one had to describe in a phrase the character of Rupert Pupkin, one might say that he is constituted by empathy. It is an abstract gift that runs as it were in an unimpeded current, from his expressiveness about having a well-digested life to the other person's identical expressiveness. No intervention is allowed from the specific density of events and feelings. He meets by chance a young woman, Rita—a beauty he has admired since high school who works now at a bar and is resigned to being a nobody—and when, after a dinner date, she asks what he wants, his reply is pure empathy. "I love you," he says. "I want to help change your life." But this is the same thing as pure publicity: "What if I set something up between me, you, and Jerry?" He has met Jerry once in a taxi. Rupert gave Jerry his personal card and Jerry told Rupert that if he wanted a career in stand-up comedy, the bottom was the place to start. On the strength of this meeting Rupert tells Rita he will take her to Jerry's summer house. The inner life has been evacuated: it would be a nuisance anyway, and nobody ever told him about it. The frightening premise of the film is that such empathy or adaptability is consistent with the character of a good-natured conformist, or a young man on the make, or a violent psychopath.

The story has its climax in Rupert's kidnapping of Jerry Langford: a hostage whose ransom becomes the ceding to Rupert of that night's opening monologue. This plan to be made real by publicity succeeds. The monologue is delivered to a solid ration of applause before he is picked up by the police. A coda invites us to believe, and we are surprised to find how far we can believe, that after serving his time in prison Rupert will come back all the better for the exposure. His fame will turn out to be renewable, and his choices have scarcely left him any cause for regret. He would do it again.

The most disturbing moment in *The King of Comedy* is not the kidnapping. It is the interlude in which Rupert actually does bring Rita to visit Jerry at his summer house. All things in his mind have passed into the currency of television. A famous running joke on the show about the house guests Jerry finds himself perpetually having to put up has been taken by Rupert to mean that anyone who encounters the famous host will be vaguely included in the invitation. In their one meeting and in his reveries, Rupert must have called him Jerry hundreds of times. Obviously, the deftness of the host will take care of any detail Rupert missed, and everything at the house will go well. By the rules of television reality, it should. But when they arrive in their slick party outfits, Jerry is on the golf course, and the butler in the empty house, confused by the unfamiliar guests, telephones him in a panic. Jerry comes back in his shorts and sweater, with golf club in hand, and is livid with anger. Rupert offers him a drink from his own stock: "What's your pleasure?" The late-night Jerry—played to the last ooze of expertise by Jerry Lewis—has always been the most accessible of public persons. In this light, Rupert's inability to take the hint is a kind of homage. And yet, on his private estate, Jerry's sense of himself becomes identical with a possessive pride in what he owns. The point is emphasized by a visual joke. Rita, who is not likely to see such a place again, slips into her handbag an exotic paperweight. On her way out, she then profusely apologizes for Rupert, who at first disowns her ("She's a girl who works in a bar. She wants to spoil everything.") and only at last understands that he is being ejected. "I have a life, OK?" says Jerry. "Well," says Rupert, "I have a life, too." "*That's not my responsibility!*" Jerry's last words are an indignant shout. One may have noticed in this scene that the face of Jerry Langford at home is lined and puffy and cruelly definite. It has a trace of a snarl. A face that bears the dimmest likeness to the image Rupert has spun out from the public glaze of television hospitality.

Irving Feldman is an American poet who has written deeply about the way publicity makes people real. I have in mind particularly a satire that resists summary, "In Theme Park America," and a shorter poem, "Interrupted Prayers," which I will quote in part from Feldman's book *The Life and Letters*. In structure, "Interrupted Prayers" is a monologue with commentary. There are three characters: a listener to a radio call-in show, Don; the host of the show, Larry; and a hidden listener, Irving. All first names of course. The opening lines establish a night-long stage set of broadcast intimacy, an apocalyptic communion of the lost where self-hatred is anointed by self-love:

> The sun goes, So long, so long, see you around.
> And zone by zone by zone across America
> the all-night coast-to-coast ghost café lights up.
> Millions of dots of darkness—the loners,
> the losers, the half-alive—twitch awake
> under the cold electronic coverlet,
> and tune in their radios' cracked insomnia.
> A static craziness scratches and buzzes
> inside the glowing tombstones of talk
> —some crossed wires' hodgepodge dialogue,

of Morse and remorse of garbled maydays
of prayers shot down by Heaven's deaf ear.
Heaven itself is crashing tonight.

The host, Larry, is a successful stew of affability and puni-
tive scorn—an accurate detail since the worldly success of
the call-in host is often a motive of the call-in conversations. Beyond the equality of the listeners in communion,
there stands one hierarchy untouchable: the ultimate
divide between the man or woman at the microphone and
the petitioners who meekly approach to solicit advice or
encouragement. Their hopes are at once raised and hum-
bled by the knowledge that in an instant their prayers
could be interrupted and the line go dead at the whim of
success.

It seems a fertile breeding ground for resentment, but
the anger never quite breaks through. Here is Don from
Cleveland, "longtime listener, first-time caller," who has "a
comment and a question" and is told to come to the point.
"What is your question?"

"My comment, Larry, is just this: Larry,
if anyone's out there, I mean, anyone at all,
who's contemplating suicide—don't do it, please!
I tried it once. It's not worth it—believe me.
So please, I beg you, please get help, get help fast!
See a counselor, a minister, a *therapist*!"
The marvelous T-word sizzles on his tongue.
"I can't emphasize this enough. But Larry,"
he segues smooth as a pro, right on beat,
"I'm really phoning in to ask you this.
Historically, twenty-two major leaguers
have played in four different decades in the Bigs.
Larry, can you tell me how many of them

are active now? And can you tell their names,
Larry—please?"

Which was the ulterior motive of Don's call, the comment
or the question? The nature of broadcast intimacy makes
it impossible to decide.

The words uttered by Larry the host are minimal. They
convey the punctual aggression suitable to so compressed
a format, though it comes in various disguises. Transparent hype: *"'Touch all the bases, baby! / Go, go, go! Go for it,
guy!'"* Admonishment: *"'I haven't got all night, sir. / I have
other callers on the line.'"* A rebuff: *"'What are you, some kind
of wacko, sir?'"* And a conciliatory farewell: *"'Hey, Larry,
am I right? or am I right?' / 'When you're right, you're right,
baby.'"* Larry's remarks in italics, like the comment and
question by Don, fit into an all-purpose tenor of saluta-
tion. What can it mean? The poet draws back near the end
to observe:

> Larry's voice holds Don off at lash's length
> —not to be contaminated by loser taint.
> And certainly success owes this to itself,
> to go on being successful,
> and always be wanting more—not like ghosts,
> who have to hunger for Larry's hunger,
> who call and call in, hoping to please him,
> because losers can't please themselves.
> From admiration, we break our bones,
> we hold the shattered stemware up to him,
> we say, For you, this toast. I am nothing.
> But drink my marrow—and be everything!

The poem closes after a last exchange, but not before the
poet has awakened in the small hours to hear Don's call

replayed on tape. The idea that hell may be nothing but an infinite repetition of life's humiliations, is a shared fantasy of pagan and Christian theologies, and the nightmare of talk radio is that everything is said endlessly. As Hart Crane wrote: "The phonographs of hades in the brain / Are tunnels that rewind themselves."

"Interrupted Prayers" brings into startling focus a strain of masochism that now pervades American popular culture and that sometimes appears to be its central unspeakable motive. Though scholars such as Carol Clover and Mark Edmundson have had interesting things to say about the persistence of the Gothic imagination in popular culture, we still lack a historical account of the origin and aim of masochistic programming. For the American culture of publicity did not acquire its present texture by accident. Well-designed patterns of financing and a corporate personality type of specifiable habits and background have presided over the emergent authority of high-fashion photography, video games, slasher movies, and gangster rap: genres more closely interlinked than their precursors in the media of thirty years ago. The methods in force and people in charge need to be carefully tracked before they can be named and the truth told of their works without fear of slander.

The masochism of our current recreations and entertainments cannot be separated from the broader therapeutic culture with its glamorous, garish, and finally abject dogma that in every life there are *wounds* that need healing; that the unhappiness of life comes down to an avoidable trauma or series of events to investigate and anatomize; and that experience may be reduced to *experiences*—on the understanding that bad experiences often happen early and always occur as side effects rather than as signs of inveterate character. These beliefs, in their gathered force, exhibit the corruption of a truth about personal freedom. They aim to divide the dignity of the person from the pathos of responsibility. Indeed, among the leading purposes of the therapeutic culture is the giving of assurance to the morally helpless. Does the responsibility weigh too much? Then it was a mistake for anyone to ask them to bear it. At this point one is brought back inevitably to the question of social class. Publicity may have become for us what political economy was said to be for an earlier age, "a gospel preached to the poor." Or rather, it is now a gospel preached to the people Nathanael West called the "profoundly humble," with their "inarticulate cries of genuine suffering."

Readers of Herbert Marcuse's *One-Dimensional Man* will recall that book's unsettling picture of two opposed versions of social liberation. The first possibility is a regime of "non-repressive sublimation," where the free play of aesthetic imagining is emancipatory for society in action as well as in imagination. Individuals would approach their projects in life with the kind of interest that artists bestow on works of art. The other possibility is a regime of "repressive desublimation": unlimited pleasure, but in the absence of political or personal autonomy. The current Fox TV miniseries *Temptation Island* calls for real-life couples to be sequestered on an island under the camera's eye while they resist or succumb to a corps of unattached tempters who have been assigned real-life supporting roles. The couples know what they are getting into. They have placed themselves in the line of the betrayals or self-betrayals that are a hazard of every life—only they have done it in conditions of formalized, almost dreamlike, predictability. Nothing is new in the problems of will and the field of action that are presented here. The puzzle is why even the most pandering and besotted of the media, and the most naive of the bodies yearning to be made real, should have bargained for an exposure quite so exacting. The president of Fox Enterprises, Gail Berman, described the show as "a terrific, unscripted soap opera," and the choice of metaphor is revealing. Conventional fiction itself has become too fake, too scripted. The solution is to turn reality itself into an organized fake. In this way, the new sort of fake, steeped in the clichés of soap opera, takes on a peculiar pungency because it is also infallibly real. The interest now lies not in the plot but in the consequences for the lives of the actors that will stay changed long after the show is over.

The great modern allegorists of the self traduced by exposure, Kafka in *The Trial* for example, never traveled this far in imagining self-desertion. By the rules of the game to which the contracting couples have submitted, every public act in the real-life story will count a second time as a private act in someone's life. The temptations and responses that pass on-screen cannot be effaced from the lives off-screen, since, ultimately, these people have no part to play except themselves. By the same token, every private act counts a second time as public, and to that extent can no longer be reckoned a personal act in the familiar way. The idea of such a calculus is as bizarre and psychically taxing as the notion that the experience you dream is true because you dreamed it. This last is a common *dread* of the sane: the relief of waking up is to recognize that it was unfounded. But once people's lives have been framed by the options of on-screen reality, there is nothing left to wake up to, just as there is no work left for the imagination. To ask whether we can live without privacy is to ask whether we can live without imagination.

Privacy is an aristocratic idea. The most private of novels and one of the greatest is *The Princess of Cleves*. The action there turns on a feeling whose proof is a deed not done and a communication in open sight that is hidden from all but the person who sends and the one who receives. Feelings today still pass between people, with the same subtlety and depth of implication, but the fact that they do has become a secret. The obvious explanation is a craving for stimulus—anything, however brutal or degraded, to rouse the mind from inertia. But could it be that a kind of resentment also underlies the extremity of the change? Privacy should not have been incompatible, it was not initially incompatible, with the coming of democratic manners in the nineteenth century. It was an idea whose arrival could seem in keeping with the spirit of the age, as it was for the great practitioners of the realist novel: Turgenev, Tolstoy, Flaubert, James. What seems to have cut off the reserve of manners and judgment the novelists took for granted is the permanent ascendancy of plebiscite and market surveillance. How do *we* know who *you* are unless we know the things you like, and why you prefer those things to certain other things? And you can help us to learn by answering just a few questions. The morale of advertising in American democracy says: "Let us make you more comfortable by giving you more and better choices, since we know that all people want comfort and indeed want it in ways they have scarcely imagined." What my friend was saying when the phone rang was an affront to the indecencies of the market. He declined to share the premise itself about the good of sharing. "I did not," he was really saying, "invite you into this room and into my life, not even for one moment. My saying nothing to you until you called was not permission to call. My not knowing you was not an indication that I probably want to know you. It was quiet here before; your question left us where we were, before any kind of beginning; and that is where we should stay for now. Strangers, unless we agree to do something together."

What have we lost? A certain spirit of unpresumingness. A generosity of personal distance, which had its roots in chivalry, but which there were reasons to expect democracy could discover its own version of. When Walt Whitman said, "What I assume you shall assume," he implied an acknowledgment between two people before the rest of the conversation began. It was an acknowledgment of equality, but that did not mean it went without saying. The culture of mediation has been clamoring for a long time to effect once and for all the good it wants: faster beginnings, more efficient paths all the way into our lives. After all, it says (and doubtless this is true), your comfort depends on your acceptance. This culture has not yet won exclusive control of American manners, but, in the past two decades, it has gained ground alarmingly. Whether a regime of publicity could ever be congenial to the interests of political democracy properly understood, is a separate question, and one that we may prefer not to put to an ultimate test. It does seem to me that privacy may be one of those checks or balances of democratic life necessary to its public success—as necessary as the existence of courts in which each member of every jury holds a dialogue of conscience for the length of a trial and longer, without so much as a tremor of a wish to speak to a reporter. "Were we even there," the voices might well complain, "if we never saw our names in the paper?" Do our private opinions count as opinions at all unless we see them associated with our image in full view? It is hard to say for sure; it always has been hard. But one kind of moral life depends on the possibility that, even in what we do not say, in what we do not come to be known for, we remain interesting to ourselves.

2001

CHAPTER 9

THE SELF-DECEPTIONS OF EMPIRE

"Nations," wrote Reinhold Niebuhr, "will always find it more difficult than individuals to behold the beam that is in their own eye while they observe the mote that is in their brother's eye; and individuals find it difficult enough." The last six words crystallize the thought. Niebuhr's political writings are an exhortation—part history, part criticism, part sermon—to hold nations as closely as possible to the individual standard; to make them recognize that even when they oppose a great evil, what they themselves embody still includes much evil. All of the good that a nation can do by violence is contingent; the evil is real and palpable. "Nothing is intrinsically good," Niebuhr remarks, "except goodwill." Hence the need for the discipline of prayer, a wish for the purity of heart to sustain the attention necessary for good will. "God, give us the grace to accept with serenity the things that cannot be changed, courage to change the things that should be changed, and the wisdom to distinguish the one from the other": Niebuhr's own most famous prayer imagines a life of patience and fortitude in which a great many satisfying actions have been refrained from, and strength has been shown in a fight against many evils, not all of them external.

He was born in 1892, in Wright City, Missouri, the son of a German pastor. His religious calling found him early—he was ordained in his mid-twenties—and he worked as a pastor in Detroit from 1915 to 1928, where he supported the efforts of Ford workers to organize. He helped to found the Fellowship of Socialist Christians and later served as an editor of the liberal magazine *Christianity and Crisis*. In the years of his prime, at Union Theological Seminary from 1928 to 1952, Niebuhr was the pre-eminent American Protestant thinker. And "thinker" is the only possible word: his range comprised theology, political theory, foreign policy, and the tactics of social reform. His views were disseminated in pamphlets, columns, book reviews and polemics, in religious and academic publications, but also in the *Atlantic Monthly*, the *Nation* and the *New Republic*. He achieved wide renown with his arguments against the Christian pacifism that had been the dominant strain in Protestant intellectual circles in the 1930s; a teacher of Dietrich Bonhoeffer and an associate of Paul Tillich, he worked with as single a mind as theirs to draw the German people away from Hitler's party. By the spring of 1940, when the lend-lease policy for Britain was first discussed by President Roosevelt and his advisers, Niebuhr was a firm supporter of American intervention in the European war. But not even at the height of the war, in 1942 and 1943, did Niebuhr cast himself as a "war preacher." No argument from necessity, no certainty that the other side was worse, could wipe clean the fact that war is legal murder. In 1946, he helped to draft, and signed, the statement by the Federal Council of Churches which judged that "the surprise bombings of Hiroshima and Nagasaki are morally indefensible," and added:

Even though the use of the new weapon last August may well have shortened the war, the moral cost was too high. As the power that first used the atomic bomb under these circumstances, we have sinned grievously against the laws of God and against the people of Japan.

In a life of public acts and public speaking, Niebuhr gave a concrete sense to the work of seeing the beam that is in your own eye.

He did it characteristically by asking what we have in common with our unlucky brothers. How did the state, in Germany under Hitler and in Russia under Stalin, achieve so tight a hold on modern societies? What is the enchantment of such collective entities for people who are capable of thought but liable in critical times to lapse from citizens into subjects? A striking passage of *Moral Man and Immoral Society* (1932) gave an answer Niebuhr would reiterate in his later writings:

> Patriotism transmutes individual unselfishness into national egoism. Loyalty to the nation is a high form of altruism when compared with lesser loyalties and more parochial interests. It therefore becomes the vehicle of all the altruistic impulses and expresses itself, on occasion, with such fervour that the critical attitude of the individual toward the nation and its enterprises is almost completely destroyed. The unqualified character of this devotion is the very basis of the nation's power and of the freedom to use the power without moral restraint. Thus the unselfishness of individuals makes for the selfishness of nations.

This analysis is not, as it is sometimes taken to be, a melancholy defense of the necessary selfishness of nations. It is a lament for the fall of man.

The projection of the generous instincts of self-sacrifice from the individual to a collective object is a psychological jump that contributes a new and unnecessary evil to the life of society—unnecessary because it goes beyond the minimum necessary evils of regulation, coercion, and punishment. The allure of the gregarious satisfaction—as if a team by a victory did more than a person through love—makes a promise only fantasy can deliver, against which reason is helpless and conscience cannot find itself. In action on behalf of the group, I do for my kind (whether they need it or not) what I will not do for a stranger: an inversion of the parable of the Good Samaritan. Yet a large portion of the other-regarding energies which seem a fortunate condition of social life, could never be summoned without the substitution by which I donate my conscious will to a larger and unthinking not-me. The process, indeed, is close to the fictive transfer of properties that we come to know in allegories and in dreams; and there is no doubt, says Niebuhr, that this "combination of unselfishness and vicarious selfishness" is the main element that goes to form the sentiment of nationalism. *Vicarious selfishness*: what a troubling thought lies buried in that phrase. And it has the temperamental accent of Niebuhr, striving against the flattery of the cheap comfort.

In Gandhi alone among modern thinkers, Niebuhr detected a possible method for averting the transfer of unselfish sentiments to the state and the consequent downward sublimation of fellow-feeling into national loyalty. Non-violence, taken as a principle, may counteract the most pernicious of collective fictions, because it robs enmity of its sting. By exposure to the tactic and to the underlying principle of non-violence, the oppressor is made to see his own actions in a starker light. Also,

Niebuhr observes, the method of non-violence works to "rob the opponent of the moral conceit by which he identifies his interests with the peace and order of society." Who is disturbing the peace when a policeman assaults with a club a man and a woman standing quietly in a boycott line? Niebuhr speculated in 1932 that "the emancipation of the Negro race in America probably waits upon the adequate development of this kind of social and political strategy." As it fell out, many of the civil rights leaders who worked closely with Martin Luther King had been trained by Niebuhr's students, or were conversant with his thinking. King's great "Letter from Birmingham Jail" would mention Niebuhr as a source of the precept that "groups tend to be more immoral than individuals."

For King himself, according to his biographer David Garrow, *Moral Man and Immoral Society* was an early and crucial influence. It turned him away from the social-gospel Christianity that looked on war as a unique enemy of progress; Niebuhr, by contrast, taught that war was only one manifestation of that selfishness by which the more benevolent instincts are narrowed and misprized. Yet—and the reservation is typical—much as Niebuhr admired Gandhi for the deliberateness of his campaign to lift the oppression of an empire without reliance on cruelty or revenge, he took care to add that non-violent resistance was often itself a case of the lesser evil. Some of its acts of willing self-sacrifice called for the sacrifice of unasked persons elsewhere: "Gandhi's boycott of British cotton results in the undernourishment of children in Manchester. . . . It is impossible to coerce a group without damaging both life and property and without imperiling the interests of the innocent with those of the guilty."

His argument against the self-justifications offered by a righteous nation at war is, *a fortiori*, an argument against empire: "No nation has ever made a frank avowal of its real imperial motives. It always claims to be primarily concerned with the peace and prosperity of the people whom it subjugates." Nor is any political or economic system exempt from this corruption of the will. *Moral Man and Immoral Society* saves its deepest scorn for the idea that there *could* be a society free of selfishness and the wish to dominate. Nikolai Bukharin, the theoretician of world Communism, supposed that a war between two Communist states was "an impossibility by definition." Niebuhr quotes the Bukharin axiom and comments that such self-overcoming is improbable for Communism and equally improbable for capitalism: "A trading civilisation is involved in more bitter international quarrels than any civilisation in history." Better-paid functionaries than Bukharin, in the commercial democracies today, have excogitated the theory that two democracies by definition can never go to war: a deduction all history is said to confirm. Niebuhr recognized that such maxims of social science were a fiction devised by juggling the names of classes of governments and classes of events. If Athens and Sparta were democracies in 431 BC, the theory is false.

If you want a nearer instance—and a case Niebuhr had plainly considered—look at the political character of Germany in the mid 1930s. Starting on March 23, 1933, Hitler enjoyed the powers, as Konrad Heiden put it, of a "dictator, created by democracy and appointed by parliament." As late as 1935, Winston Churchill could speak of Germany as a democracy that had strayed from itself; and he could wonder if Hitler might yet prove the leader to bring Germany back "serene, helpful and strong, to the forefront of the European family circle." When, on March 7, 1936, German troops marched across the Hohenzollern Bridge to occupy the Rhineland—an act of war in defiance of the Versailles Treaty—the bloodless infraction could appear a correction by armed forces of a glaring international wrong. You would think it so if you wanted to think it so. One might more truly call it an act of war by a confident but poisoned democracy against a weak and nerveless democracy. The political arrangements of democracy, as Niebuhr took pains to say, carry with them no built-in immunity against such selfish acts.

Niebuhr was dismayed by the coming of the Cold War, as only a disappointed socialist could have been dismayed. The Second World War, he wrote in his pamphlet *The Children of Light and the Children of Darkness* (1944), appeared to signal a drastic reform of bourgeois society. He thought this both necessary and good; and he believed that Britain was better adapted than America to the "social friction and convulsion" that would ensue. America had given to "bourgeois illusions" an outsize plausibility, but soon it would be generally understood that "property rights" inevitably "become instruments of injustice." This was only a slight modification of the hope, expressed in *Moral Man and Immoral Society*, that "perhaps Communism will furnish the criticism which will save parliamentary socialism from complete opportunism and futility." The need remained for a current of thought to oppose capitalism: this did not end with the Second World War and the discovery of non-denominational evil in the totalitarian menace. Every nation is subject to a massive complacency: no group, therefore, which "does not stand partly outside of the nation" will ever "criticise the nation as severely as the nation ought to be criticised." Niebuhr was at most a contingent nationalist, and American history as he saw it was to be judged without giving the benefit of the doubt to national good intentions. On the contrary, the United States, in *The Irony of American History*, is presented as a nation possessing the usual attributes of nations. It is the ascendant power in 1952, and the world could do far worse, Niebuhr implies; but it shows the characteristic deformations of every proud and aggrandizing country.

The Irony of American History treats America as the self-unknowing protagonist of a new struggle. Soviet Russia is taken to embody the greater evil about which little need be said. The book—drawn from two series of lectures, given in May 1949 and January 1951—instructs Americans to use our power when necessary in order to defend the freedom we value for good reasons; but we are warned not to suppose ourselves disinterested or free from corruption. Niebuhr's socialist beliefs have survived the twenty years of depression and war with impressive integrity. He declares as a strength of postwar American life the broad acceptance of organized labor and of the justice of collective bargaining; it remains a far from happy circumstance that "the debate in the Western world on the institution of property was aborted in America." The book presses hard against the assumption of native virtue and the dangerous pride of a nonexistent innocence. Americans like to think good things have happened to us without greed, that our conquests were entailed on us without the lust of dominion. This defect of self-knowledge mars our capacity for intelligent action, but chiefly, according to Niebuhr, in foreign rather than domestic policy; in the latter, Americans "know ourselves to be less innocent than our theories assume": at home, we have "builded better than we knew because we have not taken the early dreams of our peculiar innocency too seriously." He draws a strong contrast here with Soviet Communism, which believed its own dream of "a frictionless society" within its borders. (*Frictionless* is a pejorative word that recurs interestingly in the book; the anti-utopian skepticism of Niebuhr's analysis is matched by a positive belief in the clash of ideas.)

The U.S. differs from the Soviet Union, he thinks, in looking to achieve its ends "by moral attraction and imitation." In the years of the Marshall Plan, this was true to a degree that subsequent policies have made easy to forget. Niebuhr alludes just once to a darker possibility: "Only occasionally does an hysterical statesman suggest that we must increase our power and use it in order to gain the ideal ends, of which providence has made us the trustees." But he brings up the convergence of idealistic reasons and imperialist aims only to dismiss it: so long as the stakes of a miscarried war remain as high as they appear, no leader will succumb to such a delusion. Half a century later, he can hardly be held to answer for that notable underestimate. Yet even for the time, he pours a curiously misplaced vehemence into an attack on what he calls the "temptation" of "isolationism." It was, in truth, not much of a temptation in the last months of the Truman administration and the second full year of the Korean War. What explains this turn of the argument? It seems possible that the warning against isolationism is a veiled reference to McCarthyism (which kept foreign nationals out of America, but did not keep American troops out of foreign countries). If that is the point, the tactic is oversubtle. Another odd detail, when you look at the rhetorical economy of the book, is that Senator Joe McCarthy is never mentioned by name—though Niebuhr in fact did much in these years, both in public and in private, to protect old friends and associates from the slanders of the anti-Communist hunt. A likelier target in the attack on isolationism is the diplomat George Kennan. His name does come up, and Niebuhr mostly agrees with the "containment policy" of which Kennan was the architect. He rather dislikes the fatalism with which Kennan resigned himself to letting the Soviet Communist threat burn itself out. Not the policy but the rhetoric of containment was too moderate for Niebuhr's taste. It comes to a difference of shading, perhaps, without practical consequence; but one may feel in retrospect that Kennan's fatalism has worn surprisingly well.

Niebuhr's advice to shun an "isolationism" that constitutes a moral "temptation" closes the argument before his reasons can be entered into. He seems to have wished for a policy that was bold, but not too bold; an encouragement to militant friends of the U.S. but not a provocation to wars. A temptation ought to be resisted—the foregone conclusion belongs to the definition of the word. Niebuhr might have faced a harder climb had he renamed his isolationist opponent an "anti-interventionist" and declared himself in favor of an interventionist policy that stops short of imperialism. In this stretch of the polemic, he may be collapsing the American mood of 1952 with the mood, a world apart, of 1936. A year after his book was published, the CIA fomented the coup against Mossadegh in Iran; a year after that, the coup against Arbenz in Guatemala: covert interventions whose success would make for an utterly different temptation. Yet Niebuhr seems still in search of a eulogistic cover for interventionist policy when he writes that "human life is healthy only in relationship." Why accord relationship so peculiar a value among nations unless you are (as Niebuhr was not) a cosmopolitan quietist of the school of Hume? This looks like importing into collective psychology a value that has its significance only in the life of the individual: precisely the fallacy that *Moral Man and Immoral Society* had warned against. It must be added that the wider motive for his use of "relationship" turns out to involve a useful warning. Nations ought not to be judges in their own cause. If they want judges who are adequate and not hostile, they had better keep up international relations.

In all his political books, Niebuhr works out his thoughts by a condensed paraphrase of the thinkers who have helped him—both those whom he admires, like Kierkegaard and Burke, and those he largely rejects such as Dewey and Rousseau. His favorite device is the capsule narrative of intellectual debates juxtaposed with recent historical events. But there is a second, quite distinct, mode of persuasion that becomes very marked in *The Irony of American History*. The prose sometimes rises to an intensity that is close to prayer. These moments are infrequent, and they arrive suddenly; the context offers no preparation for a paragraph like this:

> Nothing that is worth doing can be achieved in our lifetime; therefore we must be saved by hope. Nothing which is true or beautiful or good makes complete sense in any immediate context of history; therefore we must be saved by faith. Nothing we do, however virtuous, can be accomplished alone; therefore we are saved by love. No virtuous act is quite as virtuous from the standpoint of our friend or foe as it is from our standpoint. Therefore we must be saved by the final form of love which is forgiveness.

It is a warning against empire and, more generally, a reminder of the futility of hoping for moral effects from political action. No italics mark the place, but most readers of the book will certainly pause.

If one could abstract a single idea from Niebuhr on the corruption of morality by politics, the thought would come to this. Only the guiltless deserve to wield power; but the guiltless do not exist in politics, for power makes the powerful guilty. No man can rule innocently, and what is more, none can stay innocent for two moments in dealing with hostile powers, or even with friendly rivals. What Americans have construed as our goodness was always, to an embarrassing extent, the result of good fortune and the advice of prudent framers. Nothing about the nature of the United States will guard Americans from the self-deceptions of empire; these are an evil incident to the conquests of war, and every nation "is caught in the moral paradox of refusing to go to war unless it can be proved that the national interest is imperiled, and of continuing in the war only by proving that something much more than national interest is at stake." The process of exaggerated reason-giving breeds a popular susceptibility to new threats where none exist. "Perhaps the most deleterious consequences of imperialism," Niebuhr concludes, occur in "the spiritual rather than the economic realm." He means what imperialism does to the colonizer as much as to the colonized.

Most of the world's evil is conceived and executed not by wicked persons but by dedicated officers and time-servers. "This might be myself" seems, therefore, an apt response to any glimpse of the workings of a brutal system; and Niebuhr, casting his eye over the Soviet renditions and camps under Stalin in the 1940s, makes a point of saying, not in a subordinate clause tucked into a penultimate chapter but in a staring sentence on page three:

"One has an uneasy feeling that some of our dreams of managing history might have resulted in similar cruelties if they had flowered into action." Fortunately, he adds, no set of Americans will ever ascend to anything like the control over unchecked power that has become possible in the Soviet system. But the crucifixion is reenacted in every age and in every society; and the cause is not only cruelty but blindness—the instructed and thoughtless compliance of judges of every nation, and priests of every sect.

> Christ is crucified by the priests of the purest religion of his day and by the minions of the justest, the Roman Law. The fanaticism of the priests is the fanaticism of all good men, who do not know that they are not as good as they esteem themselves. The complacence of Pilate represents the moral mediocrity of all communities, however just.

When Niebuhr searches for an example of a political actor who exhibits true forbearance and charity, he finds only one, Abraham Lincoln; and if we are looking at the leaders of larger powers in times of war, Lincoln is perhaps the only example modern history affords. Niebuhr admired Churchill as most Americans did and do, but he seems to have recognized that Churchill was thrilled by war and always lived for a contest of some sort. Churchill, too, was apt to suppose that the children of light were not much streaked by darkness. How could one relish the fight while burdened by the reservation? Lincoln, somehow, led his country in a war without coming to love war in any way at all; and when the Civil War neared its end, he gave an explanation of its moral causes in the Second Inaugural. There was wrong on both sides: if a God was at work in the war, he must have sent its sufferings as a punishment to both sides—the North for its connivance at oppression and the South for its active extension of the evils of slavery. And this is the note struck by Niebuhr in the peroration of his book. Near the start of the Cold War, the message he believes most worth sending to the rulers of the United States is that there is wrong on both sides.

"Irony" is a word that grows more elusive and complex as this argument advances. In the irony of American history (sense one), the United States was rescued from the evils of individualism by the excesses of individualism, which created the necessity for large-scale economic reforms in the 1930s. Americans were thereby saved from the illusion that their way of life was so good that it ought to spread everywhere; yet what saved them was the emergence of an idealism opposed to theirs. Communism, on this view, is a monstrous growth of the utopian germ in democracy itself; and America now confronts a system exhibiting "evils which were distilled from illusions, not generically different from our own." A steady theme of the book is that the kinship between liberalism and Communism may help us to forgive the development by which Communism became the greater evil, and make us less self-congratulatory about the crossing of fate with character by which America was spared the success of the Communists. But *they* are never alien, for Niebuhr. *Their* idealism, without distortion, would be an extension of recognizable American beliefs. That your enemy resembles yourself is the primary lesson to be extracted from the irony of the Cold War. Besides, America, in the behaviorist ideology of the social sciences, and in the rationalizing theory of the rational market, has produced its own version of bad utopianism. "Whether or not we avoid another war, we are covered with prospective guilt. We have dreamed of a purely rational adjustment of interests in human society; and we are involved in 'total' wars."

The practical teaching of the later chapters centers on the maxim that in order to retain international power, a country must use it with consistent restraint. A more particular lesson may be learned, Niebuhr believes, through the spectacle of a hero entangled in "pretensions which result in ironic refutations of his pride." The point is forcibly made in the preface, with a rolling cadence of indignation that cools the fervor of Kipling's "If": "If virtue becomes vice through some hidden defect in the virtue; if strength becomes weakness because of the vanity to which strength may prompt the mighty man or nation; if security is transmuted into insecurity because too much reliance is placed upon it; if wisdom becomes folly because it does not know its own limits—in all such cases the situation is ironic." So irony (sense two) differs from tragedy, for Niebuhr, because it springs from unconscious weakness and not completed action; and once brought to light, "an ironic situation must dissolve, if men or nations are made aware of their complicity in it." There will be "an abatement of the pretension, which means contrition." He wrote the book with the aim of producing such an "abatement."

Yet Niebuhr finally speaks of an irony (sense three) that springs from the gradual perception of the faults not of a situation but of a system, and indeed of any system. We laugh initially at Don Quixote because we can penetrate the illusions he takes for realities; only later do we laugh "with a profounder insight at the bogus character of knighthood itself." The allegory hardly requires translation: Niebuhr is pointing to the inappropriateness of commercial democracy as a gospel for the world. This was not a pleasant reflection to offer the Truman administration, and it would have been even less happily received by the Clinton administration. The fall of Communism, as Niebuhr all but prophesied, has permanently deadened the capacity for irony among those who took credit for the triumph. Power, as John Adams wrote in a passage Niebuhr cites,

> always thinks it has a great soul and vast views beyond the comprehension of the weak; and that it is doing God's service when it is violating all His laws. Our passions, ambitions, avarice, love and resentment, etc., possess so much metaphysical subtlety and so much overpowering eloquence that they insinuate themselves into the understanding and the conscience and convert both to their party.

Good intentions are the watchword of the approving ego. And in American discussions of foreign policy, the good intentions of the United States are assumed.

Niebuhr hoped Americans would become chastened heroes—Quixote at the end of his story, as seen by the reader, not Quixote at the beginning as seen by himself. But for that to happen, we must become enlightened spectators of ourselves. And what has this to do with Christianity? Niebuhr says that "the Christian faith tends to make the ironic view of human evil in history the normative one." The only judge he can imagine who would forgive the contending parties in a world-historical agon in which both are wrong, is God. If history were a novel, we could say the judge was the author—Tolstoy in *War and Peace* is Niebuhr's example. But however we imagine the necessary distance of the accusing and forgiving judge, an ironic view "is achieved on the basis of the belief that the whole drama of human history is under the scrutiny of a divine judge who laughs at human pretensions without being hostile to human aspirations." The opposite of the honest judge is the person who says of his social group, "We are good." From such a person nothing good can ever be expected.

Niebuhr's anti-messianism might seem a form of skepticism if his doubts were not so plainly qualified by a belief in two things: the good of knowledge achieved by self-examination, and the good of prayer as an act of attention that carries beyond the utterance of the words. A member of the Evangelical and Reformed Church, a "quasi-Congregationalist," he was never a parochial Christian. Twice in this book, he speaks appreciatively of Bertrand Russell, and he alludes to "A Free Man's Worship" to indicate an attitude of humility close to his own. His daughter, Elisabeth Sifton, in her affecting memoir *The Serenity Prayer*, quotes an exchange with Felix Frankfurter in which the distinguished lawyer and family friend said once to Niebuhr, after hearing him reason and espouse: "May a believing unbeliever thank you for your sermon?" Niebuhr replied: "May an unbelieving believer thank you for appreciating it?"

Most American liberals today—and let us agree to mean by this: believers in the improvement of the world through free trade and the triumph of appropriative man—are sure that they know the people who ought to run things. Stringent checks on the power of such people are beside the point; they will do the job well. They also firmly believe that, all things taken together, America is to the world of nations what the right people are to the world of people. This feeling cuts across party lines. It was Bill Clinton and not George W. Bush who first withheld the U.S. from recognition of the authority of the International Criminal

Court: America was too important, its constabulary duties too serious and far-flung, to allow us the time or patience to submit to every complaint or passing injury imputed by a citizen of Salvador or Sudan. What the good require, in order to become better, are not, according to this liberal creed, checks on their power but rules to guide their policies and actions. Hence the utility of the academic codification of just wars, first strikes, and so on. Liberals cannot conceive that the right people with the right policies could be fundamentally questionable; they do not credit the idea of an original sin of politics, or believe that the foreseeable deadly consequences of war are part of a war's intention in the eye of conscience. They believe in good intentions and good outcomes too much to nurse a deep distrust of power because it is power.

The answer to their self-confidence is all over Niebuhr's writings. Yet it has always been possible to emphasize his tactical argument against isolation, and to forget his central warning against the fallacy that might makes right. Niebuhr therefore held a partly misleading prestige among the practitioners of liberal anti-Communism, from the Berlin airlift to the Vietnam War. He was an attractive hero to persons for whom the year was always 1938 and diplomacy was always Munich. Yet the interventionists of three generations have found him in the long run a difficult ally. In 1965, he deplored the mistaken assumption of an old friend, Hubert Humphrey, in "claiming my anti-Nazi stance of the 1930s for the present war." The truth was that Niebuhr in retirement judged Vietnam a catastrophe—not a failure of democratic persuasion and military planning, but, rather, a case of the sheer destructiveness that springs from the arrogance of power. Lately some opinion makers who urged the moral necessity of the

Iraq War have brought up the name of Niebuhr to suggest that the spirit of intervention may yet be purified. In an essay in the *New York Times Magazine* in 2006, Peter Beinart took Niebuhr to be saying that even though Americans "fight evil," this "does not make us inherently good." But for Beinart "paradoxically, that very recognition makes national greatness possible. Knowing that we, too, can be corrupted by power, we seek the constraints that empires refuse. . . . The irony of American exceptionalism is that by acknowledging our common fallibility, we inspire the world." But Niebuhr, with reason, was very sparing in his references to national greatness. And "American exceptionalism"? There were no exceptions in morality; none at all.

The jacket of a 2008 paperback reprint of *The Irony of American History* carries a comment by Barack Obama that attempts a summary of Niebuhr: "There's serious evil in the world, and hardship and pain. And we should be humble and modest in our belief we can eliminate those things." That is a fair digest, considering that it was extracted by a columnist on the run. But in Obama's comment, too, something is missing and the something is not small. Niebuhr said that there is evil in the world; also, that there is evil in ourselves. Only if you take the second point with the first will you discern the depth of the madness in the claim by President George W. Bush, on September 14, 2001, that Americans are now in a position to "rid the world of evil." Irony can turn into tragedy, and Niebuhr addressed that possibility in the last sentence of his book: "If we should perish, the ruthlessness of the foe would be only the secondary cause of the disaster. The primary cause would be that the strength of a giant nation was directed by eyes too blind to see all the hazards of the struggle; and the blindness would be induced not by some accident of nature or history but by hatred and vainglory." *The Irony of American History* was written as a sermon for Americans, a warning by a man of mind to the men of power whose habits of thinking he knew well. It has a more than historical interest today for all who wonder how closely the hazards have been reckoned, and with how much self-knowledge, by a nation whose vainglory fifty years ago seemed considerable but corrigible.

2008

FOUR

CHAPTER 10

WHAT IS THE WEST?

CIVILIZATION WAS ONCE A POPULAR SUBJECT. WILL AND Ariel Durant's *Story of Civilization*, published between 1935 and 1975, told the history of the arts and sciences and the major events of political history from "Our Oriental Heritage" through "The Age of Napoleon." Sir Kenneth Clark's *Civilisation* was a memorable TV documentary, aired in 1969 in thirteen parts, which guided viewers to monuments of art, architecture, and philosophy from the Dark Ages to the "heroic materialism" of the mid-twentieth century. Clark made a book out of the show, but the appeal of the series lay in the combination of spoken words and camera shots. It took as its unit of interpretation the career rather than the isolated deed, thought, or masterpiece. As a venture of high popularization, the series set a standard that the next generation has yet to meet.

Niall Ferguson mentions Clark in his opening pages, and not without self-consciousness. Like Clark's book, *Civilization: The West and the Rest* derives from the script of a documentary conceived for television; but where Clark confined himself mainly to the visual arts, Ferguson has aimed to cover a much wider field. The political, economic, military, and technological bases of civilization are his subject, including other civilizations besides that of the West. His disposition, however, toward the civilizations of

China and Islam is indicated by his decision to call them "the rest." Works of art make an early appearance but are soon given up.

Since Ferguson regrets what he calls the *de haut en bas* authority that Clark exemplified, he has taken precautions not to sound too high. He moves from artifact to structure to event, from king to president to imam, with a relentless horizontality. The book has a spiffy, jazzed-up, knowing air, which says to the reader: "You, too, can possess this kind of knowledge; you can make your own connections—the levers are in your grasp." The tone is well adapted to the link culture of laptops and iPads, and it suits the message of the book: a dominant civilization must not hesitate to sing its own praises.

As his guide to the philosophy of history, Ferguson invokes R. G. Collingwood, the polymath philosopher and historian of early Britain. Collingwood in his *Autobiography* described the work of the historian as a reimagining of the mind of the past: "the re-enactment of a past thought." The process could succeed only when one put a question to the partly resistant materials and had the patience to coax an answer in terms not wholly dictated by present concerns.

The further one reads in Ferguson's book, the more incongruous this opening citation from Collingwood appears. Ferguson has not, in fact, launched his inquiry into the rise and fall of civilizations from an inward mastery of the named virtues or values of any particular civilization. Rather, his questions, and the answers that sometimes seem to hit before a question is asked, are dictated by habits, traits, and products of the very recent West, framed in an idiom strongly associated with American schools of management. The almost-personified West

whose triumph he celebrates, and whose future he prog-
nosticates, was shaped from the first, Ferguson wants us
to believe, by six "killer apps": elements comparable to
the applications you download to enhance a smart phone.

The killer apps are "competition" (which, to make a
proper "launch-pad" for states and economies, requires
"a decentralization of both political and economic life"),
"science," "property" rights, "medicine," "the consumer
society," and the "work ethic." These make an absurd catalogue. It is like saying that the ingredients of a statesman
are an Oxford degree, principles, a beard, sociability, and
ownership of a sports car. Ferguson's killer apps of the
West—both the idea and the phrase—in less than a decade
will date the book as reliably as the adoption by a pop
psychologist in 1966 of the word "groovy."

If for several centuries, as Ferguson believes, the West
has enjoyed an "edge" on the rest, what should we mean
by the West? It is "much more than just a geographical
expression"; one must think rather of "a set of norms,
behaviours and institutions with borders that are blurred
in the extreme." A key word that occurs quite early is "dominance." Ferguson locates the decision points or historical
residues of dominance by writing about a landmark, crux,
or monument (the author being filmed in the historically
significant place). He backs his claim for its importance
with statistics and charts, where relevant, and cuts to
another comparable place or thing. In this presentation,
pictures are all-important. Unhappily, in the book version
we do not have the pictures. The added value may be that
the book contains more words than the television series.

Then again, a second drawback is that the words were
punched in with images in mind. In a passage like the
following, for example, the on-screen continuity is plainly

meant to cut from the environs of the Yangzi River to the Thames:

> The Black Death—the bubonic plague caused by the flea-borne bacterium *Yersinia pestis*, which reached England in 1349—had reduced London's population to around 40,000, less than a tenth the size of Nanjing's. Besides the plague, typhus, dysentery and smallpox were also rife.

Poor sanitation, Ferguson concludes, made London "a death-trap." Two pages later comes a paragraph on Breughel's *Triumph of Death*. The images may make all this vivid, as the words do not.

A contrary-to-fact premise with which Ferguson occasionally teases us is that China could have dominated the West. Sanitation was on its side, and the place was full of inventions: "Chinese innovations include chemical insecticide, the fishing reel, matches, the magnetic compass, playing cards, the toothbrush and the wheelbarrow." Great little things, and yet: "By comparison with the patchwork quilt of Europe, East Asia was—in political terms, at least—a vast monochrome blanket." This was because it lacked the first killer app, "competition": an active virtue that the West came to understand in the age of exploration. Early on, Ferguson sums up his conclusion in favor of the West: "As Confucius himself said: 'A common man marvels at uncommon things. A wise man marvels at the commonplace.' But there was too much that was commonplace in the way Ming China worked, and too little that was new."

Evidence of Western ascendancy is made to issue from data of the most various kinds. For example: "The average height of English convicts in the eighteenth century was 5 feet 7 inches," while "the average height of Japanese soldiers in the same period was just 5 feet 2½ inches." So, "when East met West by that time, they could no longer look one another straight in the eye." This is a curious deduction from an unexpected comparison. Another sort of commentator might infer that the Japanese soldier, keeping guard on the English convict, would be compelled to learn a new dexterity in the martial arts: to swing his rifle butt *upward*, in a chopping motion, which would lead to the refinement of jujitsu—an art that cross-fertilized the Western mind after the Second World War. Ferguson ignores the eccentric invitations that lie in his path, and cannot be trusted to realize how an asset like height might be turned against the advantage of its owner.

The triad of goods familiar to Americans—life, liberty, and the pursuit of happiness—appeared in Locke's *Second Treatise on Government* as life, liberty, and property. Ferguson prefers the no-nonsense Lockean version, and says of the American Revolution: "At root, it was all about property." At root, all about. This sort of locution pervades the book. Again: "In the end, of course, the anomaly of slavery in a supposedly free society could be resolved only by war." Of course? The end might have been a long way off had Stephen Douglas won the election of 1860. At-root motivations and of-course developments and in-the-end inevitabilities suggest the grip of teleology: the turn of mind that tells us things had to come out the way they did because they were always leading to us, and how can we imagine "progress" toward something different from ourselves?

For all his jumps, Ferguson sticks to a largely familiar subject matter framed by conventional judgments. The American Revolution stands for true progress, and the French Revolution for counterfeit progress. The latter, he believes, put into practice the political philosophy of

Rousseau: it went astray by a literal adoption of the doctrine of the general will. This discovery Ferguson credits to Edmund Burke, but the truth is that Burke wrote very little about Rousseau, and never commented on the doctrine of the general will. He criticized the cult of Rousseau among the revolutionists for non-theoretical reasons: because it *was* a cult, a mask for collective egotism.

In *Reflections on the Revolution in France*, Burke charged that the wildness of Jacobinism had a British rather than a French source. It came from the post-1688 development of the radicalism of natural rights. Though he does not cite the name, Burke certainly does mean Locke, among others. What was wrong with Locke, or with supposing that the Glorious Revolution really was a revolution? Burke thought British liberty a tradition that England and perhaps America were able to digest; but "the old Parisian ferocity" was too little practiced in the arts of self-restraint to be trusted with so volatile a mixture. This emphasis, if acknowledged, would spoil the simplicity of Ferguson's reading—the good individualist Locke versus the bad collectivist Rousseau. But history comes out of just such accidents as violate our cherished allegories.

Finally, when Ferguson writes about "Rousseau's pact between the noble savage and the General Will," he can only mislead. There is no character called the "noble savage" in the writings of Rousseau; there is, rather, an image of man in a pre-social state, which Rousseau invents to clarify his ideas of law and convention in the *Discourse on Inequality*; but the *Discourse* is a different book, which advances a separate argument from the *Social Contract* with its doctrine of the general will. The distortion here goes beyond the compression that is necessary in a work of popularization. It is a falsification of intellectual history.

No scholar looking in from outside would guess that the foregoing materials are all brought forward in a chapter on "Medicine." The rest of the contents of that chapter give a fair suggestion of the capriciousness that the killer-app divisions have forced on this book. "Medicine" alone takes us past the eighteenth-century revolutions, through the Napoleonic Wars, to the French Empire, with a passing remark on Indochina (since Ho Chi Minh was a follower of the French Revolution). Still tracking what he calls medicine, Ferguson recounts the numbers that perished by tropical diseases in French West Africa, and comes to a temporary point of rest at the German prison camp on Shark Island.

A section on the imperialist scramble for Africa leads, eventually, to a contrast between the numbers of West Africans who fought with France in the First World War and the Indian soldiers who fought with the British. The mortality rate of British soldiers was twice that of British Indians. Of the French colonial soldiers, "one in five of those who joined up" died, says Ferguson, whereas "the comparable figure among French soldiers was less than 17 percent." Reading this, one nods and sighs, but hang on: less than 17 percent is another way of saying sixteen-point-something, which means that roughly one in six French soldiers died in the war. How stark a contrast does that make with the "one in five" French colonials who died?

The chapter on medicine runs fifty-five pages. It stands at the heart of the book, and it ends with these words: "By 1945, it was time for the West to lay down its arms and pick up its shopping bags—to take off its uniform and put on its blue jeans." We are thus prepared for the chapter on consumption: "What is it about our [Western] clothes that other people seem unable to resist?" And it is here that the main lines of an overarching narrative can be felt to emerge. Ancient Chinese civilization and medieval Muslim civilization were ahead of the West but, lacking command of the killer apps, they were set back almost permanently. Yet luxury, inattention, and a fatal indifference to the depth of our own resources have marred the vitality of the West. China will win, if it does win, by having successfully copied the North Atlantic commercial democracies; also, because plenty of Protestant missionaries went there to plant seeds of competition, science, and work.

The third "rival" among the civilizations, Islam, in Ferguson's view is not an active and energetic civilization at all, but a "cult of submission" whose only imaginable influence is destructive. A consolation for the West may be drawn from the fact that we have been through all this before. The Japanese were emulators of Western consumption at the start of the twentieth century, just as the Chinese seem to be at the start of the twenty-first. "Unsure," says Ferguson, about the secret of Western power, "the Japanese decided to take no chances. They copied everything." Constitutions, economies, military drills, school systems, and most revealing of all: "The Japanese even started eating beef." The humor of the book sits uncertainly on the page; but this detail may go well with a hearty delivery and pictures of beef.

Still, in whatever medium, Ferguson is limited by his choice of the gimmick of killer apps. Having resolved to speak about much of the twentieth-century as a history of "consumption," with a subplot on the export of textiles from West to East, he cannot resist the temptation to treat the rise of fascism as a matter chiefly of clothes:

> With the exception of Mussolini, who wore a three-piece suit with a winged collar and spats, most of those who

participated in the publicity stunt that was the March on Rome were in makeshift uniforms composed of black shirts, jodhpurs and knee-high leather riding boots.

Six pages later, the textile and political themes must somehow be brought together in the Second World War, so we get a paragraph beginning with the wide-eyed sentence: "Everyone, it seemed, was in uniform." (Montage over military music: khakis, blackshirts, navy whites, a line of paratroopers ready to jump.) Near the close of the chapter, Ferguson avows his belief that the atomic bomb was "one of the greatest creations of Western civilization"; for, whatever one might say about Hiroshima and Nagasaki, "the Bomb's net effect was to reduce the scale and destructiveness of war, beginning by averting the need for a bloody amphibious invasion of Japan."

The last sentence comes from justifications of the dropping of the bomb offered by Truman and Churchill. Among those who disagreed, in August 1945 or later, were Generals Eisenhower and MacArthur, and Admirals Nimitz and Leahy. General Curtis LeMay, who commanded the American firebombing of Tokyo and other Japanese cities, estimated that even without the atom bomb the war would have ended in September 1945. Why does Ferguson turn the self-justification of a nation at war into a fact about the history of civilization? Somewhere close to the heart of his purpose is the felt need to confer on the triumph of the West an air of inevitability, and also a clear conscience.

A long, ambitious, partly speculative chapter on "work" examines the thesis of Max Weber in *The Protestant Ethic and the Spirit of Capitalism*. Was there a strong correlation between Protestant asceticism and what we now call the "work ethic"? Ferguson, for reasons that are obscure, treats Weber and his argument with a shade of contempt. Yet he agrees with Weber, lodging only one major reservation: that the thesis underrated the civilizing influence of Christianity itself. The chapter closes with miscellaneous reflections and charts about the comparative rates of churchgoing in Europe and America. The sources of American "dominance," thinks Ferguson, have something to do with regularity of Christian observance. Chesterton, Waugh, and C. S. Lewis are quoted here; they were on to something about God and the Americans get it, while Europe, idle and dissolute, is now a vanquished supremacy.

But merely to recite the conclusion is not to convey the flavor of an extraordinary extended passage. One paragraph on "work" begins with the coat-trailing question "Who killed Christianity in Europe, if not John Lennon?" and ends with another question: "Was the murderer of Europe's Protestant work ethic none other than Sigmund Freud?" The train of association that places John Lennon in the first sentence may elude even a close reader of Ferguson; the meaning of the reference to Freud becomes clearer in the paragraphs that follow. Ferguson has in mind *The Future of an Illusion*, where Freud analyzed all religion as a form of neurotic dependency that condemns mankind to perpetual immaturity.

Is it true that Freud "set out to refute Weber"? The reader may suppose that Freud had read with care and argued against Weber's theory; but Weber's theory is never mentioned in *The Future of an Illusion*; indeed, there is not one entry under Weber in the index to the twenty-four volumes of the Standard Edition of Freud's writings. The false hint planted by the phrase "set out to refute" turns out to be only Ferguson's way of dramatizing a belief that grips *him*: Weber made allowance for the good that might come from non-rational motives, while Freud, in his treatment of religion, failed to do so.

There follows a celebration of American dominance and churchgoing. Here, finally, the book spins out of control. How many churches are in Springfield, Missouri? Well, it is "the town they call the 'Queen of the Ozarks' and the birthplace of the inter-war highway between Chicago and California, immortalized in Bobby Troup's 1946 song, '(Get Your Kicks on) Route 66.'" Picture this:

> There are 122 Baptist churches, thirty-six Methodist chapels, twenty-five Churches of Christ and fifteen Churches of God—in all, some 400 Christian places of worship. Now it's not your kicks you get on Route 66; it's your crucifix.

The argument here—that the vitality of a civilization may be measured by the number of well-attended churches—is not new; though nothing in the preceding 273 pages has quite prepared for this rhapsody. But there is something odd about the smart-aleck riff at the end. "Now it's not your kicks you get on Route 66; it's your crucifix." That verbal jiggle-and-stomp would not be conceivable by a person with an ounce of real piety. If Ferguson has any idea what actually happens in the wide range of churches he mentions, there is no sign of it in these comments. One is led to conclude that he is a detached and vicarious proselytizer. He is praising religion from a place outside religion. And he aims to encourage Christian belief only in the broadest sense: a sense so broad that it includes Jews (though not Muslims or Hindus). Christian belief is a good thing, more vital to civilization than we ever realized, but it is good *for them*.

The kicks and crucifix have been forgotten just a page later, in a comforting haze of commercial uplift. And commerce does matter to Ferguson. The good thing about "competition between sects in a free religious market," he says, is that it "encourages innovations designed to make the experience of worship and Church membership more fulfilling." The appeal to the free religious market radiates a spirit of unity. He is describing the cement that binds the altars and the stock markets of the West.

Why then does the book close on a note of lament? "Not only are the churches of Europe empty," but, says Ferguson, we have lost confidence in the value of our civilizing inheritance:

> We also seem to doubt the value of much of what developed in Europe after the Reformation. Capitalist competition has been disgraced by the recent financial crisis and the rampant greed of the bankers. Science is studied by too few of our children at school and university. Private property rights are repeatedly violated by governments that seem to have an insatiable appetite for taxing our incomes and our wealth and wasting a large portion of the proceeds. Empire has become a dirty word, despite the benefits conferred on the world by the European imperialists. All we risk being left with are a vacuous consumer society and a culture of relativism.

Two pages later, Ferguson ushers in the furies who will dine on our self-neglect: Al Qaeda and the Muslim Brotherhood.

Civilization: The West and the Rest is a rich, undercooked, and finally inedible gumbo. Almost any name is apt to be found floating in it somewhere—Mozart, Polybius, Lincoln, Atatürk, Breughel, Thomas Cole, Adam Smith (Smith a little more than the others). And yet, after several hours spent with Ferguson and his killer apps, one may be uncertain what his definition of civilization is. To judge by the contents of the book and its intermittent approaches to argument, the answer runs somewhat as follows. Civilization is a system of financial profit, founded on self-discipline, some of whose opulence goes to support the arts. Its desired effect is to render human life more comfortable and more complicated, but not too soft. This end civilization achieves by affording political and economic support to the exertions of individual genius. It sustains itself by a regime of liberal and scientific education, whose highest achievements are modern medicine, advanced weaponry, and communications technology. The final reward of a consummated civilization is to have persuaded a billion or more persons, on more than one continent, to see it as it sees itself and to have pushed to the side and uprooted less competitive ways of life.

Niall Ferguson is a patriot of the West. He aspires to be a calmer and a more reflective writer than he is. That has to be the meaning of his (evidently sincere) invocation of R. G. Collingwood in the opening pages. He cherishes a desire to become a historian of the virtues of the West, and he has some of the necessary equipment: he is a quick study, endlessly resourceful with lists, numbers, and juxtapositions. But he lacks patience. He wants to arrive at a formula, a master clue, a quotable phrase, and to get there fast.

In the present book, he has also partly concealed a passion that played a large role in guiding him to the study of history: admiration for the achievements of British imperialism. He was less reluctant to mention this motive in some of his previous writings. In an essay in the *New York Times Magazine* of April 27, 2003, on the heels of the American conquest of Baghdad, he declared himself "a fully paid-up member of the neoimperialist gang," and said of the antecedents of the Iraq War:

> The reality is that the British were significantly more successful at establishing market economies, the rule of law and the transition to representative government than the majority of postcolonial governments have been.

Perhaps because he is writing for an international audience, or because of the less vibrant condition of the American empire in Asia today, he confines his shows of sentiment in *Civilization* to a few digressions and muttered asides.

A partial exception is the thirty-page conclusion, appended to his final chapter on the killer apps. Here Ferguson attempts to judge the contest of the current imperial "rivals," and he finds comfort in the thought that a deep and immitigable "clash of civilizations" has not yet occurred. Of the main contenders—the West, China, and Islam—he lays odds on China while striking the attitude of a disappointed lover of the West.

What is missing in this coda, and missing throughout the book, is an awareness of a sense of "civilization" that mattered to John Ruskin, the teacher of Collingwood. It meant to Ruskin a pattern of duties and manners whose performance was scarcely conscious. It fostered habits of gentleness and obedience, as well as command, without a thought of profit or reward. It imparted a reverence for the good as a thing apart from cash value. This perspective is bound to be lost if one thinks of civilizations by race, region, and religion. It is doubly lost if one goes over the strategies of winning teams in the past in order to prognosticate the scramble for continents in the future.

2011

HOLY TERROR AND CIVILIZED TERROR

THE FIRST AND OFTEN THE ONLY THING ONE KNOWS ABOUT a suicide bomber is that he is someone with more to die for than to live for. That such a person would make use of his own readiness to suffer quickly, horribly, and finally, is not a recent development in the history of nations. Nor does it exhibit a peculiarly modern form of evil. Terrorism, the murder of persons of no political or military status in order to achieve a political end, goes back at least to the Shia assassins of the twelfth century, and probably further back than that. It is apt to occur wherever a religious or political ideal takes hold that has the power to absolve believers of the wrongs they commit in its name. Suicide bombing is a more desperate and in some settings a more cunning adaptation of terrorism, but any terrorist is a hunted man who knows that his death may soon follow that of his latest victim. Only a messianic politician, at the mercy of his own wildness and simplicity, could suppose it possible to conduct a worldwide purge of terrorism until one by one the guilty are subtracted and "all of the terrorists are dead."

Around the end of the Cold War, there arose a school of semiofficial comforters who taught that we were living at the end of history. They said that present-day America was the intended climax of human endeavor through the ages. A residue of this enthusiasm prompted many to look on suicide bombing, and on terrorism more generally, as a knot to be untied in the passage from the era of tyrannies to the everlasting age of the global market. As if these killings were something that wandered out of another script and into ours. As if, once they were removed, we could return to our promised ending.

But history is not the sort of thing that ends. It did not pause for long when a corps of grand strategists made the discovery that there was only one great power left in the world, and that the United States could now dominate without fighting the lesser powers. That false dawn was darkened by the savagery of the attack on the World Trade Center. The hope was discredited a second time by the violence that greeted the American occupation of Iraq. Meanwhile, out of the failure of the end of history, a vast field of exercise had opened up for the philosophy of current events (to borrow a useful phrase from Vincent Descombes). This new pamphlet literature, appearing at the rate of dozens of books each month, affords an echo of the pamphlet wars of the 1790s: the impressive debate about the principles of politics that emerged in Britain in response to the French Revolution. A significant difference is that the pamphlet-writers today show little interest in reading one another. Lawyers, therapists, journalists, divines, moral philosophers, literary critics, and scholars-without-portfolio at think tanks produce their results almost unconscious of the existence of fellow inquirers, and most of the books are easily forgotten, but memorableness is not the point. A world-terror pamphlet should make its readers feel thoughtful, panicked, and prepared.

Terry Eagleton is a literary critic with strong political and theological interests, whose first writings were contributions to radical Catholicism in the wake of Vatican II. Eagleton identifies terrorism with the wholly irrational—an intuition that sounds like common sense but is not therefore infallible. His choice of a theme dictates his choice of texts, and the most substantial part of *Holy Terror* is an interpretation of a single work, *The Bacchae*. Other works of imagination are treated in passing—*Measure for Measure*, *Women in Love*—but it is the strangely ironic tragedy by Euripides that matters most to Eagleton's analysis. The play turns on a dramatic standoff between the legitimate king of Thebes, Pentheus, a keeper of public order, and the god and guru Dionysus, who knows that people love to be out of their minds. "Anarchy and absolutism," Eagleton says, "are the recto and verso of each other. Both suspect that chaos is our natural condition. It is just that absolutists fear it, whereas anarchists revel in it." This familiar insight Eagleton varies a little by calling the current recto and verso "Texan" and "Taliban": names that, a few years after the World Trade Center attack, already sound glib and dated. Still, he is right that the absolution guaranteed by religious fanaticism has smoothed the way for the killers of innocents. Fanatics in every faith "have their dreams, wherewith they weave / A paradise for a sect." A man who believes himself to be the chosen instrument of God is capable of infinite mischief and infinite destructiveness. He will always forgive himself and will always believe himself forgiven by God.

Simple and submissive minds accordingly will read theology in an orthodox way and cultivate belief in a fearful God who asks for human sacrifice. Simple and rebellious minds will revolt against that God. So, too, with the recto and verso reactions to secular authorities who make demands that are comparable to the demands that come from God. There are modern people who deprecate religious faith as blindly as fanatics resent the tolerance of liberal society. Such people, says Eagleton, are "bound to see [God] as an unholy terror, rather as those who deny justice in political affairs are likely these days to provoke carnage and chaos." Orthodox theology issues in orthodox counter-theology. Each is linked to a politics that cuts down charity and mistakes revenge for atonement.

Under this dubious symmetrical argument lies a genuine recognition. Political violence comes from above as well as below—from those who have power and aim to keep it, and from those who crave power and will do anything to get it. A plan of national security designed to preserve a nation, and the insurgent imperative to create a nation, are antithetical alibis for such acts. The common feature is the idea of the nation; and George Orwell in "Notes on Nationalism" performed a service to intellectual clarity when he applied the word "nationalism" to religious and political phenomena alike. People endow the nation with the power to absolve them of guilt for crimes they commit on behalf of the nation. As for the broader psychology of nationalism, Orwell memorably called it "power hunger tempered by self-deception"—a motive always opaque to itself, which ministers to the collective self-love of society.

If a liberal constitution is the work of a moral imagination, the idea of the nation, any nation, is in large measure the work of a non-moral imagination. To say it another way: imagination is closely related to a power of fantasy that cannot contain itself. The emergency state of mind tends to suppress our awareness of this fact; and to the extent that Eagleton's strictures on theology are an extension of Orwell's, his warning is salutary. Yet his idea that the image of power necessarily "provokes" the powerless is facile. It reduces to cause and effect a more elusive fact about the relationship between hardened enemies. Once the opposing sides begin to do to each other all that hatred allows, terrorism on the one hand and war on the other have in common a passion that stops at nothing short of death.

Unbounded passion is Eagleton's real subject. He takes what may seem an academic turn by dealing with it under the heading of "the sublime," but he is pointing to a fact that less metaphysical writers have noticed, too. What disturbed many people about the phrase "Shock and Awe"—the Pentagon nickname for the process of massive bombing and missile attacks in the first days of the onslaught on Iraq in March 2003—was that the two words suggested aesthetic admiration for a spectacle of destruction. Eagleton has this in mind when he places in the category of the sublime everything "perilous, shattering, ravishing, traumatic, excessive, exhilarating, dwarfing, astonishing, uncontainable, overwhelming, boundless, obscure, terrifying, enthralling, and uplifting." Eagleton looks to get some help in explaining the motives of terrorists from Edmund Burke on the sublime. Yet Burke wisely stayed out of these depths. He paused, instead, at the implications of a surface phenomenon. The feeling of the sublime comes from something we fear, something distant enough for the fear to be experienced without practical risk. The satisfaction that follows an explosion from a shell you have fired, or from the devastation of a city that you look upon without a thought of the inhabitants—these partake of the emotions of the sublime. The feeling that your own house is about to be bombed, or that you are about to blow yourself up, belongs in a different category. It puts the spectator too close to be entertained.

That many people much of the time seek out violent sensations for no reason is among the puzzles of human nature. It shows the extent to which right and wrong do not inhabit our most elemental motives of action; and one strength of Burke is that he is an observant guide to that limited truth. Eagleton misses the point by trying to pump it up: "Burke thinks that we need a therapeutic dose of terror every now and then to prevent society from growing enervated and effete." Burke did not say that, and he did not think it. We are drawn to scenes of violence and ruin not as therapy, but in obedience to an appetite. The appetite, however, is compelling only so long as we are out of danger. This goes some way to explain the vogue of American pilgrimages to Ground Zero—a journey undertaken by many who would have been content never to see those buildings in their glory. It offers a clue as well to the emotions of the bombardier who dropped the atom bomb on Nagasaki, who spoke later of the terror of the explosion but added that this moment gave him "the greatest thrill of my life." It would be absurd to suppose an identity between the minds of such spectators and the person who detonates a suicide bomb. Such a person at such a time is a paralyzed will in motion.

A fairer analogy for suicide bombers might be found among "just assassins," such as the Russian revolutionists of 1905 (the killers of the Grand Duke Sergei), who preferred hanging to clemency toward themselves when the world's injustices had been augmented by their own acts. But the Russian analogy also misses the mark. Suicide bombers may resemble the just assassins in that they kill and choose to die. But the Russians were not suicide bombers: they loved life and parted with it only to condemn their own deeds. They chose their target and wished him dead and, even so, felt remorse and a need for expiation. They did not contrive to be absolved. Partly because of their severe belief in the moral law, it is hard to imagine a party of just assassins serving as the vanguard of a movement of popular rebellion.

If recent suicide terrorists have found popular support in Sri Lanka, Palestine, Iraq, and elsewhere, a reason may be that they embody the only highly visible protest against a hated authority. Eagleton speaks of "the lack of organized political resistance to the present system [of global capitalism], of the kind to which socialists have traditionally been dedicated, which encourages it to trample upon the weak, thus stimulating the growth of terror." But the disappearance of an international party for social justice is probably a minor cause of the outbreaks of the past twenty-five years. More telling, as Robert A. Pape suggests in *Dying to Win*, are such local causes as religious enmity, linguistic difference, a rebellion in progress, and an army of occupation. Pape has taught political science at the University of Chicago and at the U.S. Air Force School of Advanced Airpower Studies, and over the first several years of the twenty-first century he completed an exhaustive database on suicide terrorists.

Once you add it up, this evidence leads to an understanding Americans have worked hard to conceal from ourselves. Allowing for all the differences, there is a strong continuity between terrorism and war. A soldier shooting at soldiers may be a different moral entity from a terrorist who smuggles a bomb into a restaurant. Yet so long as the incantation of war, terror, mission, evil, world, freedom, and humanity invites our acquiescence by those cadences that thrill the blood, sanity requires that we subdue the glow around the words. All but the most insensate terrorists believe that their victims include as many as possible of the guilty. They even make up stories to prove this, to their own satisfaction, such as the story that everyone who worked in the World Trade Center was an agent of American imperialism. All but the most wanton soldiers believe that they are killing as few as possible of the innocent. The innocent dead in both cases are equally dead. To the person who has lost a husband or wife or child or friend, revenge is equally tempting if the killer was wearing a dynamite pack or seated in a cockpit at twenty thousand feet and aiming at the wrong building. To inflict death is the purpose of the suicide bomber. Assassination or "targeted killing"—with some untargeted almost sure to be hit—is the purpose of the bomber pilot or of the unmanned drone that in American engagements is gradually replacing the pilot. It is no use trying to enforce a philosophical distinction between the terrorist and the agent of state terror by means of euphemistic phraseology such as "collateral damage." This is an area in which elaboration soon becomes casuistry. It may be plausible but it is not honest to cry up war as a perennial test of the manliness of nations while denouncing terrorism as a barbarity that must be fought tooth and nail.

The motives for suicide terror may be roughly divided into (1) religious fulfillment; (2) revenge; (3) founding a state; and (4) resistance to occupation. *Holy Terror*, when one looks at the details, is concerned rather narrowly with (1) and (2). *Dying to Win* suggests that the terrorism of the past two decades, and especially the suicide bombings, have emerged saliently as instances of (4), with (3) often a discernible secondary motive. (1) and (2) in Pape's view are always-possible exacerbating causes, but as he reads the evidence, they have not excited vengeful or ecstatic persons to the length of killing others by killing themselves.

Pape's argument is limited by a social-scientific emphasis. This comes out in the assumption that terrorists may be analyzed as rational actors. But our usual tendency has been to assume the opposite without proof: that they act out of hot resentment, indifferent to circumstance and consumed by a generalized hatred of the West. Thus, Vice President Cheney, in various statements of the years 2004–2006, plucked a word of menace, "Caliphate," from an anti-Islamist primer and used it to suggest that an actual Caliphate might soon girdle the globe from Jakarta to Manhattan. By contrast, *Dying to Win* touches on the known extremes of a recognizable world.

If people tend to become suicide terrorists to resist a foreign occupation, and if they use the tactic only where they think it has a strong chance of success, we should be able to understand the logic of their acts inductively. It will be written all over what they say and do, and interpretable from what they do not say or do. The idea that a terrorist hopes to merge with God is not susceptible of proof. Who knows what they think of what they read and chant? Marching orders are a different matter. We will learn in the next few years, or whenever the United States no longer garrisons thousands of troops on Muslim soil, whether Pape is right to say that suicide terrorists mainly act for a community with which they identify themselves; that they press hardest against an occupying army from a country whose religion is different; and that they direct their attacks more at democracies than at despotic regimes. The Kurdish suicide bombers struck Turkey but spared Iraq under Saddam Hussein. It must be added that occupation—as with the U.S. in Saudi Arabia after the First Gulf War, and the U.S. in Iraq after the Second—is a matter of fact as well as a matter of belief.

The almost colorless language of Pape's account has its own drawbacks, but it serves as a counterirritant to the rhetoric of the usual pamphleteers. His purpose, he says, is to work out a strategy for eliminating the present generation of terrorists without supplying the political and imaginative soil for another generation to grow. Admittedly, this is a strategy that lacks the emotional satisfaction of a pledge to go on killing until you have killed them all. But that pledge is a fantasy. It takes the enemy to have the permanence of a species in nature—as if our own actions exerted no influence on the numbers of new recruits. The problem any society faces about such people is how to be rid of them; but it is not forbidden to understand who they are.

Terrorism has been a tactic chiefly adopted by partisans or resistance fighters, or by an insurgency that sees itself as a nation struggling to be born. The acts are done to achieve a political end, and they are evil—a word that should be used sparingly to avoid diminishing its force. Acts of terror, then, are an aberration that must not become a pattern. But the acts are performed by human beings. These separate truths need to be held in a single thought; and the whole truth is even stranger. A terrorist began life as a person, and may go back to being a person. It happened in France, after the terror of *les armées révolutionnaires*, and in Santo Domingo after the rebellion of the Black Jacobins. It happened in America after Bleeding Kansas and the Missouri raids of the James brothers. It happened in Israel after independence, and in South

Africa after full emancipation. It has happened in Northern Ireland. Human beings do such things, but sometimes they stop doing them, and sometimes they stop and regret.

By the time he wrote his book, Pape had collected all that was known about 315 suicide attacks from 1980 through 2003. His archive on the motives, the agents, and the circumstances of these attacks convinced him that nationalism was the leading motive of suicide terror. The attackers are not for the most part religious, nor, he says, particularly Islamist. They cover a wide range: some college-educated, some illiterate; some well off, others poor; the youngest fifteen, the oldest fifty-two. The picture of Islamist terrorism as the offspring of a unified ideology Pape believes to be essentially false. You may arrive at that view by reading their theology and taking to heart their apocalyptic promises, but this is to proceed by the a priori method, whereas Pape works from the data to a likely conclusion. The various fundamentalist movements do not recognize one another's authority, and their collaborations thus far have been episodic and expedient. All are anti-Western in some way, and several call for imitation of the Islam of the Prophet. But politically, as movers of violent action and self-sacrifice, they have waited for moments when they could appear as the conspicuous opposition to an imperial threat made vivid by a foreign army of occupation. The way then lies open for their soldiers to become martyrs in the cause of national liberation. This posthumous fame is all-important. "An individual can die," observes Pape. "Only a community can make a martyr."

An important case study, for him, is the Israeli occupation of Lebanon. News reports at the time made much of the Islamic identity of the attackers, and it was widely supposed that Islamic fundamentalism had driven them.

After a year-long review of the evidence, Pape found that twenty-seven of the forty-one suicide attackers "were Communists or socialists with no commitment to religious extremism; three were Christians. Only eight suicide attackers were affiliated with Islamic fundamentalism." The common motive of those willing to take their own lives was fear of "a religiously motivated occupier," and the actions were mainly intelligible as "extreme self-sacrifice to end the occupation." A similar result emerged from his examination of Al Qaeda suicide terrorists. Among the seventy-one who killed themselves in the years 1995–2003, twice as many came from Muslim countries with a significant fundamentalist population as from those without it; and yet, an Al Qaeda suicide bomber was ten times more likely to come from a country occupied by the United States than from an unoccupied country. A coercive foreign presence intensifies the injured pride, rage, and indignation that lead to suicide attacks. For this reason Pape concludes that the United States made a mistake "by embarking on a policy to conquer Muslim countries." Conquest is not, of course, the avowed policy of the United States, but the evidence of the senses tells a story that few in the region doubt, and Pape will not presume to correct them until the evidence changes.

He dismisses cult suicide and anomic suicide—the action of the brainwashed and the psychologically adrift—as irrelevant to most of the cases he studied. Team suicides are the rule: an expression of solidarity, since the killer martyrs are signaling their loyalty to a small community that stands for a larger one. "Members of the group typically go to great lengths to deepen their social ties, to participate actively in social institutions, and to adopt customs that display communal devotion." Thus, beginning in 1982, Hezbollah drew much sentimental gratitude for its 130,000 scholarships and aid to 135,000 families, along with the granting of interest-free loans. The organization also paid for sewing courses to enable the self-support of the handicapped, and, through a cover charity, it built two hospitals. Hamas has taken up the same pattern of subsidy, "deeply embedded in the surrounding society, supporting an extensive network of more than forty social welfare organizations"; and with the Tamil Tigers, again, one sees a philanthropy that is at once unselfish and cynical: "food, water, resettlement housing, health services, and interest-free loans." Bin Laden's humanitarian off-shoots had names like Human Concern International and Mercy International as well as the Islamic International Relief Organization. They did what the names promised, while they remained bin Laden's creatures. Concerning the Benevolence International Foundation and the Global Relief Organization, the 9/11 Commission found (in its own words) "little compelling evidence that either of these charities actually provided financial support to Qaeda." The profit they yielded was moral prestige.

Together with the heterogeneous profiles of suicide killers, something new that emerges in *Dying to Win* is the alternation of moral postures among those who order the acts of self-destruction. One sees a spirit of reverential glorification suitable to heroes of sport and war: a Tamil Tiger discourse says that the martyrs "die in the arena of struggle with the intense passion for the freedom of their people," a field where "the death of every martyr constitutes a brave act of enunciation of freedom." Equally marked, however, is an almost opposite trait, a calculating single-minded discipline: the Ayatollah Fadlallah, the spiritual leader of Hezbollah, observed once that "the self-martyring operation" should never go forward unless "it can convulse the enemy." A more refined calculus now and then appears, by which "the believer cannot blow himself up unless the results will equal or exceed the loss of the believer's soul." The trade-off, charred bodies for lost souls, turns into a question of pure utility when an interviewer asks a Hamas spokesman why they do not just plant a bomb and run. The spokesman answers: "There are more fatalities in a suicide attack."

"War on terror" is a stirring phrase. There was a moment in 2005—two days, maybe three—when it seemed that the Bush administration had stopped talking about the war on terror. The office of Donald Rumsfeld spun out a few substitutes that were found wanting in salt and savor. Once people have grown used to a violent order, it is hard to wind them down; and the idea of a war on terror remains even when the words have become a ghostly presence. How absurd to expect the security elite to give it up. Three words, bristling sharp and bright, that make the passive listener feel himself to be remarkable. An administration that stands firm in the conviction of its own innocence is scarcely equipped to fight without a phrase like this. The belief, meanwhile, that we are good (as President George W. Bush has said all Americans are good) assures us that whatever we do, we will be absolved in our own eyes.

Carl Schmitt observed in *The Concept of the Political* that the division of friend and enemy defined the nature of politics itself; the only people who would deny this, he guessed, were liberals—liberals in the largest sense of a tradition that includes most of Europe and North America. Liberals, Schmitt thought, believe that all people are potentially their friends and that their party encompasses nothing less than all humanity. But if that is so, their enemies cannot be mere enemies. After all, who could oppose someone who fights for the human? Only the inhuman. And if I am fighting against the inhuman, I must allow no limit on what I am permitted to do to the enemy—or (for that matter) what I may do to my own country in order to get at the enemy. In this sense, liberalism, or, to give a name closer to home, evangelical democracy, is itself an apocalyptic faith.

An episode of the descent into war on the inhuman was recounted by Dexter Filkins in a startling essay in the *New York Times Magazine* on October 23, 2005. Filkins told of the fall from valor of Lieutenant Colonel Nathan Sassaman, in actions around Samarra in 2004. Sassaman, wrote Filkins, who was "adored" by his superior officer Major General Raymond Odierno "for the zeal with which his men hunted down guerrillas," did what was expected of him and more. "He sent his men into the Sunni villages around Balad to kick down doors and detain their angry young men. When Sassaman spoke of sending his soldiers into Samarra, his eyes gleamed. 'We are going to inflict extreme violence,' he said." Notice the words *adored* and *gleamed*—words that carry a religious and aesthetic charge, finely caught by a reporter who has seen firsthand the intoxication of battle. That adoration and that gleam may be admirable when applied to fitting objects; but something different happened in Balad. This soldier, who had shown so much courage and efficiency, was ordered by superiors to "increase lethality"—a vague command like "extract information," which has been used in Iraq both to induce atrocities and to screen the responsible from public view. Sassaman followed the cue of a half-defined categorical command. When his men abused two of the enemy, within the apparent allowable limits of torment short of death, by forcing them to jump into the Tigris River at night, the experiment in "increased lethality" seems to have miscarried. One of the victims disappeared, and it is probable that he drowned.

The pity of war—that such adoration should be so mis-used—is connected with the terror of war. Organized violence injures the virtues by contaminating them with vices that are their doubles—as, for example, the aggression of brutality resembles the assertiveness of courage. This is in itself a reason to avoid wars. But does not everyone wish to avoid every war? Nothing could be more false. War is a glut of exultations. It always has been. In all of Shakespeare's plays that picture war, ordinary people are shown greeting the coming of war in a festive mood. It is the mood of people who do not guess that they will be hurt. A nation that feels omnipotent in arms is perpetually at risk from the effects of that mood.

Man is a self-justifying animal. And the justifications pile on: since 2001, we have been asked to agree that the threat of terror exposes the United States to perils more dreadful than any we have endured before; that in view of the unprecedented danger, we ought to trust our leaders to "protect" us, even if it means suspending all previous understandings of civil liberty. But there have been times of the world far more dangerous for the United States. The Cold War is still within living memory.

Terrorism is not the same as war, but war stands on a continuum with terror. It is said that American commanders in Iraq watched *The Battle of Algiers* to help them understand what they were up against. They could have told their civilian chiefs to look at another work from the same time and place, an essay by a doctor who got to know the victims of torture, Frantz Fanon's "Colonial War and

Mental Disorders." To have been "tortured night and day for nothing," Fanon wrote, "seemed to have broken something in these men," but there was another consequence for the survivors and their friends: total indifference to all moral arguments, indifference that closed in the belief that "there is no just cause. A cause which entrains torture is a weak cause. Therefore the fighting strength [of the FLN insurgency] must at all costs be increased; its justness must not be questioned. Force is the only thing that counts." Torture of the FLN in Algeria was the means by which state terror was integrated with state power in a "war on terror." This was, of course, justified by the French as an emergency tactic. But in a time of perpetual emergency, in a war expected to last a generation or more, all tactics become emergency tactics and all are justified.

And yet emergencies end, but memory does not stop. Other eyes will see what we have done. There are practices that cannot be defended, and we must say so without casuistry. The terrorist is one kind of criminal and the torturer is another kind. They are not the same because no two evils are identical. Yet both perform work that a humane society cannot countenance. If we aim for a world that has been freed from terrorism as well as state terror, the revenge of the powerless and the revenge of the civilized, the end that we look to must be legible in the means that we use to get there.

2006

CHAPTER 12

COMMENTS ON PERPETUAL WAR

CHENEY'S LAW

October 20, 2007

MIDWAY THROUGH THE *FRONTLINE* DOCUMENTARY *CHENEY'S Law*, which aired last Tuesday on PBS, a journalist, Ron Suskind, paraphrases a judgment the vice president in his hiding place conveyed to listeners during the hours after the attacks of September 11. *We will probably*, Cheney is reported as saying in other words, *have to be a country ruled by men rather than laws in this period.* The credibility of the report is vouched for by everything we have seen since 2001. "This period" (he implied) would last a long time; so the conclusion had all of the Cheney markings: cool, complete, defying contradiction. What is astounding is how quickly he arrived at it.

With the testimony of witness after witness, *Cheney's Law* establishes an alarming fact. For nearly seven years, starting not on 9/11 but at the moment this administration ascended to power, the vice president has worked tirelessly, almost selflessly, in silence and seclusion, to destroy the American system of constitutional checks and install an executive government whose levers are operated by a few. In the new system (except where its builders are caught at their work and delayed) there is to be no restraint, no oversight, no accountability.

The Cheney mutation, in every instance, has had two characteristic steps. In the first, authority is usurped in secret, and power is transferred from its ostensible holder to an agent controlled by the Office of the Vice President. Power having thus changed hands invisibly, a custom-built justification is filed away, to be produced only if the trespass is discovered and questions are asked.

Aggrandizement of the executive by a sequence of shifts and transfers of power, underwritten by a rationale that is held in reserve: this has been the method; a protocol without a precedent in the history of democracy. It is in the nature of the engine to push and push again. Its forward motion has occasionally been slowed, by a court decision or a piece of actual legislation, but the delays have never lasted long.

Americans were brought up to think about a person mistreated by authority (however lawful the authority): "You can't do that to him!—a man's got his rights." The goal, in morals and manners, of the Cheney mutation is to replace that libertarian presumption with a timid, resigned, and docile acceptance: "Too bad; he must have done something wrong if they're doing this to him." The reform of manners is not yet complete, but, every day, bad laws assist the process of coarsening and brutalization.

"Conspiracy" is a word that Americans trained by our respectable culture tend to reject. We acknowledge, because history tells us, that there were conspiracies in the distant past, among the assassins of Julius Caesar for example, or the Privy Council of Charles II, whose members owed their nickname, "the Cabal," to the surnames Clifford, Arlington, Buckingham, Ashley, and Lauderdale.

And there was the Night of the Long Knives. But there has not been an important conspiracy close to our time; certainly not in America: that is the doctrine. We need another word, then, to describe a series of actions concerted by men of power, executed with elaborate concealment for a determined end, in violation of all the ordinary procedures of government and in deliberate defiance of the law.

Such was the path of the change devised in 2001–2002 for the prisoners captured in the field in Afghanistan. The vice president and his lawyer, David Addington, held that captives were to be transported without notice to a prison sealed off from the jurisdiction of American laws, or any other system of laws. There they would be sorted and processed into Special Tribunals.

All discussions of the meditated change excluded the responsible officials in the department of state. Pierre-Richard Prosper, interviewed in *Cheney's Law*, reports that he studied the question for Colin Powell and reached a conclusion at variance with that of Cheney and Addington. He should have seen their proposal, but he never did. Rather, the executive order was routed through the corridors of the White House with the stealth of a burglar on a well-cased street. By the time it passed under the president's pen, it had changed hands four times; and these were not the usual hands. John Bellinger, the lawyer for the national security staff, never set eyes on the new understanding. Colin Powell first heard of it on the television news.

Warrantless wiretaps were meant to pass quietly into law by a similar circuit of evasion; but Cheney and Addington were tripped up by one of those accidents that haunt the most cunning of stratagems. A sick man in a hospital bed, who happened to be the attorney general, remembered he had sworn an oath to uphold the laws; and when he took that oath, he had not made a private reservation that the laws he upheld might just as well be laws contrived in secret. Cheney and Addington did not predict the cussedness or the integrity of John Ashcroft. Still, in the assault on FISA, it took the threat of more than thirty resignations from the justice department to convince the president to back down and compromise.

James Comey, the acting attorney general, fought off Cheney and Addington by physically blocking the path of their agents, Alberto Gonzales and Andrew Card, beside the bed of the attorney general. We would be living in a different country today if at that critical time, John Yoo, author of the redefinition of torture requested by the vice president, had become, as he aimed to become, the head of the Office of Legal Counsel. But in October 2003, the position went to Jack Goldsmith: a friend of Yoo's, like him an authoritarian conservative and a young dogmatist of the Federalist Society, but one whose ideas were complicated by the possession of a conscience regarding accountability and the law.

So assiduous were Yoo's exertions to curry favor with authority that he came to be called by Ashcroft himself "Dr. Yes." Yoo was infinitely obliging. He would go any length to find any reason that Cheney and Addington asked him to find. No reach of sophistry was beyond his grasp. No horror of tyranny curbed his appetite for "making new law" to supplant the outmoded refinements of democracy.

Addington (a large man, a fast thinker, and a shouter in closed meetings) declined to be interviewed by *Frontline*. Yoo, by contrast, now a professor of law at U.C. Berkeley, was willing to defend his recommendations. One is curious to see the man who wrote the torture memos; and the encounter quickens as the camera reveals a momentary shadow on Yoo's eager and expressionless public face. It happens when he is mocking the objections to the treatment allowed against prisoners at Guantánamo—as if, says Yoo, we should "read them their Miranda rights," as if we should let them "talk to a lawyer." A flicker of sadism—or is it nothing but a sneer?—crosses his face and slips halfway into his voice.

When the tortures at Abu Ghraib were brought to light, John McCain said unforgettably: "We should never simply fight evil with evil." And again: "This isn't about who they are, this is about who we are." And yet, on this issue too, Cheney and Addington pushed and bit by bit their opponent gave way. McCain won an overwhelming vote in the Senate for his bill prohibiting the use of torture; but then the vice president in person walked him through a special exemption for the CIA, and then an agreement that Guantánamo was off the map of the law. Since his capitulation in this matter, so close to his own experience, John McCain has not been the same man.

The pressure behind the new laws has never stopped. It makes a new conquest with every presidential nominee. "If waterboarding is torture," said Michael Mukasey two days ago, "it's not in the Constitution." Of the treatment of prisoners generally, Mukasey added: "If it amounts to torture, it is unconstitutional." These queer, para-logical formulae, spoken in his own voice by the nominee for attorney general, bear the signature of David Addington. Everything depends on the meaning of "if" in the first sentence above, and on the meaning of "amounts" in the second. Mukasey was really saying that our understanding of right and wrong may legitimately be warped by the executive branch. So, a cruel practice which the world regards as torture, and which we taught the world to regard as torture, and which the makers of the eighth amendment would have recognized as torture: this, in our endless emergency, may not amount to torture after all.

In the old Soviet Union, which neoconservative legal counsellors have closely studied and learned from, the goons and thugs ran everything. Everything: from the machine of the state bureaucracy to the reasons given by obedient judges for the smallest humiliation extorted from a hapless citizen by a police detective or a customs official. Good people were kept out of public life, and out of public service, because Lenin's Law and Stalin's Law had no conceivable place for them. In our society, there have been goons and thugs, of course, but something about American democracy, a something that includes the reading of Miranda rights, seemed to give assurance that they would always be a furtive minority. The manners of the society itself discouraged overt hard-heartedness and cruelty.

Wrote Emerson: "Yes, we are the cowed,—we, the trustless." Why has "protect" become a favorite verb among our leaders, and "safe" a favorite adjective? How many of the trustless are willing to work the new machine? How many, with Comey and Goldsmith, will refuse? The offer the vice president and president have extended to all Americans is, from one point of view, as generous as it is benign. They want to be our protectors. All they ask in return is unlimited power. Yet this offer reveals a judgment that is indelibly mixed with contempt for something besides the law.

Euphemism and Violence

March 5, 2008

In Tacitus' *Agricola*, a Caledonian rebel named Calgacus, addressing "a close-packed multitude" preparing to fight, declares that Rome has overrun so much of the world that "there are no more nations beyond us; nothing is there but waves and rocks, and the Romans, more deadly still than these—for in them is an arrogance which no submission or good behavior can escape." Certain habits of speech, he adds, abet the ferocity and arrogance of the empire by infecting even the enemies of Rome with Roman self-deception:

> A rich enemy excites their cupidity; a poor one, their lust for power. East and West alike have failed to satisfy them. . . . To robbery, butchery, and rapine, they give the lying name of "government"; they create a desolation and call it peace.

The frightening thing about such acts of renaming or *euphemism*, Tacitus implies, is their power to efface the memory of actual cruelties. Behind the façade of a history falsified by language, the painful particulars of war are lost. Maybe the most disturbing implication of the famous sentence "They create a desolation and call it peace" is that apologists for violence, by means of euphemism, come to believe what they hear themselves say.

On July 21, 2006, the tenth day of the Lebanon War, Condoleezza Rice explained why the U.S. government had not thrown its weight behind a cease-fire:

> What we're seeing here, in a sense, is the growing—the birth pangs of a new Middle East, and whatever we do, we

have to be certain that we're pushing forward to the new Middle East, not going back to the old one.

Very likely these words were improvised. "Growing pains" seems to have been Rice's initial thought; but as she went on, she dropped the "pains," turned them into "pangs," and brought back the violence with a hint of redemptive design: the pains were only *birth pangs*. The secretary of state was thinking still with the same metaphor when she spoke of "pushing," but a literal image of a woman in labor could have proved awkward, and she trailed off in a deliberate anticlimax: "pushing forward" means "not going back."

Many people at the time remarked the incongruity of Rice's speech as applied to the devastation wrought by Israeli attacks in southern Lebanon and Beirut. Every bombed-out Lebanese home and mangled limb would be atoned for, the words seemed to be saying, just as a healthy infant vindicates the mother's labor pains. Looked at from a longer distance, the statement suggested a degree of mental dissociation. For the self-serving boast was also offered as a fatalistic consolation—and this by an official whose call for a cease-fire might well have stopped the war. "The birth pangs of a new Middle East" will probably outlive most other phrases of our time, because, as a kind of metaphysical "conceit," it accurately sketches the state of mind of the president and his advisers in 2006.

The phrase also marked a notable recent example of a turn of language one may as well call *revolutionary euphemism*. This was an invention of the later eighteenth century, but it was brought into standard usage in the twentieth—"You can't make an omelet without breaking eggs"—by Stalin's apologists for revolution and forced modernization in the 1930s. The French Revolutionist Jean-Marie Roland spoke of the mob violence of the attack on the Tuileries as *agitation* or *effervescence*, never as "massacre" or "murder"—improvising, as he went, a cleansing metaphor oddly similar to Rice's "birth pangs."

It was natural, said Roland, "that victory should bring with it some excess. The sea, agitated by a violent storm, roars long after the tempest." The task of the revolutionary propagandist, at a temporary setback, is to show that his zeal is undiminished. This he must do with a minimum of egotism; and the surest imaginable protection is to invoke the impartial authority of natural processes.

If one extreme of euphemism comes from naturalizing the cruelties of power, the opposite extreme arises from nerve-deadening understatement. George Orwell had the latter method in view when he wrote "Politics and the English Language":

> Defenceless villages are bombarded from the air, the inhabitants driven out into the countryside, the cattle machine-gunned, the huts set on fire with incendiary bullets: this is called *pacification*. Millions of peasants are robbed of their farms and sent trudging along the roads with no more than they can carry: this is called *transfer of population* or *rectification of frontiers*. People are imprisoned for years without trial, or shot in the back of the neck or sent to die of scurvy in Arctic lumber camps: this is called *elimination of unreliable elements*. Such phraseology is needed if one wants to name things without calling up mental pictures of them.

Orwell's insight was that the italicized phrases are colorless by design and not by accident. He saw a deliberate method in the imprecision of texture. The inventors of this idiom meant to suppress one kind of imagination, the kind that yields an image of things actually done or suffered; and they wanted to put in its place an imagination that trusts to the influence of larger powers behind the scenes. Totalitarianism depends on the creation of people who take satisfaction in such trust; and totalitarian minds are in part created (Orwell believed) by the ease and invisibility of euphemism.

Before launching their response to Islamic jihadists in September 2001, members of the administration of George W. Bush and Dick Cheney gave close consideration to the naming of the response. The President is reported by Bob Woodward and Robert Draper to have said to his staff that they should all view the September 11 attack as an "opportunity." His sense of that word in the context is hard to interpret, but its general bearings are plain. Imaginative leadership, the President was saying, must do far more than respond to the attack, or attend to the needs of self-preservation. Better to use the attack as an opportunity to "go massive," as Donald Rumsfeld noted on September 11. "Sweep it all up. Things related and not." A similar sense of Bush's purpose has recently been recalled by Karl Rove. "History has a funny way of deciding things," Rove said to an audience at the University of Pennsylvania on February 20, 2008. "Sometimes history sends you things, and 9/11 came our way." But so, all the more pressingly: how to name the massive and partly unrelated response to a catastrophe that was also an opportunity?

The name must admit the tremendousness of the task and imply its eventual solubility, but also discourage any close inquiry into the means employed. They wanted to call it a war; but what sort of war? The phrase they agreed on, the *Global War on Terrorism*, was at once simple-sounding and elusive, and it has served its purpose as nothing more definite could have done.

The Global War on Terrorism promotes a mood of comprehension in the absence of perceived particulars, and that is a mood in which euphemisms may comfortably take shelter. There is (many commentators have pointed out) something nonsensical in the idea of waging war on a *technique* or *method*, and terrorism was a method employed by many groups over many centuries before Al Qaeda—the Tamil Tigers, the IRA, the Irgun, to stick to recent times. But the "war on crime" and "war on drugs" probably helped to render the initial absurdity of the name to some degree normal. This was an incidental weakness, in any case. The assurance and the unspecifying grandiosity of the Global War on Terrorism were the traits most desired in such a slogan.

Those qualities fitted well with a style of white-lipped eloquence that Bush's speechwriter Michael Gerson had begun to plot into his major speeches in late 2001. It made for a sort of continuous, excitable, canting threat, emitted as if unwillingly from a man of good will and short temper. Gerson, from his Christian evangelical beliefs and journalistic ability (he had written for *US News & World Report* and ghostwritten the autobiography of Chuck Colson), worked up a highly effective contemporary "grand style" that skated between hyperbole and evasion. The manner suggested a stark simplicity that was the end product of sophisticated analysis and a visionary impatience with compromise.

This was exactly the way President Bush, in his own thinking, liked to turn his imaginative vices into virtues; and he intuitively grasped the richness of a phrase like "the soft bigotry of low expectations" or "history's unmarked grave of discarded lies"—resonant formulae which he approved and deployed, over the challenges of his staff. What did the phrases mean? As their creator knew, the mode of their non-meaning was the point. Like "pacification" and "rectification of frontiers," these markers of unstated policy were floating metaphors with a low yield of fact. But they left an image of decisiveness, with an insinuation of contempt for persons slower to move from thought to action.

Euphemism has been the leading quality of American discussions of the war in Iraq. This was plain in the run-up to the war, with the talk of *regime change*—a phrase welcomed by reporters and politicians as if they had heard it all their lives. Regime change seemed to pass at a jump beyond the predictable either/or of "forced abdication" and "international war of aggression." Regime change also managed to imply, without saying, that governments do, as a matter of fact, often change by external demand without much trouble to anyone. The talk (before and just after the war) of "taking out" Saddam Hussein was equally new. It combined the reflex of the skilled gunman and the image of a surgical procedure so routine that it could be trusted not to jeopardize the life of the patient. It had its roots in gangland argot, where taking out means knocking off, but its reception was none the worse for that.

Are Americans more susceptible to such devices than other people are? Democracy exists in continuous complicity with euphemism. There are so many things (the staring facts of inequality, for example) about which we feel it is right not to want to speak gratingly. One result is a habit of circumlocution that is at once adaptable and self-deceptive. "Their own approbation of their own acts," wrote Edmund Burke of the people in a democracy, "has to them the appearance of a public judgment in their favor." Since the people are not always right but are by definition always in the majority, their self-approbation, Burke added, tends to make them shameless and therefore fearless. The stratagems of a leader in a democracy include giving the people a name for everything, but doing so in a way that maintains their own approbation of their own acts. Thus a war the people trust their government to wage, over which we have no control, but about which we would prefer to think happy thoughts, gives the widest possible scope to the exertions of euphemism.

There has sprung up, over the past five years, a euphemistic contract between the executive branch and mainstream journalism. "A short, sharp war," as Tony Blair was sure it would be, has become one of the longest of American wars; but the war-makers have blunted that recognition by breaking down the war into stages: the fall of Baghdad; the Coalition Provisional Authority; the insurgency; the election of the Assembly; the sectarian war. In this way the character of the war as a single failed attempt has eluded discovery; it has come to seem, instead, a many-featured entity, difficult to describe and impossible to judge. And to assist the impression of obscurity, two things are consistently pressed out of view: the killing of Iraqi civilians by American soldiers and the destruction of Iraqi cities by American bombs and artillery.

Slight uptick in violence is a coinage new to the war in Iraq, and useful for obvious reasons. It suggests a remote perspective in which fifty or a hundred deaths, from three or four suicide bombings in a day, hardly cause a jump in the needle that measures such things. The phrase has a laconic sound, in a manner popularly associated with men who are used to violence and keep a cool head. Indeed, it was generals at briefings—Kimmitt, Hertling, and Petraeus—who gave currency to a phrase that implies realism and the possession of strong personal shock absorbers.

A far more consequential euphemism, in the conduct of the Iraq War—and a usage adopted without demur until recently, by journalists, lawmakers, and army officers—speaks of mercenary soldiers as *contractors* or *security* (the last now a singular-plural like the basketball teams called Magic and Jazz). The Blackwater killings at Nissour Square in Baghdad, on September 16, 2007, brought this euphemism, and the extraordinary innovation it hides, suddenly to public view. Yet the armed Blackwater guards who did the shooting, though now less often described as mere "contractors," are referred to as *employees*—a neutral designation that repels further attention. The point about mercenaries is that you employ them when your army is inadequate to the job assigned. This has been the case from the start in Iraq. But the fact that the mercenaries have been continuously augmented until they now out-number American troops suggests a truth about the war that falls open to inspection only when we use the accurate word. It was always known to the Office of the Vice President and the department of defense that the conventional forces they deployed were smaller than would be required to maintain order in Iraq. That is why they hired the extracurricular forces.

Reflect on the prevalence of the mercenaries and the falsifying descriptions offered of their work, and you are made to wonder how much the architects of the war actually wanted a state of order in Iraq. Was this as important to them as, say, the assurance that "contracting" of all kinds in Iraq would become a major part of the American economy following the invasion? We now know that the separate bookkeeping and accountability devised for Blackwater, DynCorp, Triple Canopy, and similar outfits was part of a careful displacement of oversight from Congress to the vice president and the stewards of his policies in various departments and agencies. To have much of the work of this war parceled out to private companies, who are unaccountable to army rules or military justice, meant, among its other advantages, that the cost of the war could be concealed beyond all detection. What is a contractor? Someone contracted to do a job by the proper authority. Who that hears the word "contractor" has ever asked what the contract is for?

There was a brief contest over *surge*—so ordinary yet so crafty a word. The rival term emphasized by critics of the war was "escalation," which owes its grim connotations to Vietnam. The architects of the surge, Frederick Kagan and Retired General Jack Keane, fought hard to stop the mass media from switching to *escalation*. Their wishes were granted almost without exception, and to clinch the optimistic consensus, the *New York Times* on July 30, 2007, published an Op-Ed by Kenneth Pollack and Michael O'Hanlon extolling the progress of the surge. The authors, supporters of the war who were permitted falsely to describe themselves as skeptics, wrote, as they confessed, after an eight-day army-guided tour, from which they had neither the enterprise nor the resources to step out and seek information on their own. But it now seems likely that, with the help of the surge, the word as much as the thing, 2008 will end with as many American troops in Iraq as 2006. Meanwhile, as the mass media approved of the surge, they lost interest in Iraq, and that was the aim. The strategists of the surge may have taken some pleasure in putting across a word that sounds like a breakfast drink but that insiders at the American Enterprise Institute, the Brookings Institution, and the Pentagon would recognize as shorthand for counterinsurgency.

When Seymour Hersh broke the story of Abu Ghraib, Secretary of Defense Rumsfeld was keen on excluding the word *torture* from all discussions of the coercive interrogations and planned humiliations at the prison. His chosen word was *abuse*: a word that has been devalued through its bureaucratization in therapies against spousal abuse, child abuse, and so on. "Torture," by comparison, still sets one's teeth on edge, and the word had been avoided for a long time.

Yet there were many, in the panic months after September 2001, who eagerly approved the breaking of old restrictions to fight the Global War on Terrorism. Alfred McCoy in *A Question of Torture* recalls that in late 2001 and early 2002 "a growing public consensus emerged in favor of torture." And lawmakers were not to be outdone by legal theorists; Representative Jane Harman said, "I'm OK with it not being pretty." What did the new tolerance encompass? "Interrogation in depth" was one way of putting it; "professional interrogation techniques" were spoken of (perhaps with a view to the professionalism of the contractors). With the apparent acceptance of torture, the inversions of euphemism began to be extended to grammar as well as diction. Thus Alan Dershowitz argued in January 2002 for "torture warrants," to be issued by judges, and later spoke of the legitimation of torture as "bringing it within the law" (where, he implied, the torturer, the tortured, and the law would all be more secure). By bringing torture within the law, what Dershowitz meant was breaking the law out of itself to accommodate torture.

This argument was always about two things: the truth of words and the reality of violence. The statements to House and Senate committees, in late January and early February 2008, by Attorney General Michael Mukasey and Director of National Intelligence Mike McConnell oddly converged on the following set of propositions. A method of interrogation known as "waterboarding" would feel like torture if it were done to them (Mukasey and McConnell offered different but parallel versions of the same personal formula, pretty clearly in coordination). The method had been used by American interrogators after September 11, 2001, they said, but it was not in use at present. Whether it constituted torture was a matter under investigation—an investigation so serious that no result should be expected soon— but authorization of the practice was within the powers of the president, who reserved the right to command interrogators to waterboard suspects again if he thought it useful. The attorney general added his assurance that, in the event that the practice was resumed, he would notify appropriate members of Congress, even though Congress had no legal authority to restrain the president.

It would be hard to find a precedent for the sophistical juggle of these explanations. The secret in plain view was not a judgment about present or future policy, but an imposed acceptance of something past. President Bush, in 2002 and later, sought and obtained legal justifications for ordering the torture of terrorism suspects, and it is known that American interrogators used methods on some suspects that constitute torture under international law. If these acts had been admitted by the attorney general to meet the definition of torture, those who conducted the interrogations and those who ordered them, including the president, would be liable to prosecution for war crimes.

Because the legacy of the Nuremberg trials remains vivid today, the very idea of a war crime has been treated as a thing worth steering clear of, no matter what the cost in overstretched ingenuity. Thought of a war crime does not lend itself to euphemistic reduction.

Yet "waterboarding" itself is a euphemism for a torture that the Japanese in the Second World War, the French in Indochina, and the Khmer Rouge, who learned it from the French, knew simply as the drowning torture. Our American explanations have been as misleading as the word. The process is not "simulated drowning" but actual drowning that is interrupted. Clarifications such as these, in the coverage of the debate, did not emerge from reports on the Mukasey and McConnell testimony; they had to be found in the rival testimony, either in public discussions or before Congress, of opponents like Lieutenant Commander Charles D. Swift (the JAG Corps defense counsel who was denied promotion after his public criticism of the Guantánamo tribunals) and Malcolm W. Nance (a retired instructor at the U.S. Navy SERE school).

The contrast between the startling testimony of men like these and the speculative defense of waterboarding offered by semi-official advocates such as David B. Rivkin, the Reagan justice department lawyer and journalist, has been among the most disquieting revelations of these years. A group of men who think what they want to think and pay little attention to evidence have been running things; and they are guided not by experience but by words that were constructed for the purpose of deception.

Americans born between the 1930s and the 1950s have a much harder time getting over the shock of learning that our country practices torture than do Americans born in the 1970s or 1980s. The memory of the Gestapo and the GPU, the depiction of torture in a film like *Open City*, are not apt to press on younger minds. But the different responses are also a consequence of the different imaginings to which people may fall prey. Many who fear that their children might be killed by a terrorist bomb cannot imagine anyone they know ever suffering injustice at the hands of the national security state.

This complacency suggests a new innocence—the correlative in moral psychology of euphemism in the realm of language. And if you take stock of how little *general* discussion there has been of the advisability of pursuing the Global War on Terrorism, you realize that this country has scarcely begun to account for its own effect as an ambiguous actor on the world stage. Those who said, in the weeks just after the September 11 attacks, that the motives of the terrorists might be traced back to some U.S. policies in the Middle East were understandably felt to have spoken unseasonably. The surprising thing is that six and a half years later, when a politic reticence is no longer the sole order of the day, discussion of such matters is still confined to iconoclastic books like Chalmers Johnson's *Blowback*, and has barely begun to register in the *New York Times*, in the *Washington Post*, or on CNN or MSNBC. Ask an American what the United States may have to do with much of the world's hostility toward us and you will find educated people saying things like "They hate the West and resent modernity," or "They hate the fact that we're so free," or "They hate us because this is a country where a man and a woman can look at each other across a table with eyes of love." Indeed, the single greatest propaganda victory of the Bush administration may be the belief shared by most Americans that the rise of radical Islam—so-called Islamo-fascism—has no relationship to any previous action by the United States.

Nothing can excuse acts of terrorism, which are aimed at civilians, or those acts of state terror in which planned civilian deaths are advertised as "collateral damage." Yet the uniformity of the presentation by the mass media after 2001, affirming that the United States now faced threats from a fanaticism with religious roots unconnected to anything America had done or could do, betrayed a stupefying abdication of judgment. The protective silence regarding the 725 American bases worldwide was one obvious symptom. Also taken in without remark was the fact that fifteen of the nineteen September 11 hijackers were Saudis. The five thousand American troops on Arabian soil, left over from the First Gulf War, had been deeply resented. To gloss over or ignore such things can only obstruct an intelligent discussion of the reaction likely to follow from any extended American occupation of the Middle East. "Baghdad is calmer now; the surge is working." The temporary partial peace is an effect of accomplished desolation, a state of things in which the Shiite "cleansing" of the city has achieved the dignity of the status quo, and been ratified by the walls and checkpoints of General Petraeus.

"The surge is working" is a fiction that blends several facts indistinguishably. For example: that Iraq is a land of militias and (as Nir Rosen put it) the U.S. Army is the largest militia; that in 2007 we paid eighty thousand "Sunni extremists" to switch sides and call themselves The Awakening. Americans have suggested this militia is a warlord version of our own "neighborhood watch," and have assigned it cover-names such as Concerned Local Citizens and Critical Infrastructure Security. A *Washington Post* story on February 28, 2008 indicates that the Sunni gunmen are increasingly unhappy about their ties to the American military.

"If a Power coerces once," wrote H. N. Brailsford in his great study of imperialism, *The War of Steel and Gold*, "it may dictate for years afterwards without requiring to repeat the lesson." This was the design of the American Shock and Awe in Iraq. Looking back on the invasion, one is impressed that so clear-cut a strategy could have evaded challenge under the casual drapery of "democracy." But say a thing often enough, so as to subdue the anxiety of a people and flatter their pride, and, unless they come to know better with their own eyes and their own hands, they will accept the illusion. "History begins today" was a saying in the Bush White House—repeated with menace by Deputy Secretary of State Richard Armitage to the director of Pakistani intelligence Mahmoud Ahmad—a statement that on its face exhibits a totalitarian presumption. Nothing so much as language supplies our memory of things that came before today; and, to an astounding degree, the Bush administration has succeeded in persuading the most powerful and (at one time) the best-informed country in the world that history began on September 12, 2001. The effect has been to tranquilize our self-doubts and externalize all the evils we dare to think of. The changes of usage and the corruptions of sense that have followed the Global War on Terrorism are inseparable from the destructive acts of that war.

WILLIAM SAFIRE: WARS MADE OUT OF WORDS

October 1, 2009
"There were no thrills while he reigned, but neither were there any headaches. He had no ideas, and he was not a nuisance." What Mencken said of Coolidge can be reversed in the case of Safire. There were plenty of thrills, and after

the thrills, the field was littered with casualties. And he had tons of ideas. He was keen to share them as soon as he thought them up. The career that took him from public relations to propaganda to column-writing was a single seamless progression. He treated these different lines of work as the same work; and under his hand, they were. He was interested in words, yet he has left behind no sentence or sentiment that people will quote in the future merely because it is true.

He never stinted his approval of wars. He did all that he could to drum up several wars beyond the psychological means of his country and the world; and his disappointment could turn to spite when a war that he wanted failed to materialize. Jimmy Carter's refusal to bomb Iran in the years 1979–1980 was the greatest defeat of Safire's life. His record on Vietnam (both during and after), on El Salvador and Nicaragua, and on Iraq would be worth combing the archives of the *New York Times* to recover, simply as an exhibition of savage consistency. Safire was not the originator of the psychology of the self-righteous onslaught, "ten eyes for an eye"—human nature found it long ago—but he was the American of his generation who almost made it respectable. Did a terrorist set off a bomb in a café and five Americans die? Send in the air force and demolish a foreign capital somehow connected with that terrorist. The flash of the violent gesture, for Safire, was more important than the justice of the action.

He became the leading practitioner of the gestural politics of journalism. And in doing so, he revamped the accepted manner of the *New York Times* columnist. No more the reserve and formality and magisterial airs of a James Reston; everything now had to be fast and sharp: keep the pot boiling and the gags popping. He was the first man of the right to leaven his moralism with jokes. With fun and "pace," with plenty of euphemisms, and with calculated self-depreciation he did more than anyone else to legitimate a reactionary president, Ronald Reagan, as a new kind of centrist. A considerable sleight-of-hand.

His columns fashioned from dialogues with Richard Nixon when living, and his channeled mock-dialogues with Nixon when dead, were a prodigy of bad taste. A related genre he pioneered, the imaginary monologue of the man of power that aimed to reveal the motives of the powerful, betrayed Safire's curious want of invention. He made no effort to convey the manner and savor of the person he ventriloquized. The monologues all came out sounding like Safire (just as the quoted persons in a Woodward political chronicle all sound like Woodward). But this insider genre fitted the new *Times* like a glove.

Perhaps the ruling passion of his life was a need for violent stimulants. He sought, and craved, excitement— the thrill of the battle of everyday politics, the thrill of the slander and smear, the thrill of wars. He was equally drawn to wars of the past, wars simmering at present, and wars in the future. This love of gross sensations he sought to impose as much as possible on his readers. More important, he aimed to impose it on the men of power whom he wished to influence. And often enough he succeeded. Kenneth Starr, on the brink of quitting the Whitewater investigation, was rebuked by Safire in such humiliating terms that, rather than defy the columnist, he launched the country on the long march toward the impeachment of Bill Clinton.

Safire attended to Nixon's post-retirement fame by shining as decent a light as could be thrown on it, and he kept Nixon's posthumous fame in as good repair as the facts allowed. These exertions suggest a large investment of his own amour-propre. He would not let anyone forget that he was part of the Nixon White House, but he encouraged readers to suppose that time spent there had been happy and not shameful. Among living politicians, he cultivated a particular admiration for Ariel Sharon. Has the oddness of this relationship ever been adequately noticed? A general who became the head-of-state of a foreign power, implicated in a brutal massacre, was puffed as a wise man by a popular American journalist. Safire wanted to persuade Americans that the adventurer of the Lebanon War was our old friend "Arik." His reports of phone conversations with Sharon, like the columns he devoted to the elevation of Sharon's achievements, have no precedent in American journalism, not even in the high days of Anglophilia when Winston Churchill evoked sentimental feelings beyond any warrant from his conduct.

In person, it seems that Safire was not a brawler; no fighting stories about him have surfaced. But he had the fondness of the born propagandist for "bloody noses and cracked crowns." He served in the army as a correspondent, during a time of peace, yet he loved the idea of combat. The higher the stakes, the more zest it added to life. He smashed hard without a second thought, and could be wrong with impunity, as Wen Ho Lee, Mohamed El-Baradei, and a multitude of others can attest. And yet we are told that he was a pleasant fellow, and was known in after-years to dine with his victims.

As a writer, Safire is most often associated with the short bursts he wrote in speeches given by Vice President Spiro Agnew, before Agnew was forced to retire under a cloud of charges by the U.S. Attorney in Baltimore: extortion, bribery, tax fraud, and conspiracy. "Nattering nabobs of negativism" was a phrase in a speech of November 13, 1969. It suggested that critics of the Vietnam War were as rich as nabobs and as mindless as chattering apes. A trick from the lower drawer of Kipling, it served its reckless purpose in heating the resentments of the time. Safire's other best-known phrase, "an effete corps of impudent snobs," had been given to Agnew to speak just a month earlier at the time of the October 15 peace moratorium. Here the effect bordered on punning—a favorite device of his for disarming criticism—since "effete" brings "elite" into the ear without having to pay for the echo. He turned out other squibs in the same mood that helped to corrupt the public mind, and to break the public peace in America at a time of internal strife. His picture of the defense of civil liberties as "pusillanimous pussyfooting on the critical issue of law and order" has the true Safire touch—clever, punchy, alliterative, demagogic.

This pattern, by which zealous accusations are dealt out sharply, but mixed with a vein of buffoonery, is a staple of the far right in America that has never been properly described or accounted for. It has been with us at least since the time of Senator Joe McCarthy; and it would be surprising if William Safire in his early days did not nurse an admiration for McCarthy. More polished than McCarthy or Nixon, and by the time of his death a lion of the establishment, Safire is the link that across four decades connects the political style of McCarthy with that of Rush Limbaugh.

Under the heading "William Safire's Finest Speech," it is now possible to locate online a speech Safire wrote for Nixon which offers the most perverse imaginable illustration of political opportunism. It was written to order for an occasion that never arose. It said what Nixon ought to say in case the astronauts of Apollo 11 were stranded on the moon. In this counterfactual elegy, drafted on June 18, 1969 and sent to Nixon's aide H. R. Haldeman, the author of *Safire's Political Dictionary* worked fast to bury the dead while they were living. "Fate has ordained that the men who went to the moon to explore in peace will stay on the moon to rest in peace." Thus, in the time he could spare from enlarging a war half a world away, Safire contrived to speak for the people of the planet to mark a truce in outer space: the astronauts would "be mourned by a Mother Earth who dared to send two of her sons into the unknown." A final blessing was uttered on behalf of a species now at last united in our prayers to the sky: "Every human being who looks up to the moon in nights to come will know that there is some corner of another world that is forever mankind." A superstition, a kind of piety maybe, would have restrained many speech-writers from undertaking a preposterous assignment like this, no matter how warmly it was urged, no matter by how powerful a boss. Yet the dying fall of the final clause epitomizes Safire's facility.

Rupert Brooke, a poet of the First World War, wrote in the opening lines of a poem that Safire must have learned in school, "If I should die, think only this of me; / That there's some corner of a foreign field / That is for ever England." Compare "some corner of another world that is forever mankind." He fished up the sob of the shining line from his stock quotations to send the astronauts to their eternal rest. But consider the deeper poetry of the moment. The man most gifted in his time at summoning a literate audience to twitch, heave, and submit to the voice in the megaphone without regard to the man behind the curtain, had been asked to bury the first explorers of space. And what came into his mind? A paean of self-sacrifice lifted from the high age of Europe's empires. The astronauts, as Safire saw them, were soldiers of the next empire. It is good that they lived to make this speech unnecessary. But it is good, too, in a way, that we have this speech—a touchstone and a warning of the limitless ambition of words.

WHAT 9/11 MAKES US FORGET

September 10, 2011
The piety attached to a collective memory can be used to assist forgetting; and this is especially so when the facts are stark and engraved on every mind. Nineteen terrorists, acting on the design of a political-religious fanatic, murdered three thousand Americans. All of the killers are now dead. The danger in the commemorations around September 11 is lest the date should blot out previous history and numb our awareness of ourselves as agents of our own fortunes.

It suits some people to have things that way. "History begins on 9/11" was the message conveyed by the Bush-Cheney administration in the later days of September and early October 2001. "9/11"—thus marked, rarely lengthened to a phrase—was seen as a uniquely uncaused cause. The first and almost the last word about the event was "evil." The agents of evil hated for hate's sake. They were people capable of destroying America precisely for what is best about America. To rid the world of that evil, as President Bush said, would be to "rid the world of evil" itself. This was the task the United States should undertake in the twenty-first century.

One thing the shorthand "9/11" inclines us to forget is that the 1990s incubated a powerful sect of strategists who regarded the fall of Communism as a letdown for the United States. Great powers need great enemies. The moment an empire contracts the scope of its ambitions is the moment it ceases to think itself an empire. It may then revert to a more modest condition: that of a free republic, or one power among others. The essence of empire, by contrast, is the spirit of militarism embodied in a policy of endless expansion. That understanding lay behind the neoconservative pamphlet *Rebuilding America's Defenses*, a full-scale policy memorandum produced for the Project for the New American Century, published in September 2000 and running seventy-six pages in two columns.

Its author, Thomas Donnelly, took counsel from an advisory committee that included Stephen Cambone, Donald Kagan, I. Lewis Libby, Gary Schmitt, and Paul Wolfowitz. The "report," as it called itself, contained a sentence that has acquired a separate fame. "The process" (said the strategists at PNAC) of America's complete transformation into an unchallenged global superpower "is likely to be a long one, absent some catastrophic and catalyzing event—like a new Pearl Harbor." One year later, the catalyzing event arrived. Among the reasons Dick Cheney was so quick off the starting blocks after a surprise attack was that he had long been preparing for such an incitement. Unlike most Americans, he knew exactly how to use it.

What history began on 9/11? American "force projection" in the Middle East and Southwest Asia. This meant the bombing and (where plausible) occupation of Iraq, Syria, and Iran; and, with the successes there, control over the dome of oil in the region and "the oil-rich Horn of Africa." Also, improved security for Israel; political advantage for the administration in charge of the quest; a geopolitical base from which to push (with assistance from the former Soviet republics after the "color revolutions" subsidized by the U.S.) against any possible resurgence of Russian power. These gains in political dominance and economic hegemony might prove useful, too, as a wedge against China in South Asia.

Such were the long-term goals. The necessary short-term method for dragging America in consisted of lies supported by other lies, half-truths, forgeries, a docile press, and a clutch of reliable journalists and opinion-makers. Few analysts were so prescient as to get the whole story or almost all of it right. Two who did were Chalmers Johnson in *The Sorrows of Empire* and George Kateb in "A Life of Fear."

In the procession from 9/11 to an unprovoked war on Iraq, neoconservatives propagandized and led. Neoliberals endorsed, apologized, explained, and followed. Some neoconservatives whose opinions and votes supported the new history: Richard Perle, Robert Kagan, John McCain, William Kristol, Victor Davis Hanson, Kenneth Adelman, David Brooks, Douglas Feith, Paul Wolfowitz. Some neoliberals who differed from the above in tone but not in substance: Bill Keller, Leslie Gelb, Kenneth Pollack, Joe Lieberman, George Packer, Peter Beinart, Fareed Zakaria, Hillary Clinton, Thomas Friedman.

In brutality of sentiment, no neoconservative ever topped the explanation Thomas Friedman gave to Charlie Rose of why the U.S. had to smash the electrical grid, strangulate the water supply, demolish the major administrative centers of Baghdad and much of the rest of Iraq and kill tens of thousands of civilians. The details and justification hardly mattered, said Friedman. "What we had to do was go over to that part of the world . . . and take out a very big stick . . . [and say]: *Suck. On. This.*"

What was most disgusting in the fever-time that lasted from October 2001 through 2003 was the seamless consensus that prevailed among mainstream journalists, high-profile scholars, and men of power. It was a Middle-East scholar, Bernard Lewis, and an independent strategist, Henry Kissinger, who advised Dick Cheney—to considerable effect, by Cheney's own account—that after Afghanistan the U.S. ought to hit hard at Iraq. The academic experts concurred with the vulgar maxim: Arabs understand something better when you do it twice.

Those years proved beyond any doubt the bankruptcy of the foreign-policy elite in thought and action. The twisted understanding crossed party lines. After the 2006 election, when the Democrats won a majority in both houses of Congress, Patrick Leahy inherited the Senate judiciary committee, Jay Rockefeller the intelligence committee, Joe Biden the committee on foreign relations, and none of them held inquiries or hearings of any substance. And this, though Leahy and Rockefeller had come very close to calling the Iraq war a swindle and Guantánamo a crime. Compare the searching hearings on the Vietnam War, chaired by Senator Fulbright in 1966, and the decline in the evidence of civic conscience is staggering.

Barack Obama, in his 2008 campaign, gave some promise of clarification and partial reversal, but he lacked the knowledge, the penetration, the stamina, and the political courage to effect a shadow of the change the campaign had suggested, and in his passivity he was abetted by a choice of advisers utterly confined to adherents of the pro-war consensus. So we are still in a history that began on 9/11. The war the U.S. left behind, in Iraq, has been replaced by less visible wars in Yemen, Somalia, and Libya, and a Black Ops archipelago that circles the globe.

What Cheney innovated and Bush signed off on, Obama has ratified and made normal. By doing so, he has anaesthetized the spirit of opposition as no Republican could have done. His declared determination to "look forward as opposed to looking backwards" was a calculated insult to the very idea of accountability.

The consequences of that evasion will long outlast his presidency. Today, a decade later, 9/11 has become the name of a path as much as the name of an occurrence. Until we search out the tributary paths that fed the catastrophe, we will not begin to master the alternative course to which it might lead. There are ways that we could commemorate the unknowing and blameless dead of that day without casting our country in the role it has committed itself to play ever since: the largest of victims, seeking revenge; the world's sole superpower, intoxicated at its discovery of a new enemy who will last "more than a generation."

The Snowden Case

June 21, 2013
Most Americans who know anything about the National Security Agency probably got their mental picture of it from a 1998 thriller called *Enemy of the State*. A lawyer (Will Smith), swept up by mistake into the system of total surveillance, suddenly finds his life turned upside down, his family watched and harassed, his livelihood taken from him, and the records of his conduct altered and criminalized. He is saved by a retired NSA analyst (Gene Hackman), who knows the organization from innards to brains and hates every cog and gear that drives it. This ally is a loner. He has pulled back his way of life and associations to a minimum, and lives now in a desolate building called The Jar, which he has proofed against spying

and tricked out with anti-listening armor, decoy-signal devices, and advanced encryption-ware. From his one-man fortress, he leads the hero to turn the tables on the agency and to expose one of its larger malignant operations. Michael Hayden, who became the director of the NSA in 1999, saw the movie and told his workers they had an image problem: the agency had to change its ways and inspire the trust of citizens. But in 2001 Hayden, like many other Americans, underwent a galvanic change of consciousness and broke through to the other side. In the new era, in order to fight a new enemy, he saw that the United States must be equipped with a secret police as inquisitive and capable as the police of a totalitarian state, though of course more scrupulous. Gripped by the same fever and an appetite for power all his own, Dick Cheney floated the idea of Total Information Awareness (soliciting Americans to spy on their neighbors to fight terrorism), but found the country not yet ready for it. So he took the project underground and executed it in secret. Cheney issued the orders, his lawyer David Addington drew up the rationale, and Hayden at NSA made the practical arrangements. Eventually Cheney would appoint Hayden director of the CIA.

Americans caught our first glimpse of the possible scope of NSA operations in December 2005, when the *New York Times* ran a story by James Risen and Eric Lichtblau on massive warrantless surveillance: "Bush Lets US Spy on Callers without Courts." The government was demanding and getting from the telecoms all the records it wanted of calls both to and from their customers. But the feed had been deliberately routed around the court set up by the Foreign Intelligence Surveillance Act to issue warrants for searches of this kind. The *Times*, at the urging of the Bush

White House, had held back the story for a year, across the significant divide of the 2004 presidential election. Even so, James Risen, who protected the source for his leak, was threatened with prosecution by the Bush justice department, and under Obama that threat has not been lifted. As a candidate in 2007 and early 2008, Obama took an unconditional stand against data mining and warrantless spying, which he softened, well before the election, into a broad commitment to oversight of the existing programs by the inspectors general of the relevant departments and agencies. Over the past five years, Obama's reduction of the pledge to a practice had largely been taken on trust.

Such was the background of almost forgotten anxiety and suspended expectation when, on June 6 and 7, the *Guardian* struck with its stories on U.S. data mining and Internet surveillance. The collection of "to" and "from" numbers and the duration of phone calls had, it turned out, not only continued but expanded under Obama. The government reserves in storage and taps (on occasion) the emails and Internet activity of the customers of nine major companies including Google, Apple, and Microsoft. The major difference from the Cheney machinery seems to be that general warrants are now dealt out, rather than no warrants at all, but general warrants fail to meet the requirement of "probable cause" or the specification of the place to be searched and items to be seized. The Bill of Rights wanted not to make things too easy for the police. Now, on the contrary, the government gets the data wholesale, secure in the knowledge that a gag order prevents the corporate channels from speaking about the encroachment, and individual targets are sealed off from any knowledge of how they are watched. A law-like complexion is given to the enterprise by the fact that the government does not delve into personal records without the consent of the citizenry; the records, instead, are held by private companies and then siphoned off by the government under legal compulsion.

Our communicative doings may be likened to a fish-pond stocked with both actual and conjectural fish. The new protocol allows the government to vacuum up the entire pond, while preserving a posture quite innocent of trespass, since it means to do nothing with the contents just then. The test comes when a discovery elsewhere calls up an answering glimmer of *terror* or a *terror-link* from somewhere in your pond; at which point the already indexed contents may be legally poured out, dissected, and analyzed, with effects on the owner to be determined.

Edward Snowden made these discoveries, among others, while working as an analyst for the CIA, the NSA, and the security outfit Booz Allen Hamilton (whose present vice chairman, Mike McConnell, is a former director of the NSA). Imperialism has been defined as doing abroad what you would like to do at home but can't. Snowden, from the nature of his work, was made to recognize with growing dismay that what American intelligence was doing to terrorist suspects abroad it was also doing to two hundred eighty million unsuspecting Americans. The surveillance-industrial complex has brought home the intrusive techniques of a militarized empire, with its thousand bases and special-ops forces garrisoned in scores of countries. It has enlarged itself at home, obedient to the controlling appetite of an organism that believes it must keep growing or die. Of course, the U.S. government cannot do to Americans what it does routinely to non-Americans. The key word in that proposition, however, is *government*. In fact, the same government can do all it likes with the *commercial data* on American citizens, so long as it obtains a follow-up warrant from the FISA court. This court is always in session but its proceedings are secret; and qualified observers say it grants well over 99 percent of the warrants requested. There is therefore no point at which the move by government from data collection to actual spying on citizens can come under genuine oversight or be held accountable.

In "this our talking America" (as Emerson called it), we prefer to talk about personalities. It could be anticipated that the "leaker" of NSA secrets, and not the trespass by government against the people, would become the primary subject of discussion once the authorities produced a name and a face. He was destined to have his portrait fixed by the police and media, blurred and smeared to look, in some vague way, probably psychopathic, and once arrested to be dispatched to trial and prison. The Obama justice department, under its attorney general Eric Holder, has in the last four years prosecuted six whistle-blowers under the Espionage Act of 1917: twice the number prosecuted by all previous administrations combined. Before he fled Hawaii for Hong Kong, Snowden kept close watch on those prosecutions, and on the treatment of Bradley Manning in the brig at Quantico and in his military trial. Snowden resolved not to endure Manning's fate. He would get the story out in his own way, and would also describe his own motives as he understood them, before the authorities published his image and tracked it over with the standard markings of treachery and personal disorder. So the first *Guardian* stories were followed, in the same week, by a twelve-and-a-half-minute video interview of Snowden, shot by the documentary director Laura Poitras. The interviewer was

Glenn Greenwald, a constitutional lawyer as well as a *Guardian* columnist, whom Snowden had sought out and who, in defiance of American journalistic etiquette, served as author or coauthor of early *Guardian* stories based on the NSA leaks. The principles that guided Snowden's thinking and something of his views could be inferred already from his choice of Greenwald and Poitras as the persons to help convey his story to the public.

I have now watched this interview several times, and have been impressed by the calm and coherence of the mind it reveals. Snowden had looked for ways of serving his country in the grim months after September 2001 (he would have been eighteen then). He joined the army, hoping to be taken on in Special Forces, but broke both legs in a training accident and then dropped out, disaffected with an anti-Arab racism in the mood that took him by surprise. He had never finished high school but had no difficulty passing the test for a diploma equivalent. Since his computer skills were prodigious and easily recognized, he was an obvious candidate for well-paying security work in the IT industry, and, by his mid-twenties, had worked his way to the highest clearance for analyzing secret data. At the same time he was educating himself in the disagreeable facts of America's War on Terror, and the moral and legal implications of the national security state. He was pressed by larger doubts the more he learned. Not all these particulars emerged in the interview, but all could be inferred; and Snowden's profile differed from that of the spy or defector (which he was already charged with being) in one conspicuous way. He did not *think* in secret. In conversations with friends over the last few years, he made no effort to hide the trouble of conscience that gnawed at him. It also seems to be true that even as he went to work and made use of his privileged access, he felt a degree of remorse at the superiority he enjoyed over ordinary citizens, any of whom might be subject to exposure at any moment by the eye of the government he worked for. The remorse (if this surmise is correct) came not from a suspicion that he didn't deserve the privilege, but from the conviction that no one deserved it.

And yet, the drafters of the new laws, and the guardians of the secret interpretation of those laws, do feel that they deserve the privilege; and if you could ask them why, they would answer: because there are elections. We, in America, now support a class of guardians who pass unchallenged through a revolving door that at once separates and connects government and the vast security apparatus that has sprung up in the last twelve years. The cabinet officers and agency heads and company heads "move on" but stay the same, from NSA to CIA or from NSA to Booz Allen Hamilton; and to the serious players, this seems a meritocracy without reproach and without peril. After all, new people occasionally come in, and when they do they enter the complex voluntarily. They do it often enough from unselfish motives at first, and among the workforces of these various institutions you may find Americans of every race, creed, and color.

Nothing like this system was anticipated or could possibly have been admired by the framers of the constitutional democracies of the United States and Europe. The system, as Snowden plainly recognized, is incompatible with "the democratic model," and can only be practised or accepted by people who have given up on every element of liberal democracy except the ideas of common defense and general welfare. A few hours after the September 11 attacks, Cheney told his associates that the U.S. would have to become for a time a nation ruled by men and not laws. But his frankness on this point was exceptional. It may safely be assumed that most of the players go ahead in their work without realizing how much they have surrendered. Those who are under thirty, and less persistent than Snowden in their efforts of self-education, can hardly remember a time when things were different.

The year 2008 brought a remission for Snowden, because the Obama campaign promised a turn away from the national security state and the surveillance regime. He cherished the warmest hopes for the presidency to come. I have talked to young men and women like him—a dozen or more who made a point of saying it that way—for whom the wrecked promise of a liberating change was worse than no promise at all. Snowden may have been especially affected because he could see, from inside, how much was not changing, and how much was growing worse. All this, it should be added, is to take his report of himself at face value; but on the evidence thus far, it seems reasonable as well as generous to do so. He took an enormous risk and performed an extraordinary action, and he now lives under a pressure of fear that would cause many people to lose their bearings. Though apparently still in Hong Kong, he says he has no intention of going to China. He knows that if he does take that step, the authorities will have no trouble making him out to have been a simple spy.

The first wave of slanders broke as soon as the video interview was released. What was most strange—but predictable once you thought about it—was how far the reactions cut across political lines. This was not a test of Democrat against Republican, or welfare-state liberal versus big-business conservative. Rather it was an infallible marker of the anti-authoritarian instinct against the authoritarian. What was distressing and impossible to predict was the evidence of the way the last few years have worn deep channels of authoritarian acceptance in the mind of the liberal establishment. Every public figure who is psychologically identified with the ways of power in America has condemned Snowden as a traitor, or deplored his actions as merely those of a criminal, someone about whom the judgment "he must be prosecuted" obviates any further judgment and any need for thought. Into this category immediately fell the Democratic and Republican leaders of Congress, Nancy Pelosi, John Boehner, Mitch McConnell, Harry Reid, along with every lawmaker closely associated with "intelligence oversight" of the War on Terror: Dianne Feinstein, Mike Rogers, Lindsey Graham—here, once again, cutting across party lines. Those who praised Snowden's action and (in some cases) his courage included the left-wing populist Michael Moore, the right-wing populist Glenn Beck, non-statist liberals such as Senator Sheldon Whitehouse of Rhode Island and Dick Durbin of Illinois, and non-statist Republicans from the West and South: Senator Rand Paul of Kentucky and Mike Lee of Utah. But there were others in dissent, more than at any time since the vote on the Iraq War, lawmakers who insisted that the secret surveillance by government was a matter of deeper import than anything about the character of Snowden himself.

Senators Ron Wyden and Mark Udall were prominent here. It was Wyden who had declared many months earlier that Americans would be stunned and angry when they learned how the government acted on its secret interpretation of its right to carry out searches and seizures. Wyden, too, had been the lawmaker who asked James Clapper, the director of national intelligence, "Does the

NSA collect any type of data at all on millions or hundreds of millions of Americans?" and received in reply the now entirely penetrable untruth: "Not wittingly." Clapper later regretted that his reply was "too cute by half." The same characterization would fit President Obama's remarks on June 7: "Nobody is listening to your telephone calls. That's not what this program's about." He let fall the cool dismissal with an assured paternal air, a camp counselor addressing an unruly pack of children. But the New York police commissioner, Ray Kelly, was still unsatisfied: "I don't think it should ever have been made secret," Kelly said on June 17, and added: "What sort of oversight is there inside the NSA to prevent [malfeasance]?" The president has said that the necessary reforms are in place: "I came in with a healthy skepticism about these programs. My team evaluated them. We scrubbed them thoroughly." But this was another verbal juggle and an economy of truth. They don't listen to your conversations unless they want to; but if they want to, they listen. Obama's "team" scrubbed the programs and took out some bad bits, but they added some of their own and then shut the door by bringing the process under the authority of a secret court. Outlines of the new proceedings are shown to eight members of Congress who are forbidden by law to say what they learn.

Of the public expressions of contempt for the man who opened the door, one deserves particular attention. The *New Yorker* legal journalist Jeffrey Toobin said that Snowden was a "narcissist," and the word was repeated by the CBS news presenter Bob Schieffer. What were they thinking? "Narcissist" is so far from capturing any interesting truth about Snowden that the slip invites analysis in its own right. In this twelfth year of our emergency, something has gone badly wrong with the national morale. There are cultured Americans who have lived so long in a privileged condition of dependence on the security state that they have lost control of the common meanings of words. A narcissist in Snowden's position would have defected anonymously to Russia, sold his secrets for an excellent price, and cashed in by outing himself in a memoir published in 2018, studded with photographs of his dacha and his first two wives. Whatever else may be true of him, the actual Snowden seems the reverse of a narcissist. He made a lonely decision and sacrificed a prosperous career for the sake of principles that no one who values personal autonomy can be indifferent to. That is a significant part of what we know thus far.

Fear must have been among the strongest emotions that penetrated Snowden when he grasped the total meaning of the maps of the security state to which he was afforded a unique access. In one sort of mind, and it characterizes the majority of those in power, the fear turns adaptive and changes slowly to compliance and even attachment. In a mind of a different sort, the fear leads to indignation and finally resistance. But we should not underestimate the element of *physical* fear that accompanies such a moral upheaval. Since the prosecutions of whistle-blowers, the abusive treatment of Manning, and the drone assassinations of American citizens abroad have been justified by the president and his advisers, a dissident in the U.S. may think of our safety machine the way the dissidents in East Germany under the Stasi thought of theirs. It watches and listens; it works in secret; it cannot be questioned. What will it do with all that it finds?

INDEX

Said, Edward, 35
Salinger, J. D.: *The Catcher in the Rye*,
    229–231; privacy of, 225–229
Salinger, Margaret, 228–229
Sassaman, Lieutenant Colonel
    Nathan, 301–302
Schmitt, Carl, 300–301
Scorsese, Martin: *The King of
    Comedy*, 231, 236–241; *Taxi
    Driver*, 236
Second World War, 62, 86, 256, 281,
    321
self-justification: Blake on, 34;
    empire and, 255; rationalizing
    conduct, 281, 302
Seward, William, 135
Shakespeare, William: *Coriolanus*,
    198; *Hamlet*, 139, 161–162,
    178–179; *Julius Caesar*, 165–167;
    Macbeth, 157, 161, 169–170, 173,
    174–177; *A Midsummer Night's
    Dream*, 4
Shelley, Percy, 12
Sifton, Elisabeth, 266
Snowden, Edward: as anti-
    authoritarian, 341–42; disen-
    chantment of with War on
    Terror, 339; and distrust of
    national security apparatus,
    339–340; as "narcissist," 343–344
Soviet system, 261–262, 309
Spinoza, Baruch, 68
strangers: communitarian
    exclusion of, 12, 253; and
    extension of idea of neighbors,
    13, 42, 86; and Good Samari-
    tan, 80–83, 86, 87, 253; justice
    toward, 14–15, 26
Swift, Charles D., 321
sympathy: culture not the proper
    object of, 41, 68; deceptive
    variants of, 11, 195; distance a
    test of, 7, 8, 82; oppression and,
    73; radical humanity of, 8; self-
    respect and, 17, 20–21

Tacitus, 310
Taney, Chief Justice Roger B.,
    123–124, 130–131
Taylor, Charles: on cultural con-
    struction of persons, 56; on cul-
    tural integrity, 61–62; on cultural
    survival, 59–50; on misrecog-
    nition, 58–59; on recognition,
    57–58
Temptation Island, 245
terrorism: definition of, 323;
    Global War on, 314, 319, 322,
    339; motives for, 291, 295, 296,
    298–300, 322; and Al Qaeda,
    298, 299, 314, 330; state and,
    294, 322; war compared with,
    293–294, 302–303
Thomas, Clarence, 225
Thoreau, Henry David, 30

Udall, Senator Mark, 342

Vietnam War, 24–25, 27, 267

Walzer, Michael: on authenticity,
    50–51; and "connected" criticism,
    42; and cultural integrity, 47–48;
    and particularism, 43–44, 48,
    51–52; and religious wars, 52–53;
    and tribal loyalty, 48–49, 52
War and Peace, 265
Warhol, Andy, 232
Weber, Max, 281–282
Webster, Daniel, 199
West, Nathanael, 234–236
Wheelwright, John Brooks,
    187–188
Whitman, Walt: *Democratic Vistas*,
    95, 97, 116–117; *Leaves of Grass*,
    92; his opinion of Fillmore and
    Buchanan, 151; preface to *Leaves
    of Grass*, 49, 94–95, 102; *Song of
    Myself*, 100–107, 126; *Specimen
    Days*, 99–100; other references,
    183, 206